SCHOOLS, CORPOR
AND THE WAR
CHILDHOOD OBESITY

Challenging the idea that the corporate 'war' against childhood obesity is normal, necessary, or harmless, this book exposes healthy lifestyles education as a form of mis-education that shapes how students learn about health, corporations, and consumption. Drawing on ethnographic research and studies from across the globe, this book explores how corporations fund, devise, and implement various programmes in schools as 'part of the solution' to childhood obesity.

Including perspectives from children, teachers, school leaders, and both public and private external providers on how children's health and 'healthy consumption' is understood and experienced, this book is divided into eight accessible chapters which include:

- Schooling the childhood obesity 'crisis';
- The corporate 'gift' of healthy lifestyles;
- 'Coming together' to solve obesity;
- Learning about health, fatness, and 'good' choices; and
- Shaping the (un)healthy child-consumer

Schools, Corporations, and the War on Childhood Obesity is the perfect resource for postgraduate students and academics working in the public health or education field, or those taking courses on the sociology of education, health and physical education, curriculum, pedagogy, ethnography, or critical theory, who are looking to gain an insight into the current situation surrounding obesity and health in corporations and schools.

Darren Powell is a senior lecturer in the School of Curriculum and Pedagogy in the Faculty of Education and Social Work at the University of Auckland, New Zealand.

CRITICAL STUDIES IN HEALTH AND EDUCATION
Series Editors: Katie Fitzpatrick, Deana Leahy,
Michael Gard, and Jan Wright

Critical Studies in Health and Education explores the sociological, critical, and political approaches to health-related issues in education. The series underscores the discussions and debates surrounding the practice of health education and the development of solutions to the new ethical, practical, political, and philosophical questions that are emerging within the field.

SCHOOLS, CORPORATIONS, AND
THE WAR ON CHILDHOOD OBESITY
How Corporate Philanthropy Shapes Public Health and Education
Darren Powell

SCHOOLS, CORPORATIONS, AND THE WAR ON CHILDHOOD OBESITY

How Corporate Philanthropy Shapes Public Health and Education

Darren Powell

Routledge
Taylor & Francis Group

LONDON AND NEW YORK

First published 2020
by Routledge
2 Park Square, Milton Park, Abingdon, Oxon OX14 4RN

and by Routledge
52 Vanderbilt Avenue, New York, NY 10017

Routledge is an imprint of the Taylor & Francis Group, an informa business

British Library Cataloguing-in-Publication Data
A catalogue record for this book is available from the British Library

Library of Congress Cataloging-in-Publication Data
A catalog record has been requested for this book

ISBN: 978-0-8153-5514-4 (hbk)
ISBN: 978-0-8153-5512-0 (pbk)
ISBN: 978-1-351-13059-2 (ebk)

Typeset in Bembo
by Cenveo® Publishers Servies

For Maddy, Harvey, and Matilda

CONTENTS

ACKNOWLEDGEMENTS

Like most aspects of life, research and writing is built on the encouragement, critiques, and support from many kind souls.

First, I need to give my deepest thanks to the one and only Michael Gard. Your work on childhood obesity is what started me on this quest, and your insights, advice, and frankness have been invaluable, both for my development as a writer and a researcher. Long may the Skype meetings with occasional guitar accompaniments continue.

Next, to my good friend and mentor Katie Fitzpatrick. I don't know where to start, but I couldn't have done this without you. In so many ways you have continued to help me grow as an academic. Your knowledge of research, theory, methods, writing, teaching, whisky – and your willingness to share – is a force to be reckoned with.

I must also thank my colleagues (past and present) at the Faculty of Education and Social Work, University of Auckland. In so many ways, shapes, and forms you have helped me navigate this sometimes strange place called academia. I especially want to acknowledge (and apologies in advance for anyone whom I've overlooked) those who have pushed my knowledge and understanding of schools, health and physical education, and critical obesity research: Wayne Smith, Alan Ovens, Rachel Riedel, Fetaui Iosefo, Jean Allen, Hayley McGlashan, Aimee Simpson, Melinda Webber, Rod Philpot, Ben Dyson, Dillon Landi, and Richard Pringle. To the 'writing group' – Lisa Darragh, Blake Bennett, Frauke Meyer, and Nike Franke – I really appreciate the feedback on my first few chapters. To Jay Marlowe – your openness and advice are truly valued. And to Helen Hedges, your unwavering support over this first part of my academic career has been marvellous.

There are also a huge number of academics whose work has inspired me, and whose kindness and humility has always made me feel welcome. Thank you to Richard Tinning, John Evans, Doune Macdonald, Martin Thrupp, John O'Neill, and Mikael Quennerstedt for your willingness to engage in my research and rants – it's certainly has provided me with a belief that I can actually do this academic thing. A special mention to three others: Deana Leahy – for your always interesting insights into the wonderful worlds of food, health, and education. Jan Wright – I am always grateful for the time you have given me, for your feedback on an earlier version of this work, and your supreme wisdom. And Lisette Burrows – it was your support over a decade ago, before I had even considered doing any type of postgraduate study, that set me on this path. As I'm sure you are told (or should be told) every day, you are amazing, a taonga, and inspire me to be a better researcher, lecturer, and person.

One of the wonderful things about this job is the opportunities to travel around New Zealand and the globe, and catch up with great people over a few drinks. Over the past few years, I've met and worked with some wonderful colleagues, whose ideas continue to push the boundaries for what is possible in this space, including the wonderful Cat Pausé, Carolyn Pluim, Eimear Enright, Rosie Welch, my doppelgänger Ben Williams, Jessica Lee, Anna Hogan, José Tenario, Kirsten Petrie, Kristy Telford, Bob Lingard, Symeon Dagkas, Brendon Hokowhitu, LeAnne Petherick, Dean Barker, Peter Korp, Irene Torres, Marie Öhman, Dorte Ruge, and Joe Piggin.

Several chapters directly draw on previously published works. Sections of Chapter 3 and 4 originally appeared in *The 'will to give': corporations, philanthropy and schools'* (*Journal of Education Policy*, 2018). Chapter 5 is based on *Assembling the privatisation of physical education and the 'inexpert' teacher* (published in *Sport, Education and Society*, 2015). Chapter 7 features ideas and excerpts from *Governing the (un)healthy child-consumer in the age of the childhood obesity crisis* (also in *Sport, Education and Society*, 2016).

To my whānau: Mum and Dad, without your unwavering love and support, from the regular babysitting and much needed sleep-ins to frequent financial handouts/help-ups, I would never have been able to start, never mind finish, this research. Mum, your passion for teaching children Māori and Pasifika children has undoubtedly shaped my career, my life, and my research. Harvey and Matilda – you are my entire world and I love how you constantly remind me that play is far more important than work. Maddy, I'm so grateful for your aroha, your belief in me, and your ability to help me switch off from academia and spend time with our two beauties. Ka nui taku aroha ki a koe.

Finally, my research would not have been possible without the support of the principals, teachers, and external providers who agreed to be part of my research. I especially wish to thank all of the children who decided to participate in this study. Your openness, honesty, warmth, smiles, and ability to challenge my own assumptions ensured that you kept me on my toes and enjoyed almost every moment of the research. I hope I have written about you in a way that does justice to your experiences, perspectives, intellect, and lives.

1

CORPORATIONS AND THE 'WAR ON CHILDHOOD OBESITY'

In 2010, I was conducting a research project with a class of children from a primary school in Auckland, New Zealand. On my first day in the school, a group of children were about to take photographs of their classmates 'in action' during one of their regular physical education lessons. I dutifully checked the cameras: batteries charged – check; camera works – check; memory blank – no. There were a series of images stored on the camera that seemed out of place; images that initially shocked me. "What's happening in these photos?" I asked Daisy, one of my nine-year-old participants. "Oh", she nonchalantly replied, "last week Ronald McDonald came to school to take us for fitness". This is when I first began to think seriously about the troubling notion that having food and drink corporations teach children in schools was a common-sense solution to childhood obesity and children's 'unhealthy' lifestyles.

I became increasingly curious about why McDonald's wanted to teach children about fitness (and, as it turned out, about health, physical activity, and the McDonald's brand). A number of other questions also emerged. What other food and drink corporations were in schools? What were they trying to teach children about fitness or health? Who else was involved? After a quick search through corporate websites, educational resources in schools, and academic literature, three things became clear. First, there were a number of private sector organisations, particularly those with links to the food and drink industry, that were producing educational resources and other types of programmes to be used in schools. Second, there appeared to be a global attempt by multinational corporations to 'teach' (or at least be seen to teach) children about health, with the expressed goal to not only make children live healthy lifestyles, but also prevent childhood obesity. And finally, there had been little criticism in the media or academic literature about this particular phenomenon. It seemed to have been passed by relatively unnoticed and unremarked on. Given the public and political backlash against 'Big Food' and its impact on children's health, I found this rather surprising. How was it that the very companies blamed for the problem of childhood obesity are now seen as part of the solution?

1

This book emerges from a research project conducted between 2011 and 2015 (see Powell, 2015). The evidence for this project was collected and analysed by using a critical ethnographic approach (Madison, 2012) with three primary schools in Auckland, New Zealand: St Saviour's School, Reynard Intermediate School, and Dudley School[1] (for further details on the approach and the three schools, see the Methodological Appendix). Critical ethnography was a productive and valuable way of conducting research that allowed me to investigate not only what those with the 'will to govern' (Li, 2007) *want to happen* (e.g. fight obesity, change marketing practices, increase consumption), but also *what actually happens* when these programmes meet their intended targets – children in schools. By gathering together a number of ethnographic methods – spending time in schools, building relationships, talking with participants, observing participants 'in action', journaling, and collecting documentary evidence – I was able to interact with members of three school communities and collect evidence about the everyday practices that occurred in these schools. It was an approach that enabled me to pay close attention to place, space, context, and individual subjects; to understand the 'realities' of these schools, teachers, and their students; and to examine the knowledge, understandings, and perspectives of those who experienced the corporate 'part of the solution' to childhood obesity. What follows is a theoretically informed analysis of the global and local 'war on childhood obesity' being fought in schools – a battle that may do more harm than good.

Supersized kids: corporations as a cause of childhood obesity

Corporations, particularly those of the food and drink industry, regularly incur the wrath of anti-obesity campaigners, politicians, public health researchers, nutritionists, children's advocacy groups, journalists, celebrity chefs, and the public. A number of popular books, movies, and television programmes have been published on the topic of food and drink corporations and their links to childhood obesity: *Fast Food Nation, Food Politics, Fat Land, Supersize Me, Food, Inc., The Weight of the Nation, That Sugar Film* – the list goes on. These critiques of the food and drink industry are based on the idea that 'junk food' companies "do everything possible to persuade people to eat more – more food, more often, and in larger portions – no matter what it does to waistlines or well-being" (Nestle, n.d., para. 1). In a nutshell, there is a shared belief that the corporate quest for profit has resulted in increasingly unhealthy lifestyles and an 'epidemic' of childhood obesity.

It is hardly surprising that the food and drink industry now rejects and refutes claims that their products and advertising strategies are responsible for *causing* childhood obesity. Various representatives and lobbyists for Big Food are now vocal about the food industry's relationship with childhood obesity and regularly provide media releases to prove their socially responsible and obesity-fighting activities, such as sponsoring sports events, reformulating products, modifying marketing practices, stopping the sale of sugar-sweetened beverages to schools (directly, anyway), and pledging to support public health initiatives. The public is routinely informed that the marketing practices of food and drink companies are already regulated, albeit only self-regulated, and do not need further government intervention. Children's health, eating, exercise, and fatness are positioned as the responsibility of children and parents, and those who bemoan the place of 'junk food' and advertising in today's society are brushed off as the 'food police' who "have forgotten the joys of childhood" (Stewart, 2014, para. 14). The food and drink industry continues to reinforce the idea that everyone is to blame for obesity. For instance, New Zealand's former Food Industry Group (now the Food & Grocery Council) stated in their 2011–2012 annual report:

> As with many of society's issues, much starts in the home and at an early age. Education needs to increase and attitudes need to change here and in all sectors of society. Only a total community response will result in people taking greater personal responsibility for food and drink intake, energy output and their long-term health. (Food Industry Group, 2012, p. 2)

As Indra Nooyi, CEO of PepsiCo, also argued: "If all consumers exercised, did what they had to do, the problem of obesity wouldn't exist" (Mangalindan, 2010, para. 6). Although food and drink companies continue to emphasise that they are not part of the problem of childhood obesity, what is rather remarkable is how they now promote themselves as part of the solution.

'Dear Dr Chan': Big Food's commitment to the World Health Organization

In 2011, the International Food & Beverage Alliance (IFBA), a formalised coalition between the CEOs of multinational giants Nestlé, General Mills, Ferrero, Kellogg's, Grupo Bimbo, Kraft Foods (now Mondelēz International), Mars, PepsiCo, The Coca-Cola Company, and Unilever,[2] wrote Dr Margaret Chan, the erstwhile Director-General of the World Health Organization (WHO):

> We all recognize that non–communicable diseases and childhood obe-sity are major public health problems that require multi-stakeholder solutions. As a member of the private sector, we firmly believe that the food industry has a role to play as part of the solution, and have committed our time, expertise and resources to do our part. (International Food & Beverage Alliance, 2011, p. 1)

This re-positioning of corporations from obesity 'causers' to obesity 'solvers' has not gone entirely unnoticed. A number of scholars have critiqued some of

the promises, pledges, partnerships, and corporate social responsibility programmes designed and/or enacted by the private sector in the name of being
'part of the solution' to childhood obesity (e.g., see Herrick, 2009; Koplan &
Brownell, 2010; Molnar, 2005; O'Dowd, 2011; Simon, 2006). Few researchers have, however, critically examined how schools or children have been
drawn into this new corporate war on childhood obesity. Of course, anyone
who dares to challenge the sincerity of the food and drink industry's attempts
to make children healthier is criticised by Big Food, its CEOs, spokespeople, and lobbyists. For instance, when Koplan and Brownell (2010, p. 1487)
criticised the food and drink industry's response to the obesity 'threat' as
primarily a means for the industry "to avoid public criticism and forestall
government intervention", PepsiCo-funded researchers (Mensah et al., 2011,
p. 361) responded that this assertion was "disingenuous in light of multiple
recent calls for the industry to engage in partnerships in the prevention and
control of obesity". Similarly, Katherine Rich, CEO for the New Zealand
Food and Grocery Council (2013, para. 6), stated that any claims that the
food and drink industry "is not interested in being part of the solution to
the obesity epidemic ... are made out of ignorance". This tension between the
official intent of Big Food – to *genuinely* be part of the solution to childhood
obesity – and my own supposedly 'ignorant' perception that it is actually the
food and drink industry that is being somewhat disingenuous was a considerable motivation to research this relatively new phenomenon: the corporate-led,
school-based 'war on childhood obesity'.

Schools, corporations, and childhood obesity

The moral and medical panics about childhood obesity and 'couch-potato
kids' have resulted in a "rapid proliferation of policies and interventions"
(Pike, 2010, p. 82), many of which target children in schools. Despite the
perception that schools are an 'obvious solution' to childhood obesity (as
well as numerous other social, emotional, health, and economic problems),
Gard and Vander Schee (2011) caution that this perspective may be naïve
and misguided as there is a long history of school-based interventions failing to shape children's body weight. Although I will more closely examine
the problematic positioning of schools as effective and appropriate sites to
fight obesity in Chapter 2, it is important to point out here the relative ease
with which schools and corporations have been brought together to fight the
so-called war.

As one example, back in 2008 and 2010, approximately one-fifth of all
primary school students in New Zealand participated in McDonald's *My
Greatest Feat*[3] pedometer programme (the reason why Ronald McDonald had
been in the primary school I mentioned earlier). This programme was widely
promoted – on the news, on television, in McDonald's restaurants, online,
and in schools. Yet there was not a single news story, opinion piece, or journal article that questioned why McDonald's wanted to 'teach' children in

schools, what children were learning, or how McDonald's has been 'allowed' into these schools. I found it astonishing that a corporation frequently criticised for worsening children's ill health could be effortlessly re-invented as both a health promoter and a health educator.

On further examination I found that the food and drink industry's new-found interest in schools and obesity was closely connected to their reconfigured policies on marketing to children. In 2009, the IFBA introduced a self-regulated *Global Policy on Marketing and Advertising to Children*, whereby each member agreed to adopt

> a *global* marketing policy to children which *covers all of the countries around the world in which it operates*. IFBA's *global* marketing approach has been shown to effectively limit how and what IFBA companies advertise to children under 12 years. (International Food & Beverage Alliance, 2011, p. 2, my emphases)

In addition to the *Global Policy on Marketing and Advertising to Children*, the IFBA members made – and continue to make – national and regional (self-regulated) 'pledges' to reduce childhood obesity and to reduce marketing to children, such as those in the *Partnership for a Healthier America*, the now defunct *Public Health Responsibility Deal* in the United Kingdom, the *EU Pledge*, and the recently launched *Healthy Kids Industry Pledge* in New Zealand. In countries where no specific pledge is made, the IFBA stated that the *Global Policy on Marketing and Advertising to Children* would still apply. This policy and the associated promises and commitments signalled a new phase in marketing to children. On the surface, this global policy was promoted as 'limiting' how and what these corporations can advertise to "children under 12 years" (even though UNICEF defines a child as someone 16 years of age and under). In fact, the Association of New Zealand Advertisers Inc.[4] (2014, p. 8) endorsed the IFBA's *Global Policy on Marketing and Advertising to Children* by stating it was "wrong to suggest that industry is not committed to responsible marketing". However, there was one industry promise that included a noteworthy exception; an exception that seemed to actually create further opportunities for the food and beverage industry to advertise to children:

> We expanded our global policy on marketing and advertising to children by adding a schools policy. IFBA members have committed, at a minimum, not to engage in any commercial communications to students related to food and beverage products in primary schools, *except* where specifically requested by, or agreed with, the school administration for *educational purposes*. (International Food & Beverage Alliance, 2011, p. 4, my emphases)

This book interrogates these so-called *educational purposes* and the purpose they might serve for corporations, schools, principals, teachers, and students.

Here I ask a number of questions that are seldom raised or answered in mainstream media or academic writing. What are the reasons schools request corporations to engage in "product marketing communications to students in primary schools"? What forms do these communications take? Why do teachers or school leaders 'employ' McDonald's and other private sector organisations to teach children in schools? What do children 'learn'? How do corporations 'win' from their relationships? And how might schools, teachers, and children actually 'lose'?

There has been much scholarly and public criticism of the impact of corporations, 'junk food' and advertising on children's health. There is a plethora of quantitative research on the 'successes' of anti–obesity interventions, both in schools and beyond. In stark contrast, there has been little debate about the ways in which corporations are using fears about fat children[5] and unhealthy lifestyles to promote their brands and their products in schools. Critiques of how the corporate 'part of the solution' to childhood obesity is shaping schools and schooling, teachers and teaching, children and learning, are also scarce. To be clear, it is not my intent to examine the effectiveness of these interventions in terms of how they may or may not have increased children's consumption of healthy food and physical activity, reduced their body weight, or changed their lifestyles. Indeed, these programmes are rarely evaluated in such ways. Rather, I want to critically examine how corporations, their partners, and adults and children in schools justified and understood the various programmes, and how these rationales act in alignment – and in tension – with the official rhetoric of corporations. My aim in this book is to analyse how certain notions of health, obesity, childhood, and education are drawn upon in corporate anti-obesity programmes; how corporations (and other organisations) are perceived as being an acceptable, even preferable, 'part of the solution'; how corporations use the war on childhood obesity to market their brand and products; how their 'solutions' are actually implemented (or not) in schools; and critically, to what effect.

Although I have attempted to write this book in a style that is accessible to a wide audience and tone down the use of theoretical language, it is important to note this research was significantly influenced by the work of the French philosopher and social theorist, Michel Foucault. Foucault's (1991) notions of government and governmentality proved to be a fruitful theoretical lens through which to analyse the phenomenon of corporations funding, devising, and implementing educational resources and activities in schools. I was particularly interested in the Foucauldian concept of government as "the conduct of conduct … a form of activity aiming to shape, guide or affect the conduct of some person or persons" (Gordon, 1991, p. 2). This provided a particular way of seeing and understanding how the corporate-backed endeavour to make children less fat actually 'conducts the conduct' of children (as well as their parents, teachers, and school leaders). These attempts do not happen by obvious force or 'top-down' oppression, but rely on, as Foucault (1982, p. 789) argued, "a total structure of actions brought to bear upon possible actions". It is, as Miller and Rose (2008, p. 16) succinctly state, "government at a distance". Indeed, my interest in this phenomenon began with a concern that these anti-obesity programmes – what I refer to in this book as 'healthy lifestyles education' programmes – were more than an attempt by corporations to "shape, sculpt, mobilize and work through [children's] choices, desires and aspirations, needs, wants and lifestyles" (Dean, 2010, p. 20), but also business strategy to serve corporations' financial interests: a strategy with unpredictable outcomes.

As I will illuminate throughout this book, corporate-influenced anti-obesity/healthy lifestyles education programmes are convoluted and messy. They are constituted by an "ensemble" (Foucault, 1991) of elements that have converged together to provide simple solutions to the complex 'problem' of children's health. A number of these elements, such as rationalities of neoliberalism and welfarism; dominant discourses of health, obesity, fatness, individual choice, and responsibility; multinational food corporations and regional charities; pedagogies of disgust, fear, and silence; and technologies of consumption, outsourcing, privatisation, and corporatisation, have been identified and critiqued in previous studies of public health and public education. However, what this book sheds light on is some of the ways that often conflicting elements – including some rather strange bedfellows – have been successfully brought together to 'fight obesity' in schools.

This is not to say, however, that this book is only relevant to the New Zealand context. As I will demonstrate, the ways in which the so-called obesity crisis is used as an opportunity for the private sector to fight obesity, shape public policy, teach children about health, and to profit is undoubtedly a worldwide issue. The following is a dual examination of how childhood obesity is being used as a weapon for powerful private sector players to shape public policy on a global scale, and importantly, how this impacts children in schools.

Overview of book

In the next chapter, I explore how public health scholars, policymakers, and the media problematise childhood obesity (and childhood) as well as provide a critique of the assumption that school-based programmes are an obvious solution to obesity. This chapter also examines how neoliberalism underpins a number of key elements that make the corporate war against obesity possible, including processes of corporatisation, privatisation, and philanthropy. Chapter 3 extends my examination of the backdrop to the corporate war on obesity, with a focus on corporate philanthropy and corporate social responsibility initiatives at transnational, national, and local levels that position the private sector as a central player. This chapter also introduces the different types of 'anti-obesity programmes' that are deployed into schools across the globe, specifically those that are devised, funded, and/or implemented by the food and drink industry, such as nutrition education resources, incentive schemes, fundraising events, sports coaching sessions, and physical activity initiatives.

In Chapter 4, I interrogate how the global war on obesity has forged alignments between a number of disparate organisations, including corporations, schools, government agencies, charities, and a mishmash of other for-profit and 'not-for-profit' organisations. This includes an exploration of how partnerships are used as an essential tactic to bring together the ambitions of corporations, charities, the state, and schools. Chapter 5 features a closer examination of the New Zealand context, in particular, how the increasing use of outsourced programmes and resources has been re-imagined by teachers, principals, and external providers themselves as an almost 'perfect' practice, albeit a practice that comes with a number of hidden dangers. In Chapter 6, I demonstrate the ways in which various corporate healthy lifestyles education programmes were actually enacted, experienced, understood, and felt by children and adults in primary schools. This includes an in-depth analysis of various resources and pedagogies that informed students about 'good' lifestyle choices, taught students about 'bad' health consequences (including 'disgusting' fat bodies), and attempted to re-place the responsibility and blame for children's health and fatness onto the children themselves. Chapter 7 looks at the attempts of corporations and their partners to mobilise children to be healthy consumers. Here I examine the numerous ways in which strategies such as product place-ment, transforming children into marketers, sponsorship, and free gifts have 'congealed' with the resolve of corporations to develop children as lifelong consumers of the corporate brand image and their allegedly healthy corporate products. This chapter draws heavily on students' voices to demonstrate that not all children are necessarily naïve or easily 'duped' into believing corpo-rate marketing and advertising tactics, as well as exploring the possibilities for educators and researchers to resist or challenge the corporatisation of health and education in schools. Finally, in Chapter 8, I provide a reminder that the school-based 'corporate assault' on childhood obesity is not benign, but poses a number of risks for schools, teachers, and children.

Given the importance of children's health and education, it is vital that all of those who care for and work with children understand how the corporate attempts to teach children about health shapes children's understanding of health, fatness, teachers, corporations, and 'healthy' consumption of corpo-rate products. My overarching concern is that the school-based corporate assault on childhood obesity is 'dangerous'. For this reason, I ask readers to seriously consider the implications of the 'war on childhood obesity'; a war that is often portrayed as inherently harmless and healthy, yet may also result in collateral damage to children, teachers, and schooling.

Notes

1 For ethical reasons, all names of schools, adults and children are pseudonyms.
2 In 2012 McDonald's became a member of the IFBA. The IFBA has a number of 'associate' members also, such as the Grocery Manufacturer's Association, The World Federation of Advertisers, and Food Industry Asia (FIA).

3 For added clarity, I have italicised the names of the specific programmes and resources implemented in schools, such as *Life Education, Iron Brion, My Greatest Feat,* and *5+ A Day.* When the name of a programme is similar to, or the same as, the organisation devising, funding, or conducting the programme, the programme will remain italicised, and the name of the organisation will not. For example, the Life Education Trust produces *Life Education* resources, and the Iron Brion character performed at St Saviour's School as part of the *Iron Brion* programme.

4 The Association of New Zealand Advertisers Inc. (ANZA) is the New Zealand advocacy group for the advertising and marketing industry (see www.anza.org.nz).

5 I use the word 'fat' throughout this book. Some readers may baulk at such phrasing, especially when used to describe fat children, as 'fat' is often employed as a way to tease, bully, and shame children and adults whose bodies do not fit within societal norms or ideals. However, fat activists and fat studies scholars have reclaimed 'fat' as a form of resistance against the medicalised categorisation (and associated demonisation and stigmatisation) of bodies as 'obese' or 'overweight' (see Rothblum & Solovay, 2009). As Marilyn Wann stated: "There is nothing negative or rude in the word *fat* unless someone makes the effort to put it there; using the word *fat* as a descriptor (not a discriminator) can help to dispel prejudice" (2009, p. xii, italics in original). In this way, my use of 'fat' (and sometimes 'fatness') is an attempt to signal the importance of fat identities in a broader political project to fight social injustices. It is also an acknowledgement that our bodies (and the values placed upon them) are socially constructed; that bodies are inscribed with meaning through their articulation with discourse and power. It is also my endeavour to make a point that the rhetoric used to define children is powerful. By re-thinking and re-placing the language that is used to talk about children – from 'childhood obesity' to 'fat children' – we can see how words matter: a 'war on childhood obesity' is also a 'war on fat children'. In a similar vein, I understand that many fat studies scholars and fat activists would disagree with me using the 'O-words' at all (especially if not used within quote marks) (see Wann, 2009). It is a conundrum I spent much time considering when writing this book. However, I have continued to employ the term 'obesity' in this book to emphasise how different authorities (e.g. corporations, external providers, charities) use the rhetoric of 'childhood obesity' – as a crisis, a sign of ill health, a disease – to achieve their disparate ambitions.

References

Association of New Zealand Advertisers Inc. (2014). *A submission from the Association of New Zealand Advertisers Inc to the New Zealand Beverage Guidance Panel: options to reduce sugary sweetened beverage consumption in New Zealand.* Retrieved from http://www.anza.co.nz/Folder?Action=View%20File&Folder_id=74&File=New%20Zealand%20Beverage%20Guidance%20Panel_%20Submission_%20May%202014.pdf

Dean, M. (2010). *Governmentality: Power and rule in modern society* (2nd edition). London: Sage.

Food Industry Group. (2012). *Food Industry Group Annual Report 2011–2012.* Retrieved from http://www.fig.org.nz/Resources/library/FIG_Annual_Report_2012.pdf

Foucault, M. (1982). The subject and power. *Critical Inquiry, 8*(4), 777–795.

Foucault, M. (1991). Governmentality. In G. Burchell, C. Gordon, & P. Miller (Eds.), *The Foucault effect: Studies in governmentality* (pp. 87–104). London, England: Harvester Wheatsheaf.

Gard, M., & Vander Schee, C. J. (2011). The obvious solution. In M. Gard (Ed.), *The end of the obesity epidemic.* Oxon, UK: Routledge.

Gordon, C. (1991). Governmental rationality: An introduction. In G. Burchell, C. Gordon, & P. Miller (Eds.), *The Foucault effect: Studies in governmentality* (pp. 1–52). Chicago, IL: The University of Chicago Press.

Herrick, C. (2009). Shifting blame/selling health: Corporate social responsibility in the age of obesity. *Sociology of Health & Illness, 31*(1), 51–65. 10.1111/j.1467-9566.2008.01121.x

International Food & Beverage Alliance. (2011). *Second progress report of the International Food & Beverage Alliance.* Retrieved from https://www.ifballiance.org/sites/default/files/IFBA_Progress_Report_2009-2010.pdf

Koplan, J. P., & Brownell, K. D. (2010). Response of the food and beverage industry to the obesity threat. *JAMA, 304*(13), 1487–1488.

Li, T. M. (2007). Practices of assemblage and community forest management. *Economy and Society, 36,* 263–293. doi: 10.1080/03085140701254308

Madison, D. S. (2012). *Critical ethnography: Method, ethics, and performance.* Thousand Oaks, CA: Sage.

Mangalindan, J. P. (2010). *PepsiCo CEO: 'If all consumers exercised…obesity wouldn't exist'.* Retrieved from http://archive.fortune.com/2010/04/27/news/companies/indra_nooyi_pepsico.fortune/index.htm

Mensah, G. A., Yach, D., & Khan, M. (2011). Industry response to the obesity threat. *JAMA, 305*(4), 361–362.

Miller, P., & Rose, N. (2008). *Governing the present.* Cambridge, England: Polity.

Molnar, A. (2005). *School commercialism: From democratic ideal to market commodity.* New York: Routledge.

Nestle, M. (n.d.). *Food politics: How the food industry influences nutrition and health.* Retrieved from https://www.foodpolitics.com/food-politics-how-the-food-industry-influences-nutrition-and-health/

New Zealand Food and Grocery Council. (2013). *Katherine Rich: Fighting the obesity epidemic.* Retrieved from https://www.fgc.org.nz/media/archive/katherine-rich-fighting-the-obesity-epidemic

O'Dowd, A. (2011). Government's public health responsibility deal is met with scepticism. *BMJ: British Medical Journal (Online), 342.* doi:10.1136/bmj.d1702

Pike, J. (2010). *An ethnographic study of lunchtime experiences in primary school dining rooms* (Doctoral dissertation, University of Hull, Hull, United Kingdom). Retrieved from https://hydra.hull.ac.uk/resources/hull:3511

Powell, D. (2015). *"Part of the solution"?: Charities, corporate philanthropy and healthy lifestyles education in New Zealand primary schools.* (Doctoral dissertation, Charles Sturt University, Bathurst, Australia). Retrieved from https://researchoutput.csu.edu.au/files/9316089/80326

Rothblum, E., & Solovay, S. (Eds.). (2009). *The fat studies reader.* New York: New York University Press.

Simon, M. (2006). *Appetite for profit: How the food industry undermines our health and how to fight back.* New York: Nation Books.

Stewart, M. (2014). *Ban on junk food gimmicks sought.* Retrieved from http://www.stuff.co.nz/national/health/9702508/Ban-on-junk-food-gimmicks-sought

Wann, M. (2009). Foreword: Fat studies: An invitation to revolution. In E. Rothblum, & S. Solovay (Eds.), *The fat studies reader* (pp. xi–xxv). New York: New York University Press.

2

SCHOOLING THE CHILDHOOD OBESITY 'CRISIS'

Childhood obesity has been declared "one of the most serious public health challenges of the 21st century" (World Health Organization, 2018a, para. 1). Over the past two decades, the rhetoric employed by researchers, politicians, the public, and mainstream media alike has increasingly drawn on discourses of a crisis (Gard & Wright, 2005), a phenomenon described as a time bomb, epidemic, pandemic, or tsunami that poses a significant threat to children's lives, national economies, national security, and even climate change.

The notion of a childhood obesity crisis has been 'sold' to us on multiple premises. The official story goes something like this: children are unacceptably fat – and getting fatter. Children today are more likely to be obese as adults. Being fat is unhealthy. Being fat is a sign of sloth and gluttony. Being fat is a drain on the economy. This generation of children will face a shorter life expectancy than their parents. Children are fat because of an 'obesogenic' environment consisting of multiple 'scourges' of modernity (Gard & Wright, 2005): increased screen time, decreased physical activity, and excessive marketing and consumption of 'junk food'. And schools are a common-sense site to wage a 'war on obesity'. Although there is an ease in which these statements are accepted as being certain 'truths', they are also assumptions that continue to be contested, critiqued, and challenged (for excellent critiques of the childhood obesity crisis and the role of schools, see Evans, Rich, Davies, & Allwood, 2008; Gard, 2011; Gard & Wright, 2005).

Foucault (1980) argued that every society has 'regimes of truth'; particular discourses that are accepted by society and allowed to function as true. The childhood obesity crisis is one such regime of truth. I am not attempting here to replace one set of obesity 'truths' with another, nor am I trying to summarise the rich corpus of research that has contested common assumptions about childhood obesity. However, that work of many critical scholars is compelling because it recognises that "definitions of the problem of overweight and obesity as well as suggested interventions are not as simplistic, straightforward, or as ideologically neutral as they appear" (Vander Schee & Boyles, 2010, p. 170). For instance, there is a 'truth' shared by politicians, journalists, teachers, scholars, celebrity chefs, and the public that there is, without a shadow of a doubt, a childhood obesity crisis; that rates of childhood obesity are not only increasing, but increasingly increasing. Gard (2011, p. 66), however, challenges this assumption by providing strong evidence "that overweight and obesity prevalence amongst Western children had flattened and, in some cases, begun to decline even before the world-wide alarm about spiralling childhood obesity had been raised". More recently, there have been a number of reports that have also cast doubts on the idea that there continues to be an increasing prevalence of childhood obesity. Childhood obesity rates have been stable in Canada for the past decade (Rao, Kropac, Do, Roberts, & Jayaraman, 2016). There were no significant changes in obesity prevalence in children (or adults for that matter) between 2003 and 2004 and 2011 and 2012 in the United States (Ogden, Carroll, Kit, & Flegal, 2014). In New Zealand, there was no significant increase in the prevalence of overweight or obese children between 2011 and 2012 and 2016 and 2017 (Ministry of Health, 2018).[1] In spite of these types of evidence, researchers and others have continued to create and maintain the indisputable 'truth' that childhood obesity rates are dramatically increasing and will continue to do so. For example, in the following excerpts from a news article in New Zealand, we can see how the 'shocking' rhetoric of increasing childhood obesity rates is deployed as a means to help manufacture a crisis:

> Auckland University obesity expert Professor Boyd Swinburn said a comprehensive approach was needed to reverse New Zealand's fast-growing childhood obesity rates.
>   Children were getting fatter around the world, but our own kids were growing obese at "an [alarming] rate". (Morton, 2016, para. 23–24)

The journalist then goes on to write that Swinburn was 'shocked' that there were no signs of the childhood obesity rates being reversed: "Many places in the US are seeing significant declines in childhood obesity, so the fact it's not happening in New Zealand means we are really not doing a good job" (Morton, 2016, para. 26–27).

Furthermore, a report on child obesity prevalence across communities in New Zealand (where Swinburn was also an author) demonstrated that over the period 2010/2011–2015/2016 most territorial authorities experienced a *decrease* in child obesity (Gibb et al., 2019). My point here is that although there is conflicting and contradictory evidence about the 'problem' of fat children and their supposedly unhealthy lifestyles, crisis discourses continue to dominate academic and public understandings of childhood obesity. These are discourses that have been manufactured both intentionally and unintentionally (Kirk, 2006), and with serious implications for policies and practices that target children. By employing the notion of childhood obesity as a crisis, what can be said, what cannot be said, and who is allowed to be an 'expert' in dealing with the causes of and solutions to the 'problem', are re-worked and re-defined (Thorpe, 2003).

Critiques of the 'truth' of a childhood obesity crisis are critical to this book for two central reasons. First, my thinking and writing about children's health, bodies, and education has been significantly shaped by scholars who sit within the 'broad church' of what is now being called critical obesity studies, including Michael Gard, Jan Wright, John Evans, Lisette Burrows, and Paul Campos. By engaging with their and others' work, my understanding of childhood obesity is that it cannot simplistically be understood as some sort of neutral biomedical categorisation of health or bodies, but it is a complex issue that is uncertain, contested, and socially constructed. In other words, a child's fatness or a fat child is far more than a medical condition to be solved through a variety of interventions. Children's bodies and health are complicated phenomena, shaped by interconnecting social, political, historical, economic, and cultural forces. Second, I share the concern that when claims relating to childhood obesity "are treated as uncontestable truths, void of any ambiguities and uncertainties ... and are uncritically welcomed as a kind of individual and cultural salvation" (Vander Schee & Boyles, 2010, p. 170), they are also uncritically welcomed into schools (as well as homes, hospitals, sports clubs, government organisations). Subsequently, no matter whether one agrees with the critiques of the childhood obesity crisis in their entirety (or at all), acknowledging that causes, consequences, measurements, prevalence, and solutions for childhood obesity are complicated and *uncertain* should force us to question what is happening to children. As Gard (2004, p. 76) notes:

> While there are doubts about the degree to which the so-called 'obesity epidemic' really is the 'global' phenomenon it is claimed to be, it has clearly become an important discursive resource in the legitimation of a number of academic disciplines, industries and public health policy agendas. Indeed, a complex feedback loop in which academics, entrepreneurs, funding bodies and governments are simultaneously constructing and responding to this alleged crisis is now in full swing. Almost inevitably, it seems, schools have been drawn into the obesity vortex.

Schools and obesity

> Schools are identified as a key setting for public health strategies to lower or prevent the prevalence of overweight and obesity ... While the schools alone cannot solve the childhood obesity epidemic, it also is unlikely that childhood obesity rates can be reversed without strong school-based policies and programs. (Story, Nanney, & Schwartz, 2009, p. 72)

As the above quote demonstrates, schools are seen as a vital site to fight obesity, both in terms of being 'part of the solution' and 'part of the cause'.

The alleged school-based causes are numerous and ever-expanding, but tend to focus on schools providing or selling poor-quality food (e.g. school meals, vending machines), irresponsible parents unwilling to send their child to school with 'healthy' lunches, 'junk food' fundraising activities such as bake sales and sausage sizzles, the failure of schools to provide adequate education (especially in regard to physical education, health education, and physical activity opportunities), teachers not being healthy role models, and even schools allowing children to eat birthday cakes – the list goes on.

At the same time, schools have been swiftly positioned as "uniquely situated to address the epidemic of obesity and sedentary behaviour plaguing our youth" (Trost, 2006, p. 183). It is hardly surprising that researchers continue to view schools as an "obvious place" to fight childhood obesity given the plethora of research that "is full of common-sense assertions about the need to start young, the amount of time children spend in schools and the relative capacity of governments to mandate policies with immediate effect in schools compared to other spheres of life" (Gard & Vander Schee, 2011, p. 82).

There are, however, significant criticisms of the 'common-sense' idea that schools and school-based interventions (e.g. physical activity initiatives, healthy eating programmes, physical education lessons, anti-obesity schemes) are effective or even appropriate sites to solve the obesity crisis. There is much evidence that school-based interventions "have a long and virtually unbroken record of failure in affecting children's body weight" (Gard & Vander Schee, 2011, p. 84). For example, in Brown and Summerbell's (2008, p. 138) systematic review of the effectiveness of 38 school-based interventions that focused on changing children's weight, physical activity (PA) levels, and dietary intake, the authors concluded that

> There is insufficient evidence to assess the effectiveness of dietary interventions to prevent obesity in school children or the relative effectiveness of diet vs. PA interventions. School-based interventions to increase PA and reduce sedentary behaviour may help children to maintain a healthy weight but the results are inconsistent and short-term.

This is not the only large-scale study to have reported similar findings. Harris, Kuramoto, Schulzer and Retallack's (2009, p. 723) meta-analysis of primary school-based physical activity interventions (18 studies involving over 18,000 children) also demonstrated that

> School based physical activity interventions did not improve BMI. Therefore, such interventions are unlikely to have a significant effect on the increasing prevalence of childhood obesity ... Variation in the duration, intensity and structure of school-based physical activity interventions had minimal effects on short-term or long-term BMI change.

Yet despite the failures of anti-obesity interventions that have been designed, conducted, and evaluated by obesity, nutrition, and physical activity researchers, there remains a steadfast conviction that school policies, teachers, curricula, and health and physical education (HPE) programmes *must* play an important role. For example, in Trost's (2006, p. 165) examination of the relationship between school physical education and children's health, he conceded that there was a "relatively weak evidence linking childhood physical activity with long-term health outcomes". However, in the same breath he argued that schools needed to provide physical education in order to improve children's bodies and health. The "scientific basis" for Trost's argument was that he believed it was "intuitively sensible to promote an active lifestyle for children as a preventive health measure" in schools. When it relates to the certainty that physical activity *will* lead children to live healthier, non-obese lives, claims often reflect more "a cherished cultural belief rather than an object for dry scientific conjecture" (Gard, 2008, p. 497).

The fields of HPE are also regularly drawn into debates about how to make children thinner and healthier. Back in 2002, New Zealand researchers argued that because children were allegedly participating in less physical education in schools – and choosing more sedentary activities – it seemed "inevitable that body weight will increase" (Hamlin, Ross, & Hong, 2002, p. 51). In a similar vein, Gordon (2014, para. 6) argued: "It would seem sensible, when considering the implications of New Zealand's growing lifestyle-related problems, to place a greater emphasis on [the health and physical education] learning area, especially in primary schools where many of our lifestyle habits are developed". The American Medical Association went one step further, claiming that because of the apparent failure of schools to teach children not to be fat, there needed to be legislation that would require yearly instruction in all public schools (from grade 1 through 12) to teach students the causes, consequences, and prevention of obesity (see Moyer, 2012). The legislation has not (yet) been passed.

Contrary to such claims for more or 'better' education about health, physical activity, and obesity, there is a large number of internationally recognised scholars who contest the idea that physical education or health education (or schooling in general) are appropriate or effective tools to improve children's health (for detailed discussions on the relationship between schools, physical education, obesity, and health, see Evans et al., 2008; Fitzpatrick & Tinning, 2014a; Gard, 2011; Gard & Pluim, 2014; Gard & Wright, 2005; Wright & Harwood, 2009). One significant argument for challenging the use of HPE to address childhood obesity is that "the discourse surrounding obesity and some of the reports, messages, policies and measures being taken to tackle it are misleading, misguided and could do more harm than good" (Cale & Harris, 2011, p. 1). This was certainly the case for scholar Cat Pausé (2019, p. 1), who recently wrote a powerful autoethnographic account of her experience of physical education as a fat child, describing it as a space where "I lost my love of movement, thanks to uniforms that did not fit, activities that had not been modified for my fat body, taunting from my peers and the anti-fat bias of my teachers". For Pausé, physical education was clearly positioned as a means "to produce weight loss, rather than being allowed to enjoy physical movement for enjoyment's sake. If I was not losing weight, then what was the point?" (2019, p. 1).

In 2003, Evans warned that if claims regarding childhood obesity are uncritically implemented in schools, it may negatively affect children's health and could actually damage the education of children and young people. Five years later, Evans and colleagues published *Education, Disordered Eating and Obesity Discourse: Fat Fabrications* (Evans et al., 2008). In this book, they clearly demonstrate how obesity discourses are mediated through education policy, biomedical science, and pedagogies in schools, discourses that are recontextualised by children and young people in highly problematic and 'unhealthy' ways, including disordered relationships with eating, exercise, and their bodies. A central rationale for my research and writing this book was to take these arguments seriously, especially given evidence that "the identities constructed for children within contemporary panics around childhood obesity especially, are 'dangerous' ones" (Burrows & Wright, 2004, p. 91; see also Powell & Fitzpatrick, 2015).

I do not claim that the failure of school-based interventions to prevent or reduce obesity, or improve children's health and well-being, means there should be no debate about the role of schools in improving children's health. On the contrary, it is the *uncertainty* of the evidence which encourages me to critically examine and provoke discussions about what is happening to children in schools in the name of fighting childhood obesity (see also Powell, 2018a). If childhood obesity critiques have any merit whatsoever, then it is imperative to ask critical questions relating to school-based anti-obesity interventions. Who has the most to gain and to lose from the current war on childhood obesity? How does the childhood obesity crisis create a space for exploitation – by corporations, academics, government agencies, charities, external providers, teachers, and children? What are the consequences of these organisations and individuals implementing anti-obesity interventions in schools? With common-sense understandings of childhood obesity as a current crisis and schools as key sites for intervention, how have public, private, and voluntary sector groups 'cashed in' on the obesity epidemic? And what sense do children make of these attempts to make them fit, healthy, and not fat?

Healthism, public health, and public education

One of the main reasons that schools are viewed as key sites to fight childhood obesity is the historical association between public schools and public health imperatives (for an excellent analysis, see Gard & Pluim, 2014). The alignment between the interests of public education and public health is not only historical, but also demonstrated in contemporary contexts by "the ease and regularity with which the work of schools and teachers is assumed by others to be an instrument of public health policy" (Gard & Pluim, 2014, p. 5). Whatever the agenda of public health – to make young people less fat, more moral, use contraception, or not use drugs – the "new public health" has resulted in "everyone" being required to improve their own and others' lifestyles (Petersen & Lupton, 1996, p. ix). This 'new' version of public health has helped to re-define health as both an individual's right *and* their responsibility. Robert Crawford (1980), in his influential article 'Healthism and the Medicalization of Everyday Life', used the term *healthism* to demonstrate the increasingly individualistic understandings of health and public health promotion, describing healthism as "the preoccupation with personal health as a primary – often *the* primary – focus for the definition and achievement of well-being; a goal which is to be attained primarily through the modification of life styles" (Crawford, 1980, p. 368, emphasis in original). In this way, the root causes of disease or ill health may be complex, yet "healthism treats individual behavior, attitudes, and emotions as the relevant symptoms needing attention" (Crawford, 1980, p. 368, emphasis in original).

A key tenet of healthism is that individuals not only *could* take more responsibility and care for their bodies, behaviours, and health, but that *everyone should*. This is not to say that people who emphasise individual responsibility for health completely ignore broader determinants of (ill)health, such as the environment or politics. However, what healthism does is re-place the responsibility for managing (un)healthy behaviours as lying "within the realm of individual choice" (Crawford, 1980, p. 368). In this way, healthism de-politicises and undermines social, collective attempts to improve health and "functions as dominant ideology, contributing to the protection of the social order from the examination, critique, and restructuring which would threaten those who benefit from the malaise, misery, and death of others" (Crawford, 1980, pp. 368–369).

Crawford (1980, p. 368) used the tobacco and food industries as examples of "those who benefit". One of my initial concerns with the corporate efforts to 'teach' children about obesity and healthy lifestyles was the way that healthism may be deployed to protect the food and drink industry from critique, disguise the social forces and processes that "systematically encourage unhealthy behaviour, often for private advantage" (p. 368), and shift the responsibility and blame for ill health onto individuals.

The dominance of individualistic understandings of health in education policies and practices has been the subject of numerous critiques (e.g. Fitzpatrick & Tinning, 2014b; Hokowhitu, 2014; Kirk, 2006; Burrows & Wright, 2004). Writing three decades ago, Kirk and Colquhoun (1989) drew on Crawford's insights into healthism to argue that physical education teachers produced and consumed the 'culture' of healthism by positioning health-based physical education as a panacea to students' unhealthy (i.e. sedentary, 'junk food' consuming) lifestyles. In this way, teachers reproduced healthism by supporting "the moral imperative to be slender ... to be fat implies loss of control, impulsiveness, self-indulgence, sloth – in short, moral failure" (Kirk & Colquhoun, 1989, p. 430).

There has been a proliferation of HPE programmes, pedagogies, and practices that reinforce the 'new public health' and the ideology of healthism by encouraging young people to obsessively monitor their bodies, manage risks, be seen to be healthy (by exercising, dieting and being thin), and be responsible (see Fitzpatrick & Tinning, 2014a). In addition, the imperatives of public health (e.g. the prevention of obesity, poor hygiene, bad posture, cardiovascular disease, drug use, teenage pregnancy, depression, suicide, and much more) are constantly re-positioned as problems for public education to take responsibility for and solve. This "'give it to schools' reflex" (Gard & Pluim, 2014, p. 5) exhibited by public health organisations and actors may be well meaning, but the impact it has on schools, teachers, and education is rarely considered.

One impact of public health with public education being interconnected is that the meaning of education (especially when it relates to HPE) is muddied, resulting in policies and practices that fail to differentiate between teaching *about* health and trying to make children healthy (for detailed discussions on these differences, see Fitzpatrick & Tinning, 2014a). Even though healthism "may not completely dominate the ideologies and activities of the gamut of groups and individuals" involved in public health, public education, and hybridisations of the two (including health promotion), it is an ideology that "is present in all of them":

> As an ideology which promotes heightened health awareness, along with personal control and change, [healthism] may prove beneficial for those who adopt a more health-promoting life style. But it may in the process also serve the illusion that we can as individuals control our existence, and that taking personal action to improve health will somehow satisfy the longing for a much more varied complex of needs. (Crawford, 1980, p. 368)

While some researchers continue to promote the idea that 'teaching' children to be individually responsible and make better choices is an appropriate and effective antidote to (potentially) fat children and their unhealthy lives, the linking of education with healthism is problematic. There are now "a number of groups who have something to gain from the notion that health is the ultimate responsibility of individuals" (Kirk & Colquhoun, 1989, p. 431), a mix of corporations, charities, public health agencies, and schools that share an interest in teaching children about health and fatness. There is, therefore, a clear need to examine how healthism is (re)produced in various healthy lifestyles education programmes, how it may advantage certain individuals and groups, and how it may further disadvantage or marginalise others. The emphasis on individualism and self-responsibility is not just an integral aspect of healthism, but another influential ideology that has shaped both public health and public education: neoliberalism.

Health Education Inc.: neoliberalism, corporatisation, and privatisation

Neoliberalism is a dominant and pervasive political rationality, an ideology, that problematises the welfare state and re-organises government to align with concepts of choice, standards, performance, efficiency, competitiveness, autonomy, enterprise, consumption, and responsibility (for critiques of neoliberalism in public education, see Apple, 2006; Ball, 2007, 2012; Boyles, 2008; Giroux, 2001; Rizvi & Lingard, 2009; Saltman, 2010). The rise of neoliberal reforms in public education "is just one manifestation of a global reworking of the economic, social, moral and political foundations of public service provision" (Ball, 2012, p. 15). The neoliberal strategy to increase corporate control and decision-making power over management, curriculum and teaching in schools has led to an array of reforms across the world, including public-private partnerships (PPPs), voucher schemes, educational management organisations, standardised testing, performance pay (which is sometimes linked to standardised test results), and charter/partnership/free schools. The 'neoliberal turn' in public education (and other responsibilities of the state, such as public health) has attempted to restrict the job of the state (although often alongside a greater regulatory role) and re-shape policy in line with key principles of market 'logic' through processes of commercialisation, privatisation, multi-sector partnerships, and outsourcing. Although proponents of the neoliberalisation of education continue to argue that the private sector is both more efficient and effective than the public sector (e.g. Green, 2005), critics argue that neoliberalism has changed the role of the state and "called into question the very aims and purposes of public education" (Codd, 2008, p. 15).

Neoliberalism re-defines education as being for the "corporate good rather than the public good ... a new conflation of corporate profit with the social good" (Saltman, 2011, p. 13) which erodes democracy and children's position as citizens. As Kohn (2002, p. 7) also argues, "when business thinks about schools, its agenda is driven by what will maximise its profitability, not necessarily by what is in the best interests of students". The meanings and purposes of schools, charities, governments, teachers, and students have been influenced by a discourse of *economism* that conflates "the public and private purposes of schooling, treating schooling like a for-profit business ... an expression of neo-liberalism [that] reduces the purposes of schooling to economic ends" (Saltman, 2009, p. 58). In this way, education is positioned as another consumable good, "simply one more product like bread, cars and television" (Apple, 2006, p. 32); a public good that is now produced, marketed, and 'sold' by the private sector – back to the public sector – for private advantage. According to Boyles (2008), Saltman (2010) and others, the responsibility of public education to promote critical citizenship has been 'assaulted' by corporations for the development of profit.

Tinning and Glasby (2002) and Lupton (1999) have also argued that the neoliberal imbued principles of the 'new public health' significantly shape curricula and pedagogical work in schools. Neoliberalism acts as part of the machinery to produce healthy citizens, where "everyone is being called upon to play their part" (Petersen & Lupton, 1996, p. ix) in being healthy, living healthy lifestyles, avoiding risks, and being more responsible. Writing specifically about the field of health education, Leahy (2012, pp. 13–14) argues that neoliberalism has, and continues to, dominate health education curricula in schools, resulting in health education resources and pedagogies that are "saturated through with neoliberalism, its rationalities and associated practices". As I will demonstrate in later chapters (in particular, Chapters 6 and 7), multiple tenets of neoliberalism dominate the corporatised efforts to 'solve' childhood obesity.

Central to neoliberalism is the belief that the market should be used to re-develop all areas of society. As Ball (2012, p. 66) argues, the promotion of "'market-based solutions' to 'wicked' social and educational problems … fits within and fosters the neo-liberal imaginary". A raft of 'problems' (including education, health, obesity and welfare) have been re-imagined through neoliberalism's 'less state, more market' mantra as opportunities for private sector organisations to solve – and profit from. One such 'wicked' problem to be urgently solved by the 'neoliberal imaginary' is childhood obesity. Organisations across all sectors of society, with a focus on private sector players, are encouraged to collaborate and be 'part of the solution' (see World Health Organization, 2018b). It is in this way that schools and governments, charities, and corporations, as well as teachers, principals, and students, have been drawn into the 'vortex' of obesity solutions (Gard, 2011).

Corporations and corporatisation

Corporations play an increasing role in funding, devising, promoting, and implementing anti-obesity programmes and healthy lifestyles interventions in schools. I use the term corporation to refer to two types of private sector for-profit organisations: publicly traded corporations (those that sell shares to generate capital), such as McDonald's and Nestlé S.A.,[2] and 'closely-held' businesses in which the company is owned by a group of people or companies but is not publicly traded. For instance, the New Zealand beverage company Frucor, and its parent company, Suntory Beverage & Food Limited, are both 'closely-held' and not publicly traded. Although in this book, the majority of corporations that take an interest in being 'part of the solution' to childhood obesity are those in the food and drink industry, they are not the only ones. Corporations from insurance, sportswear, fitness, weight-loss, professional sports, gambling, tobacco, medical, advertising, farming, pharmaceutical, gaming, academic and education industries, among others are also keen to position themselves as obesity warriors and child-saviours.

The work of corporations is already strongly evident in public education. As Stephen Ball (2012) clearly demonstrates in *Global Education Inc.: New Policy Networks and the Neoliberal Imaginary*, the private sector is increasingly involved in devising, producing, and selling education services to school and public education authorities across the globe. 'Edu-business' is now a multi-billion dollar industry that profits from selling a range of professional development, leadership, consultancy, management, IT, and policy services. Edu-business companies also devise and sell resources (e.g. online resources, software, textbooks, lesson plans), including HPE resources, to governments, universities, school districts, schools, and teachers across the globe.

A number of education scholars have interrogated the ways in which the private sector is 'corporatising' the field of public education (see Boyles, 2000, 2005; Norris, 2011; Saltman, 2000, 2010; Saltman & Gabbard, 2011). Saltman (2010, p. 13), for instance, argues that "the corporatization of schools is part of the broader assault on public and critical education and the aspirations of a critical democracy". He goes on to define the corporatisation of public education as meaning two things: "the privatization of public schools and the transformation of public schools on the model of the corporation" (Saltman, 2010, p. 13). However, this use of the term corporatisation can be misleading as it suggests that the privatisation of public education fundamentally involves corporations. As I will demonstrate in this book, responsibility for children's education and health is not shifting solely towards corporations, but a messy mix of charities, non-governmental organisations (NGOs), not-for-profits, lobby groups, industry groups, *and* corporations. For the sake of clarity, I will use the word *corporatisation* to describe those instances when a corporation (or group of corporations) is involved in the implementation of a programme to fight childhood obesity or improve children's health or education. In this way, corporatisation is a process (or more accurately, a set of processes) by which private sector companies – corporations – deliberately insert their presence and business activities into the sphere of public education in an attempt to improve their bottom line. For instance, I will sometimes use the phrase 'corporatised resources' to describe education resources that feature specific products (e.g. Coca-Cola, Just Juice, beef and lamb), are devised through corporate philanthropy (e.g. The Healthy Weight Commitment Foundation's *Together Counts* resources in the United States,[3] and Nestlé's *Be Healthy, Be Active* programme in New Zealand), and promote a corporate-friendly perspective of health and how to achieve it (e.g. resources shaped by United Fresh New Zealand Inc. and 5+ A Day Charitable Trust that aim to increase the consumption of fruit and vegetables). There are, however, other neoliberal processes at play that attempt to re-align the aims and purpose of public education (and public health) with the interests of corporations and the broader private sector.

Privatisation in and of education

Privatisation is a critical element of the neoliberalisation of public education, a process that, although inextricably interconnected with corporatisation, has distinct forms, functions, and processes that require further explanation and analysis. There is an important reason to delineate between corporatisation and privatisation. While corporatisation may be viewed as a somewhat "incidental or piecemeal involvement" (Evans & Davies, 2015a, p. 2) of private corporations in public education (e.g. outsourcing of a single healthy lifestyles programme to an external provider), privatisation encapsulates the wide breadth of strategies and plans that have increased use of the private sector in the management, government, provision, funding, organisation, and delivery of public services. As Ball (2007, p. 13) argues, privatisation is 'shorthand' for a range of *processes*: "It is more appropriate perhaps to think of 'privatisations'. There are a wide variety of types and forms involving different financial arrangements and different relationships between funders, service providers and clients".

Ball and Youdell (2007) argue that privatisation can be understood as being of two main types: endogenous and exogenous (although both have some similarities and crossovers). Endogenous privatisation refers to privatisation *in* public education, where various practices, rationales, and techniques of the private sector are imported into the public sphere, such as performance-related pay, new public management systems, the provision of school vouchers, and decentralising education administration. Exogenous privatisation is the privatisation *of* public education, "the opening up of public education services to private sector participation on a for-profit basis and using the private sector to design, manage or deliver aspects of public education" (Ball & Youdell, 2007, p. 13). This includes the use of PPPs to build and manage schools, the formation of charter schools, the outsourcing of education services (such as a payroll, testing, and assessment), purchasing digital technologies (including tablets, interactive whiteboards, and robots), providing professional development for teachers, and private teacher education organisations. Not all of these types of privatisation are obvious. Many forms of privatisation are now 'hidden' from schools, teachers, and the public (see Burch, 2009; Powell, 2019). Drawing on privatisation practices of competition, choice, and performance management, Ball and Youdell (2007, p. 11) point out that these forms of "hidden privatization ... carry ethical dangers and many examples of opportunistic and tactical behaviours are already apparent in schools and among parents within such systems".

Despite the privatisation of education accelerating the involvement of private sector players in public education contexts across the globe, there has been a relative dearth of sociological research that closely examines the privatisation processes of education and their impact on schools, teachers, and children (Ball, Thrupp, & Forsey, 2010). A key aspect of this book is, therefore, to examine concrete, everyday examples of privatisation in schools; the hidden and obvious, dangerous and benign processes by which corporations and their partners have become acceptable players in the school-based war on obesity, and the impact these forms of privatisation have on schools, teachers, and children.

There has certainly been a lack of research on the processes of privatisation that have shaped various anti-obesity, healthy lifestyles education, and HPE programmes in schools. Acknowledging this 'gap' in research, the editor of

Sport, Education, and Society published a special issue: *Neoliberalism, Privatisation and the Future of Physical Education*, with the aim to "explore the implications across the globe of privatisation of provision of physical education (PE) and its variants" (Evans & Davies, 2015a, p. 1). In this issue a number of facets of privatisation are explored, critiqued, and problematised. Evans and Davies (2015b, p. 18), for example, connect the dots between UK government rhetoric on Academies (i.e. funded by the state, but independent from local authority control – similar to charter schools), the privatisation of education, and the commercialisation of PE, warning that

> what we are witnessing here is not just the incidental outsourcing of education and PE to private enterprise ... but also the privatisation of the governance, organisation, purposes and practices of education, of its structures, processes and cultures, via the marketisation of just about everything required to make schools work.

In other papers in that special issue, Gard (2015) argued that the increasing privatisation of HPE signifies a potentially significant shift in the role of the academic, including how knowledge is produced and consumed, while Macdonald (2015) examined the concept of 'teacher-as-knowledge-broker' and interactions with neoliberalism. In addition, Penney, Petrie, and Fellows (2015) and Williams and Macdonald (2015) critically interrogated some of the practices, rationales, and processes by which teachers and principals recruit non-public sector organisations and agents to teach health education, physical education, fitness, physical activity, and sport. These analyses are all germane to this book, given that current solutions to childhood obesity/children's unhealthy lifestyles encompass a plethora of programmes and resources outsourced to corporations and their partners.

Outsourcing is a key element of privatisation and critical to any examination of the school-based war on childhood obesity. It is a process that works to blur the boundaries between privatisation *in* education and *of* education. When schools outsource services (e.g. a healthy lifestyles education programme) to external providers, they do not only employ a business strategy of the private sector (based on neoliberal notions of choice and efficiency), but also allow public education to be used as a tool for non-public organisations to strategically and financially profit (for HPE research on outsourcing, also see Blair, 2018; Macdonald, Hay, & Williams, 2008; Powell, 2014; Powell, 2018b; Powell & Gard, 2015; Sperka, Enright, & McCuaig, 2018; Williams & Macdonald, 2015).

HPE seems to be a particularly easy target and good market for a range of private and voluntary sector providers. As Petrie, Penney, and Fellows (2014, p. 25) revealed in their mapping of the external provision of HPE in New Zealand, primary school teachers are "swamped with options from external providers of resources and programmes for 'HPE'". Indeed, their research into the providers of HPE programmes in New Zealand schools identified

124 "nationwide initiatives, resources and providers of programmes designed to 'support' the delivery of HPE curriculum" in New Zealand schools (Penney et al., 2015, p. 49). It is important to mention too that these 124 programmes did *not* include smaller, local programmes and providers that were used in school settings, but only those that were found across the length of New Zealand. Furthermore, Dyson and colleagues reported in their research with teachers from 133 primary schools across six regions of New Zealand that 87% of teachers had used an external provider for physical education, and that these schools had used a total of 638 providers (Dyson, Gordon, Cowan, & McKenzie, 2016). This did not include resources that had been purchased from an external provider, but focused on those where external providers were involved in actually teaching students. In the context of New Zealand, particularly in primary schools, outsourcing teaching and curricula is rife (Dyson, Cowan, Gordon, Powell, & Shulruf, 2018).

While there is a developing evidence base that describes and/or examines the outsourcing of HPE, most research has either focused on mapping the range of programmes that are available to schools, or centred on particular programmes/external providers. There is, however, still little in-depth research into "the lived sites of educational places and spaces" (Leahy, 2012, p. 75) where education is outsourced, including research (ethnographic or otherwise) into the impact of outsourcing and privatisation on children. The privatisation literature, as it stands, appears to render children's voices mostly silent. The aim of this book, in part, is to bring children's voices – their lived experiences of education privatisation – to the fore. However, before I can provide a more detailed examination of the actual impact of these programmes on schools, teachers, and children, it is important to demonstrate the scope and scale of privatisation that takes place in the name of 'fighting childhood obesity'; programmes that are promoted by corporations as being philanthropic and socially responsible.

Notes

1 It is also important to note that although the Ministry of Health in New Zealand did report a significant increase in the prevalence of 'obese' children between the periods 2006 and 2007 and 2016 and 2017, there was no significant increase in waist to height ratios, nor was there a significant increase in the prevalence of 'overweight' children. Furthermore, over this same period there was a significant increase in the prevalence of 'thin' children, yet this has not been discussed in academic or media publications as an 'alarming' increase or even a cause for concern.

2 It is common in French-speaking countries, such as Switzerland, to use the acronym S.A. (*Société Anonyme*), loosely translated as 'Anonymous Society', which designates a certain type of corporation that employs civil law. It is similar to that of a plc (public limited company) in the United Kingdom.

3 The Healthy Weight Commitment Foundation is a "a broad-based, not-for-profit organization whose mission is to help reduce obesity, especially childhood obesity, by encouraging positive and permanent lifestyle changes among school-aged children and their families" (http://www.healthyweightcommit.org/about/).

References

Apple, M. W. (2006). *Educating the 'right' way: Markets, standards, God, and inequality* (2nd edition). New York: Taylor and Francis.

Ball, S. J. (2007). *Education plc: Understanding private sector participation in public sector education.* New York: Routledge.

Ball, S. J. (2012). *Global Education Inc.: New policy networks and the neoliberal imaginary.* Oxon, UK: Routledge.

Ball, S. J., Thrupp, M., & Forsey, M. (2010). Review of the book hidden markets: The new education privatization, by P. Burch. *British Journal of Sociology of Education, 31*(2), 229–241.

Ball, S. J., & Youdell, D. (2007). *Hidden privatisation in public education (preliminary report).* London: Institute of Education.

Blair, R. (2018). The deliverers debate. In G. Griggs & K. Petrie (Eds.), *Routledge handbook of primary physical education* (pp. 61–73). Oxon, UK: Routledge.

Boyles, D. R. (2000). *American education and corporations: The free market goes to school.* New York: Falmer Press.

Boyles, D. R. (2005). *Schools or markets? Commercialism, privatization, and school-business partnerships.* Mahwah, NJ: Lawrence Erlbaum.

Boyles, D. R. (2008). *The corporate assault on youth: Commercialism, exploitation, and the end of innocence.* New York: Peter Lang.

Brown, T., & Summerbell, C. (2008). Systematic review of school-based interventions that focus on changing dietary intake and physical activity levels to prevent childhood obesity: An update to the obesity guidance produced by the National Institute for Health and Clinical Excellence. *Obesity Reviews, 10*, 110–141. doi:10.1111/j.1467-789X.2008.00515.x

Burch, P. (2009). *Hidden markets: The new education privatization.* New York: Routledge.

Burrows, L., & Wright, J. (2004). The good life: New Zealand children's perspectives on health and self. *Sport, Education and Society, 9*(2), 193–205. doi: 10.1080/1357332042000233930

Cale, L., & Harris, J. (2011). 'Every child (of every size) matters' in physical education! Physical education's role in childhood obesity. *Sport, Education and Society, 18*(4), 1–20. doi: 10.1080/13573322.2011.601734

Codd, J. (2008). Neoliberalism, globalisation and the deprofessionalisation of teachers. In V. M. Carpenter, J. Jesson, P. Roberts, & M. Stephenson (Eds.), *Nga Kaupapa here: Connections and contradictions in education* (pp. 14–24). Melbourne: Cengage Learning.

Crawford, R. (1980). Healthism and the medicalization of everyday life. *International Journal of Health Services, 10*, 365–388.

Dyson, B., Cowan, J., Gordon, B., Powell, D., & Shulruf, B. (2018). Physical education in Aotearoa New Zealand primary schools: Teachers' perceptions and policy implications. *European Physical Education Review, 24*(4), 467–486. doi: 10.1177/1356336X17698083

Dyson, B., Gordon, B., Cowan, J. & McKenzie, A. (2016). External providers and their impact on primary physical education in Aotearoa/New Zealand. *Asia-Pacific Journal of Health, Sport and Physical Education, 7*(1), 3–19. doi: 10.1080/18377122.2016.1145426

Evans, J., & Davies, B. (2015a). Physical education, privatisation and social justice. *Sport, Education and Society, 20*(1), doi: 10.1080/13573322.2014.942624

Evans, J., & Davies, B. (2015b). Neoliberal freedoms, privatisation and the future of physical education. *Sport, Education and Society, 20*(1), 10–26. doi: 10.1080/13573322.2014.918878

Evans, J., Rich, E., Davies, B., & Allwood, R. (2008). *Education, disordered eating and obesity discourse: Fat fabrications.* Oxon, UK: Routledge.

Fitzpatrick, K., & Tinning, R. (2014a). *Health education: Critical perspectives.* Oxon, UK: Routledge.

Fitzpatrick, K., & Tinning, R. (2014b). Considering the politics and practice of health education. In K. Fitzpatrick & R. Tinning (Eds.), *Health education: Critical perspectives* (pp. 142–156). Oxon, UK: Routledge.

Foucault, M. (1980). The confession of the flesh. In C. Gordon (Ed.), *Power/knowledge: Selected interviews and other writings, 1972–1977* (pp. 194–228). New York: Pantheon Books.

Gard, M. (2004). An elephant in the room and a bridge too far, or physical education and the 'obesity epidemic'. In J. Evans, B. Davies & J. Wright (Eds.), *Body knowledge and control: Studies in the sociology of physical education and health* (pp. 68–82). London: Routledge.

Gard, M. (2008). Producing little decision makers and goal setters in the age of the obesity crisis. *Quest, 60*(4), 488–502.

Gard, M. (2011). *The end of the obesity epidemic.* Oxon, UK: Routledge.

Gard, M. (2015). 'They know they're getting the best knowledge possible': Locating the academic in changing knowledge economies. *Sport, Education and Society, 20*(1), 107–121. doi: 10.1080/13573322.2014.957177

Gard, M., & Pluim, C. (2014). *Schools and public health: Past, present and future.* Lanham, MD: Lexington Books.

Gard, M. & Vander Schee, C. J. (2011). The obvious solution. In M. Gard (Ed.), *The end of the obesity epidemic.* Oxon, UK: Routledge.

Gard, M., & Wright, J. (2005). *The obesity epidemic: Science, morality, and ideology.* New York: Routledge.

Gibb, S. Shackleton, N., Audas, R., Taylor, B., Swinburn, B., Zhu, T.,... Milne, B. (2019). Child obesity prevalence across communities in New Zealand: 2010–2016. *Australian and New Zealand Journal of Public Health.* doi:10.1111/1753-6405.12881

Giroux, H. A. (2001). *Stealing innocence: Corporate culture's war on children.* New York: Palgrave Macmillan.

Gordon, B. (2014, August 6). Healthy lifestyle as important a lesson as reading. *The Dominion Post.* Retrieved from http://www.stuff.co.nz/dominion-post/

Green, C. (2005). *The privatization of state education.* New York: Routledge.

Hamlin, M., Ross, J., & Hong, S.W. (2002). The effect of 16 weeks of regular short duration physical activity on fitness levels in primary school children. *Journal of Physical Education New Zealand, 35*(1), 47–54.

Harris, K., Kuramoto, L. K., Schulzer, M., & Retallack, J. E. (2009). Effect of school-based physical activity interventions on body mass index in children: A meta-analysis. *Canadian Medical Association Journal, 180*(7), 719–726. doi: 10.1503/cmaj.080966

Hokowhitu, B. (2014). If you are not healthy, then what are you? Healthism, colonial disease, and body-logic. In K. Fitzpatrick & R. Tinning (Eds.), *Health education: Critical perspectives* (pp. 31–47). Oxon, UK: Routledge.

Kirk, D. (2006). The obesity crisis and school physical education. *Sport, Education & Society, 11*(2), 121–133. doi: 10.1080/13573320600640660

Kirk, D., & Colquhoun, D. (1989). Healthism and physical education. *British Journal of Sociology of Education, 10*(4), 417–434. doi: 10.1080/0142569890100403

Kohn, A. (2002). *Education, Inc.: Turning learning into a business.* Portsmouth, NH: Heinemann.

Leahy, D. (2012). *Assembling a health[y] subject.* (Doctoral dissertation, Deakin University, Melbourne, Australia). Retrieved from http://dro.deakin.edu.au/view/DU:30048464

Lupton, D. (1999). 'Developing the "whole me"': Citizenship, neo-liberalism and the contemporary health and physical education curriculum. *Critical Public Health, 9*(4), 287–300. doi: 10.1080/09581599908402941

Macdonald, D. (2015). Teacher-as-knowledge-broker in a futures-oriented health and physical education. *Sport, Education and Society, 20*(1), 27–41. doi: 10.1080/13573322.2014.935320

Macdonald, D., Hay, P., & Williams, B. (2008). Should you buy? Neo-Liberalism, neo-HPE, and your neo-job. *Journal of Physical Education New Zealand, 41*(3), 6–13.

Ministry of Health. (2018). *New Zealand health survey: Annual data explorer.* Retrieved from https://minhealthnz.shinyapps.io/nz-health-survey-2016-17-annual-data-explorer/_w_453ce9aa/_w_dbe2c43e/#!/home

Morton, J. (2016). *Obesity study puts kids under lens.* Retrieved from http://www.nzherald.co.nz/lifestyle/news/article.cfm?c_id=6&objectid=11669947

Moyer, C. S. (2012). *Taxes on sugary beverages could fund obesity prevention.* Retrieved from http://www.ama-assn.org/amednews/2012/images/prhd0702.pdf

Norris, T. (2011). *Consuming schools: Commercialism and the end of politics.* Toronto, Canada: University of Toronto Press.

Ogden, C. L., Carroll, M. D., Kit, B. K., & Flegal, K. M. (2014). Prevalence of childhood and adult obesity in the United States, 2011-2012. *JAMA, 311*(8), 806–814.

Pausé, C. (2019). (Can we) get together? Fat kids and physical education. *Health Education Journal,* 1–8. doi: 10.1177/0017896919846182

Penney, D., Petrie, K., & Fellows, S. (2015). HPE in Aotearoa New Zealand: The reconfiguration of policy and pedagogic relations and privatisation of curriculum and pedagogy. *Sport, Education and Society, 20*(1), 42–56. doi: 10.1080/13573322.2014.e947566

Petrie, K., Penney, D., & Fellows, S. (2014). Health and physical education in Aotearoa New Zealand: An open market and open doors? *Asia-Pacific Journal of Health, Sport and Physical Education, 5*(1), 19–38. doi: 10.1080/18377122.2014.867791

Petersen, A., & Lupton, D. (1996). *The new public health: Health and self in the age of risk.* St Leonards, NSW: Allen & Unwin.

Powell, D. (2014). Childhood obesity, corporate philanthropy and the creeping privatisation of health education. *Critical Public Health, 24*(2), 226–238. doi: 10.1080/09581596.2013.846465

Powell, D. (2018a). Primary physical education and health. In G. Griggs & K. Petrie (Eds.), *Routledge handbook of primary physical education* (pp. 9–19). Oxon, UK: Routledge.

Powell, D. (2018b). The 'will to give': Corporations, philanthropy and schools. *Journal of Education Policy, 34*(2), 195–214. doi: 10.1080/02680939.2018.1424940

Powell, D. (2019). Revealing the privatisation of education. In M. Hill & M. Thrupp (Eds.), *The professional practice of teaching in New Zealand* (6th edition) (pp. 256–272). Melbourne, Australia: Cengage Learning.

Powell, D., & Fitzpatrick, K. (2015). 'Getting fit basically just means, like, nonfat': Children's lessons in fitness and fatness. *Sport, Education and Society, 20*(4), 463–484. doi: 10.1080/13573322.2013.777661

Powell, D., & Gard, M. (2015). The governmentality of childhood obesity: Coca-Cola, corporations and schools. *Discourse: Studies in the Cultural Politics of Education, 36*(8), 854–867. doi: 10.1080/01596306.2014.905045

Rao, D. P., Kropac, E., Do, M. T., Roberts, K. C., & Jayaraman, G. C. (2016). Childhood overweight and obesity trends in Canada. *Health Promotion and Chronic Disease Prevention in Canada: Research, Policy and Practice, 36*(9), 194–198.

Rizvi, F., & Lingard, B. (2009). *Globalizing education policy.* London: Routledge.

Saltman, K. J. (2000). *Collateral damage: Corporatizing public schools–A threat to democracy.* Oxford: Rowman & Littlefield.

Saltman, K. J. (2009). Corporatization and control of schools. In M. W. Apple, W. Au, & L. A. Gandin (Eds.), *The Routledge international handbook of critical education* (pp. 51–63). New York: Routledge.

Saltman, K. J. (2010). *The gift of education: Public education and venture philanthropy.* New York: Palgrave MacMillan.

Saltman, K. J. (2011). Introduction to the first edition. In K. J. Saltman & D. A. Gabbard (Eds.), *Education as enforcement: The militarization and corporatization of schools* (2nd edition, pp. 1–18). New York: Routledge.

Saltman, K. J., & Gabbard, D. A. (Eds.). (2011). *Education as enforcement: The militarization and corporatization of schools* (2nd edition). New York: Routledge.

Sperka, L., Enright, E., & McCuaig, L. (2018). Brokering and bridging knowledge in health and physical education: A critical discourse analysis of one external provider's curriculum. *Physical Education and Sport Pedagogy, 23*(3), 328–343.

Story, M., Nanney, M. S., & Schwartz, M. B. (2009). Schools and obesity prevention: Creating school environments and policies to promote healthy eating and physical activity. *The Milbank Quarterly, 87*(1), 71–100. doi: 10.1111/j.1468-0009.2009.00548.x

Thorpe, S. (2003). Crisis discourse in physical education and the laugh of Michel Foucault. *Sport, Education and Society, 8*(2), 131–151. doi: 10.1080/13573320309253

Tinning, R., & Glasby, T. (2002). Pedagogical work and the 'cult of the body': Considering the role of HPE in the context of the 'new public health'. *Sport, Education and Society, 7,* 109–119.

Trost, S. G. (2006). Public health and physical education. In D. Kirk, D. MacDonald & M. O'Sullivan (Eds.), *The handbook of physical education* (pp. 163–187). London: Sage.

Vander Schee, C., & Boyles, D. (2010). 'Exergaming', corporate interests and the crisis discourse of childhood obesity. *Sport, Education and Society, 15*(2), 169–185. doi: 10.1080/13573321003683828

Williams, B. J., & Macdonald, D. (2015). Explaining outsourcing in health, sport and physical education. *Sport, Education and Society, 20*(1), 57–72. doi: 0.1080/13573322.2014.914902

World Health Organization. (2018a). *Global strategy on diet, physical activity and health: Childhood overweight and obesity*. Retrieved from https://www.who.int/dietphysicalactivity/childhood/en/

World Health Organization. (2018b). *Global strategy on diet, physical activity and health: The role of the private sector*. Retrieved from http://www.who.int/dietphysicalactivity/childhood_private_sector/en/index.html

Wright, J., & Harwood, V. (2009). *Biopolitics and the obesity epidemic: Governing bodies*. New York: Routledge.

3

THE CORPORATE 'GIFT'
OF HEALTHY LIFESTYLES

Fighting childhood obesity has become a key corporate philanthropy strategy for 'Big Food', where it is crucial for food and drink corporations to *be seen* to be trying to reduce childhood obesity, change their marketing practices, and improve children's health (Herrick, 2009). I use the phrase corporate philanthropy to describe a range of business practices where corporations provide 'gifts' to schools, charities, and other organisations (see Guthrie, Arum, Roksa, & Damaske, 2008; Porter & Kramer, 2002; Powell, 2018). This form of 'giving' is varied, ranging from sponsorship of 'not-for-profit' organisations, donating money directly to schools, promotions that encourage communities to support schools, providing free educational resources, and supporting different organisations with funding and/or personnel. However, as I have argued previously (Powell, 2018) and hope to demonstrate in this chapter, corporate philanthropy is not simply altruism: those who give do so in order to receive.

This is a type of "strategic philanthropy" (King, 2006, p. 4) that is clearly visible and active in public education, public health, and other spheres. Although there are different terms used to describe this "new philanthropy" (Ball, 2012, p. 66), such as philanthrocapitalism (Edwards, 2008), a central concern shared by a number of scholars is that it is a form of philanthropy inextricably interconnected to the business interests of the private sector, where a 'hot button' topic, such as childhood obesity or breast cancer, is used to "maximize the impact of giving and to align contributions with the company's business goals and brand characteristics" (King, 2006, p. 8).

In Samantha King's (2006) insightful and provocative critique of breast cancer philanthropy – *Pink Ribbons, Inc.: Breast Cancer and the Politics of Philanthropy* – she demonstrates how corporate philanthropy is now positioned as a "morally and economically viable means through which to respond to societal needs" (King, 2006, p. xxvii). Ball (2012) describes this as a kind of neoliberal "social capitalism" (p. 66) where 'new philanthropists' (including businesses, industry groups, wealthy individuals, corporate foundations) use business strategies to target social problems. It is a strategy that means the private sector now assumes "socio-moral duties that were heretofore assigned to civil organizations, governmental entities and state agencies" (Shamir, 2008, p. 9).

However, the corporate 'will to give' (Powell, 2018) can be understood as being far more than simply a moral or social agenda, but a way for private sector organisations to receive "clear and measurable impacts and outcomes from their 'investments' of time and money" (Ball, 2012, p. 70). It is unsurprising then that a company's endeavour to be philanthropic is intimately tied to "other departments such as marketing, public affairs, and government relations; the forming of partnerships with community groups, local governments, and other companies that share a common interest in a particular concern" (King, 2006, p. 8). In the case of childhood obesity, philanthropy is used as a means for corporations to be seen as healthy and socially responsible, to successfully shape public policy, and to profit.

Health–washing: the socially responsible corporation?

Corporate social responsibility (CSR) programmes are an integral mechanism for corporations to achieve their philanthropic aims. Also called corporate citizenship or stakeholder management, CSR has become a common activity in private sector organisations across the globe. Pedersen (2006, p. 7), for example, writes: "An infinite number of scholars and practitioners sing its praise in annual reports, conference papers, journal articles and magazines …. Corporate citizenship and related terms … have swept across the world and become catchwords of the new millennium". This is perhaps not that surprising, as governments are increasingly interested in CSR due to the "emergence of a new and seductive 'truth' about CSR, namely that it is good for business and good for the economy" (Vallentin & Murillo, 2010, p. 152). However, there is much disagreement as to whether the benefits of CSR are equally shared between stakeholders and shareholders.

Advocates for CSR often promote it as a 'win–win' situation for all involved. The corporate reports/websites from Nestlé, the world's largest food company, exemplified the notion that CSR is good for shareholders and stakeholders alike. Nestlé asserted that their global CSR programme *Creating Shared Value* "is not about philanthropy. It is about leveraging core activities and partnerships for the joint benefit of people in the countries where we operate and of our shareholders" (Nestlé Singapore, n.d., para. 6). While CSR is often viewed as "simply philanthropy by a different name, it can be defined broadly as the efforts corporations make above and beyond regulation to balance the needs of stakeholders with the need to make a profit" (Doane, 2005, p. 23). Proponents of CSR programmes tend to draw on similar rationales: sustainability (environmental and social), moral appeal (a duty to be 'good citizens'), license to operate (permission from stakeholders to conduct business), and/or reputation (to improve brand, image, morale, and stock price) (Porter & Kramer, 2006).

Conversely, critics of CSR view it as a public relations strategy, designed primarily to increase shareholder value through profits. For instance, Doane

(2005, p. 25) writes that CSR "simplifies some rather complex arguments and fails to acknowledge that ultimately, trade-offs must be made between the financial health of the company and ethical outcomes. And when they are made, profit undoubtedly wins over principles". The profit-seeking motives for corporations to be strategically socially responsible are closely tied to their marketing strategies. As Blanding (2010) argues in his book *The Coke Machine: The Dirty Truth Behind the World's Favorite Soft Drink*:

> The danger of CSR initiatives is that they have become such a branding tool that they make it seem like the opposite is true – that companies are somehow investing in causes out of a motive of self-sacrifice, rather than *partnering* with causes for mutual benefit. And as branding has become the primary reason for CSR, the appearance of doing something can overshadow the benefits of doing it. (2010, pp. 136–137, emphasis in original)

In other words, the *marketing* of CSR activities is a pivotal tactic in itself. Corporations that do not promote their philanthropic, socially responsible activities and ideologies risk losing their markets to competitors who 'do' CSR 'better'. CSR and advertising are, therefore, "strategic complements" (Bazillier & Vauday, 2009, p. 1) and in the school-based war on childhood obesity we frequently witness how corporate philanthropy goes hand-in-hand with marketing strategies.

Saltman and Goodman (2011) argue that corporations like Coca-Cola, Nestlé, and BP target public education to conceal their negative impact on society and promote themselves "as a 'responsible corporate citizen' supporting beleaguered schools with its corporate philanthropy" (p. 36). Controversial issues (e.g. obesity, climate change) and somewhat disreputable industries (e.g. 'junk food', petrochemical) are the most common corporate philanthropy/social responsibility programmes implemented in schools (Molnar, 2005). In this way, we can see how CSR may act as an effective type of "reputation insurance" (MacDonald, 2008, p. 71). As Kenway and Bullen (2001, p. 100) point out: "Not only do schools offer a way to establish and maintain a high public profile, but an opportunity for businesses with doubtful reputations or bad publicity to practice some reverse psychology". For example, in the current context of global concerns about the climate change, BP and ExxonMobil have produced educational resources about mining, fossil fuels, and the combustion engine (for critiques of these resources see Norris, 2011; Saltman & Goodman, 2011). These particular types of environmental CSR initiatives are described by some authors as green-washing (e.g. see Bazillier & Vauday, 2009; MacDonald, 2008); a form of 'disinformation' about an industry's or corporation's environmental practices "from organizations seeking to repair public reputations and further shape public images" (Laufer, 2003, p. 253).

In a similar vein, the term *health-washing* may be appropriate to describe the attempts of corporations and industries to use corporate philanthropy to deflect accusations they are part of the problem of childhood obesity (and other health concerns), to repair reputations, and to position themselves as responsible organisations who genuinely want to be (seen as) part of the solution. As the International Food & Beverage Alliance (IFBA) asserted in their *2014 Progress Report*:

> IFBA companies have made responsible marketing to children a critical part of their effort to promote balanced diets and healthy, active lifestyles. In 2008, members voluntarily adopted an approach restricting how and what they advertise to children globally. This approach promotes product innovation reformulation and choice, and through education and communication, the benefits of healthy diets and physical activity among children. (IFBA, 2015, p. 32)

School-based 'anti-obesity' and 'education' programmes devised, funded, or implemented through corporate philanthropy may act as a form of health-washing by serving two important functions: diverting public attention from 'less agreeable' practices (e.g. marketing of nutrient-poor food) *and* shaping consumers' image of the corporation as an altruistic, socially responsible, health-promoting organisation. Corporations and their partners also attempt to health-wash a 'captive audience' – children in schools – through a rapid proliferation of healthy lifestyles education programmes being gifted to children all around the world.

Schools, corporations, and healthy lifestyles programmes

In the context of global anxieties about childhood obesity and children's (un)healthy lifestyles, schools, teachers, and children have been and continue to be targeted by a myriad of anti-obesity interventions. Depending upon who is designing and implementing the school-based intervention, interventions are typically used to either decrease individual children's Body Mass Index (BMI), decrease the average BMI of a population of children (e.g. in a school, a school district, city, or country), or decrease the prevalence of obesity in that population. In addition, school-based anti-obesity interventions have tended to focus on one of the three distinct, yet often overlapping, types of interventions: *physical activity* interventions to get children more physically active now, as well as 'into the habit' of being more active for the future; *nutrition* interventions, such as teaching children how to make healthy choices or restricting certain foods to be consumed within the school; and a more *holistic* interventionist approach taking into physical activity, nutrition, food marketing, school sport, physical education, active transport, playgrounds, extra-curricular activities, and other factors, which are considered to contribute to a so-called obesogenic school environment.

The types of programmes that are marketed by corporations and their partners as 'part of the solution' to childhood obesity often draw on aspects of interventionist approaches, but contain some key points of difference. For instance, the corporate-produced programmes rarely, if ever, measure the fatness of children (which in itself is a positive aspect for the children involved, given the plethora of research that has problematised the weighing of children and the use of BMI[1]). Curiously, they seldom seem to draw on notions of 'fighting obesity' in the promotional material that schools, teachers, or children receive. This is, of course, not to say that the very same programmes are not promoted to policymakers and the public as a genuine, even effective, strategy to solve childhood obesity. However, the various programmes tend to be promoted as a type of resource, event, or practice that will help teach children how to make healthy lifestyle choices (and therefore be less fat) – both now and in the future. For this reason, I refer to the programmes that corporations 'give' to schools and wider communities as a type of *healthy lifestyles education* (see also Dinan-Thompson, 2009). This is an umbrella term I will continue to use for the vast array of programmes, resources, funding, partnerships, schemes, pledges, competitions, edutainment events, commitments, sponsorships, external providers, and lessons that are related to the business strategies of corporations and attempt to shape schools, teachers, and children. As I will illustrate below and illuminate in the rest of this book, these healthy lifestyles education programmes are inextricably intertwined with both the desire of corporations to be seen to be altruistically 'fighting obesity' and their desire to profit.

The website of the IFBA provides plenty of examples of how their need to be 'part of the solution' to childhood obesity is made possible through connecting their corporate philanthropy strategies with schools and children. For instance, one of the IFBA's (2015, p. 7) commitments – to realise the goals of the World Health Organization's *Global Strategy on Diet, Physical Activity, and Health* – is to "promote healthier lifestyles and increased physical activity in communities around the world and in the workforce". In 2015 the IFBA reported on their progress in making these commitments. They wrote:

> IFBA members have been working to support hundreds of initiatives around the world in support of this commitment, including school-based programmes to raise nutrition, health and wellness awareness of school-age children and help teachers and families to promote healthy eating and active living; sporting and other athletic events and activities promoting physical activity among children and young people; and community-based programmes and targeted marketing and education campaigns that raise awareness, promote behaviour change and encourage consumers to adopt healthy habits and physical activity.
>
> Building on this long history of collaboration, in September 2014, members committed to continue their support for innovative,

community-based programmes designed to promote balanced diets and regular physical activity; and to support projects that can yield evidence-based approaches and research that can help contribute to the learning around tackling NCDs. Members also committed to help implement the strategies called for in the WHO Global Action Plan on NCDs, aimed at reducing the prevalence of insufficient physical activity. (2015, p. 40)

In this progress report, the IFBA also provides a lengthy list of case studies as 'proof' they are meeting their commitments to the World Health Organization. These healthy lifestyles education programmes employed a mixture of physical activity initiatives, sports events, incentive schemes, and nutrition education resources to target children (and adults) within and outside of schools, such as Nestlé's *United for Healthier Kids* (U4HK) in Mexico and the Philippines; Ferrero's global *Kinder+Sport* project; Mars and *Go for Kids* pedometer programme in China; the *Vitamin D Mission* with Kellogg and Danone in the United Kingdom; General Mills' *Champion for Healthy Kids* nutrition and fitness programmes in the United States; Grupo Bimbo and the *Futbolito Bimbo Soccer Tournament* in Mexico, Chile, Guatemala, and the United States; Kellogg's Gaelic Athletic Association of Ireland *Cúl Camps* (summer camps) in Ireland; Mars and *Iss bewusst und sei aktic* (eat sensibly and be active) programme in Germany (providing education to Turkish migrant children on "how to live an active lifestyle and the responsible consumption of confectionary" (p. 44)); Mondelēz International's *Health for Life* gardening and cooking programme in Birmingham, England; PepsiCo (and partners, the National Dairy Council and National Football League) implementing *GENYOUth* nutrition and physical activity programmes in the United States; McDonald's *Getting Kids Active* sports tournaments in France; and, Nestlé's worldwide *Healthy Kids Global Programme* (which, according to the report, reached 7.6 million children). Curiously, out of the 11 corporate members of the alliance, The Coca-Cola Company was the only corporation absent from the case studies. All of the programmes mentioned above drew heavily on the importance of multi-sector partnerships and the need to promote balanced diets and regular physical activity. Indeed, the implementation of physical activity and sport 'solutions' to obesity (the 'energy out' component of energy balance) tends to be favoured by the food and drink industry over programmes that teach children to reduce 'energy in'.

Before I provide in later chapters a more in-depth examination of how these programmes are taken up in schools and understood by teachers and children, it is essential to give an overview and specific examples of the types of programmes (both globally and in New Zealand) that 'count' as philanthropic solutions to childhood obesity and unhealthy lifestyles. After all, the food and drink industry made a commitment to the World Health Organization to "not to engage in any commercial communications to students related to food and beverage products in primary schools, except where specifically requested by, or agreed with, the school administration for educational purposes" (IFBA, 2011, p. 4). These programmes include incentive schemes, fundraising, sports and physical activity initiatives, and free educational resources. Some programmes are implemented by well-known multinational corporations, while others feature regional companies and not-for-profits. A number are closely related to the food and drink industry, yet others are private sector organisations that do not appear to have any obvious links to childhood obesity or children's health. Many programmes have been rolled out in different forms across the globe, whereas others have been created for a specific national context. Even though all of these healthy lifestyles-type programmes target schools and children in some way, shape, or form, their connections to meaningful educational experiences appear to be fairly tenuous.

Consumer-oriented philanthropy: fundraising and incentive schemes

Not all corporate 'solutions' to childhood obesity have an obvious connection to teaching and learning in schools. Some private sector companies have managed to come through the 'back door' of schools through a variety of fundraising and incentive schemes that encourage families to consume particular products that will supposedly benefit schools and make children healthier. Fundraising and incentive schemes tend to be less publicised as 'part of the solution' to obesity than explicit healthy lifestyles education programmes and resources, but nevertheless still constitute an important element of the overall strategy for corporations to be seen to be both philanthropic and health-promoting.

Fundraising is a school activity that traditionally was planned and implemented by an individual school and community to raise money for essential resources. In contemporary times, and with schools often underfunded, fundraising has become an increasingly important income for schools as well as an opportunity for corporations to gain access to schools, students, and parents and to improve their brand image and profit margins. Indeed, over a decade ago, Molnar and colleagues reported that the most prevalent form of food advertising in American elementary schools was through fundraising (Molnar, Boninger, Wilkinson, & Fogarty, 2008). Fundraising in schools has also been the subject of much debate based on the idea that it actually causes childhood obesity. For instance, Richards, Darling, and Reeder (2005) argued that fundraising undermines health education and endorses children's consumption of high fat/sugar foods, such as sausages and cakes. This view was echoed by Utter, Scragg, Percival, and Beaglehole (2009, p. 6) who stated that "good nutrition should have nothing to do with fundraising ... funding for schools should not be at the expense of children's health, just as schools would never be permitted to sell cigarettes or alcohol".

The decision by governments, local authorities, school districts, or individual schools to 'ban' certain types of foods to be used for fundraising has frequently been met with strong opposition. Molnar and Garcia (2005), for instance, described how such restrictions caused outrage in the media and public, with those responsible for 'unhealthy' food fundraising bans described as a 'food Nazis' and 'communists'. Recently in New Zealand, the Ministry of Education's first Chief Education Health and Nutrition Advisor, Grant Schofield, publicly called for a ban on selling chocolates as fundraisers for schools, justifying his decision based on concerns about childhood obesity and that "this may be the first generation of humans where the kids will not live as long as their parents" (Newshub, 2017). The erstwhile Minister of Health, Jonathan Coleman, replied by also drawing on the 'life-expectancy sound-bite' (Gard, 2011), stating that: "Obesity is a serious issue threatening the health of young New Zealanders, which means some of our kids could end up living shorter lives than their parents" (Wiggins, 2017). On Twitter that same day, however, Coleman tweeted: "I'm happy for schools to continue doing chocolate box fund raisers – I've sold plenty of them myself to help my kids' school". Schools in New Zealand are still allowed to fundraise by selling chocolates.

In response to worries about childhood obesity, a number of 'healthy' fundraising opportunities have opened up for schools. In New Zealand, the Heart Foundation (2018) has a "free list of fundraising ideas will inspire you to raise money while staying healthy too", which includes ideas such as green 'Hulk' smoothies with spinach, plain popcorn, and the *Adidas School Fun Run*. Adidas originally set up this school fundraising organisation in Australia, which is advertised as a "healthy fundraiser that ensures all schools have a viable alternative to junk food fundraising" (see Tuggerah Lakes Secondary College, n.d.). Brendan Hopp, General Manager of The Fundraising Group, stated that "businesses such as adidas and CUA [Credit Union Australia] are seeing the real value in being a part of the solution to childhood obesity for Australian school children .... Too often we see schools and community groups choose unhealthy fundraisers with no educational value. The *adidas* School Fun-Run offers fitness education, health messages and encourages students to get active" (Tuggerah Lakes Secondary College, n.d.). These public relations messages are repeated *verbatim* in other school websites and local newspapers. To reiterate points made earlier, the idea that the philanthropic activities of private sector companies should be 'part of the solution' to childhood obesity continues to help corporations from a range of industries – not just the food and drink industry – to get into schools, to be seen to be healthy, and to be perceived as having a vital role in the education of children.

Another type of commercialism in schools that fit in closely with the aims and *modus operandi* of fundraising are *incentive schemes*, which "provide money, goods, or services to a school or school district when its students, parents or staff engage in a specific activity" (Molnar & Boninger, 2015, p. 28). There are a variety of terms used to describe incentive schemes, including 'voucher collection schemes' (Ball, 2007), 'proof-of-purchase', and 'receipt-redemption' schemes (Molnar et al., 2008). In these programmes, parents and other members of the school community (including children and teachers) are encouraged to purchase particular brands of products, or shop at a specific store in order to collect vouchers to 'donate' to their local school. These vouchers can then be redeemed for school-related resources, services, activities, and events. These types of schemes are a form of consumer-oriented philanthropy (King, 2006), whereby consumers are encouraged to buy a certain product over others based on the notion that their purchase will, in some way, benefit a charitable cause (e.g. the use of the pink ribbon logo on packaging or marketing a promise to donate money from every purchase of a certain brand of nappies to an immunisation programme in a developing country). They are also schemes that increasingly exploit the current moral panics about children's health, lifestyles, and bodies.

In the United Kingdom, for instance, redemption schemes have been created and promoted by major supermarkets, such as Sainsbury's *Active Kids* campaign and Tesco's *Tesco for Schools and Clubs*. Tesco's promotion was 'applauded' by a Member of Parliament, Helen Grant (2011), who reported Tesco had given "over 440,000 pieces of useful equipment worth a staggering £9.3m to schools and clubs around the country". One early criticism of these voucher schemes was that parents, teachers, and even children were required to spend a significant amount of money to redeem the equipment and resources for schools. For instance, for a school to receive a trampoline in the Tesco scheme, parents and other members of the school community would have needed to spend almost one million pounds (Robertson, 2007).

The marketing of these schemes and the products that the schools/students may receive as a result of their own and the private sector's 'philanthropy' is strongly connected to concerns about childhood obesity and children's lifestyles. The corporate rhetoric reproduces the assumption that unhealthy lifestyles, poor diet, and physical inactivity are the primary cause of obesity, and that their incentive schemes will somehow 'encourage' children to live healthy lifestyle for life. For instance, Sainsbury's strategic report from 2017 stated:

> Our commitment to helping children to lead healthy, active lives is well known – we have been encouraging children, regardless of ability or impairment, to get active and lead healthier lives for the last 11 years with our Active Kids scheme. The initiative emphasizes both calories in and calories out, helping children to understand the importance of diet and exercise. (J Sainsbury plc, 2017, p. 27)

In New Zealand, children and parents are encouraged by schools and the Yummy Fruit Company to participate in the *Yummy Apples Sticker Promotion*. For this scheme, children are asked to bring stickers off certain types of fruit from particular supermarkets to school, in which they are collected and sent off in order to win a share of sports equipment: "The more you collect, the more sports gear you get so get going and start collecting" (The Yummy Fruit Company, 2019, para. 1). A connection is also made between buying apples, collecting stickers, receiving sports equipment, and making children healthier. On an earlier Yummy Apple's website, the scheme was endorsed by former international footballer Wynton Rufer: "I couldn't think of a better way to be encouraging our kids to be actively healthier Kiwis. Eating Yummy apples and getting free sports gear in return is an awesome campaign to be proactively supporting" (The Yummy Fruit Company, n.d.).

I share with Molnar (2005) an unease that the collection of box tops and vouchers, and fundraising in general, makes children more familiar with particular brands and companies stores and encourages children to develop positive attitudes towards them. This is part of the embedded nature of these activities. Children's attitudes towards brands and products are deeply connected with their emotions – in this case, feeling good about helping their school 'buy' more books and sports equipment. Additionally, the corporations advertise themselves as almost a redeemer of public education, rescuing cash-strapped schools from financial difficulties. For instance, Sainsbury's proclaim that: "With budget cuts taking effect, it is more important than ever, that we all do what we can to make sure sport continues to be a priority within schools" (Smithers, 2011). Of course, these fundraising and incentive schemes do little to challenge the fact that the reason many schools need fundraise in the first place is because of a lack of government funding. They also fail to address the powerful sociopolitical forces that shape inequities in children's health and education.

Physical activity and sport programmes

The use of physical activity and sports initiatives to 'teach' children to live healthier lifestyles is a common corporate philanthropy tactic that is also used as proof of the food and drink industry's 'commitment' to solve childhood obesity. Ferrero's *Kinder+Sport* project is one such initiative, "one of the four pillars of Ferrero's corporate social responsibility strategy" that appears to be gaining considerable traction across Europe, Asia, the Middle East, and Central and South America:

> Today 'Kinder+Sport' is a global project with a mission to facilitate physical activity, as an easy and daily practice, among young children worldwide. The project is built on a partnership model – collaborations are established with national and international sports federations, associations and institutions (currently numbering more than 90) to design specialized and innovative programmes within a framework of physical activity. Education is at the core of the programme – both in the selection of the activities and in the evaluation of innovative projects .... In 2012, the 'Joy of moving' research

project was launched – a three-year initiative, to examine how quality physical education targeted to promote the holistic development
of pre-school and primary school pupils may be realized at the local
level by means of collaborations between the public and private sector …. At the end of 2014, 'Kinder+Sport' was active in 21 countries
and 'moving' 3.8 million children. By 2018, Ferrero aims to reach
30 countries, move 5 million children and spread the 'Joy of moving'
methodology in all the countries where Kinder+Sport is established.[2]
(IFBA, 2015, p. 42)

In the above statement we can see a number of key elements that regularly
feature in these corporate designed, funded, and implemented solutions to
childhood obesity: the use of corporate philanthropy/social responsibility;
the employment of partnerships and collaboration with multiple organisations ("more than 90"); the importance of educating young children about
nutrition and physical activity; and the need to globalise these programmes.
These features of sports and physical activity programmes are also strongly
evident when they are promoted within a particular region.

The United Kingdom is one of the 21 countries that has taken up a localised version of *Kinder+Sport: Move & Learn*. This version is "a national school
project for children aged 9-10", an initiative where "children spend 45 minutes in the classroom learning about the body, nutrition and the importance
of exercise, then 45 minutes enjoying physical exercise in the form of football, dodgeball or handball" (Ferrero, 2017a). In a 2017 media release on the
company website, Ferrero (2017b) promoted their programme as one that,

> forms part of our global social responsibility commitments and is
> one of our most exciting initiatives. Designed to get children mov-
> ing by encouraging dynamic play and sports amongst young people
> and their families, we have already moved over 15 million children
> in 27 countries around the world.

The company then drew on the childhood obesity 'crisis' to further emphasise the importance of their philanthropic initiative:

> As childhood obesity levels continue to rise across Britain, Ferrero
> recognises it has a responsibility to take positive action to promote
> nutritional education and build awareness of the importance of a
> balanced diet and active lifestyle amongst children. That's why, in
> 2013, we launched Kinder + Sport in the UK.

Although the statistics of how many countries or children have participated
(or will participate) in the project do not appear to align between different
documents and public relations messages (e.g. from a total of 15 million in
2017 to 4.4. million in 2018), we can see yet again, how the same central

principles of corporate-led healthy lifestyles education programmes are reproduced: social responsibility; the need to globalise the programme; a focus on
children needing to be educated (by a chocolate manufacturer) on the importance of an active lifestyle and balanced diet; and, of course, responding to a
crisis of childhood obesity.

On the *Kinder+Sport* website, Ferrero (2017c) promotes a number of "bind-
ing rules" for the project "to ensure a universal value to the programme",
including the need to be global, responsible, consistent, educational, and
not commercial ("it has no aim to profit"). However, for a number of the
Kinder+Sport programmes, it is difficult to (a) see how they are educational,
and (b) how they are *not* commercial. The Swedish iteration, for example, is
marketed on the website as being "very active in promoting movement of
children and young adults, and has been particularly involved in promoting the sport of running" through Kinder+Sport playing "a leading role in
supporting the Stockholm Mini Marathon" (Ferrero, 2017d). According to
Ferrero (2017d), in 2016 "6,000 children aged 5–13 took part with a crowd of
over 10,000 spectators cheering them on to the finish". However, there does
not seem to be any clear educational elements to this programme. As with a
number of sports and physical activity initiatives, they appear to be based on
more of a hope that children will learn something positive from the experience, rather than any explicit teaching or pedagogical strategy designed to
develop children's skills, knowledge, or understanding. This is not to say that
children who participated in this particular event did not or will not learn
anything (positive or negative) from their experiences, but rather to draw
attention to the idea that claims of an educative value are often questionable
and lack strong evidence.

Moreover, the idea that CSR programmes are not commercial belies
the fact that corporations (and their partners) use a number of obvious and
stealthy marketing strategies to promote the corporation and the brand. I
argue that if there was no commercial aspect to a particular programme, that
there should also be no publicity, no branding, and no promotional material
that advertises the corporation's involvement. Yet the Swedish programme
was promoted on the *Kinder+Sport* website as being "particularly active with
logos on all the promotional material, including the Mini Marathon's highly
successful webpage, banners at the finishing line and welcome gym–bags and
neck warmers: participation was so high that 6,000 of each were distributed"
(Ferrero, 2017d). There are also multiple photographs on the same website
that feature the *Kinder+Sport* logo – a logo that often includes the logo of the
Kinder product brand. As mentioned previously, any CSR programme must
be closely interconnected with broader business strategies, including the marketing tactics, of the corporate 'investors'.

In New Zealand, there are numerous examples of major multinational
corporations and smaller organisations delivering – or at least supporting
the delivery – of physical activity and sports initiatives in schools. One of
the more obvious examples of a corporatised physical activity programme

was McDonald's *My Greatest Feat*. This was a physical activity/pedometer programme implemented by McDonald's in 2008 (in conjunction with the Beijing Olympics) and in 2010 (FIFA World Cup), and both in partnership with the New Zealand Olympic Committee. Schools that signed up to the programme received free pedometers and teachers could record and track the number of steps each student completed by entering students' details into the McDonald's *My Greatest Feat* website. The programme was widely promoted on the news, through children's television programmes, in McDonald's restaurants, and online. Approximately one-fifth of all primary school students in New Zealand (including home-schooled children) participated in the programme, with McDonald's claiming making it was "the largest physical activity programme ever undertaken in New Zealand" (Scoop, 2010).[3]

There are also plenty of school-based physical activity and sport programmes in New Zealand where the private sector acts or acted as a minor partner or sponsor. For example, the *ASB Football in Schools* programme in New Zealand was promoted by ASB (a bank), and was sponsored by McDonald's, Persil, Volkswagon, Nike, New Zealand Football, and the Auckland Football Federation. This "football literacy programme" included "2 × 5 week blocks of football curriculum delivered in school time as part of a typical physical education class" (New Zealand Football, n.d.). Like many other physical activity and sports programmes in schools, its rationale was one that was buttressed by the usual assumptions about children: "With physical activity levels among kids on the slide, and obesity on the rise, it is critical to get kiwi kids back on track" (Hutt City Council, n.d., para. 3).

Although some programmes had little or no involvement from food and drink corporations, for others it was not always obvious how the private sector was implicated in the funding or design of a particular physical activity or sport initiative in schools. For instance, the *Get Set Go* programme is a partnership between Athletics New Zealand and ActivePost to teach three- to seven-year-olds 'fundamental movement skills' (see Athletics New Zealand, 2018). Although developed and run by Athletics New Zealand (the national body for athletics), the programme was implemented in schools by coaches from Regional Sports Trusts (RSTs).[4] *Get Set Go* at St Saviour's School, for instance, was conducted by Jonie, a coach employed by RST Sport Auckland. The justification for *Get Set Go* was built on the assumption that children are too inactive and too fat:

> Research also shows that New Zealand children appear to be following the global trends of increasingly being more overweight and suffering obesity problems (Ministry of Health, 2003). Changes in lifestyle and technology are all contributing factors of these trends, leading to a negative impact on the overall health and wellbeing of our children, and affecting the capability for enjoyable participation and lifelong interest in sport and an active lifestyle. (Athletics New Zealand, 2013, p. 6)

ActivePost is the CSR/community wellness programme of New Zealand Post, a state-owned enterprise responsible for providing the postal service in New Zealand. State-owned enterprises are companies that function as a private business – where the focus is on being profitable – yet are owned by the state. In New Zealand, they also tend to be former government departments that were corporatised, such as the case of New Zealand Post, which was formerly the New Zealand Post Office. The only 'true' private sector player for *Get Set Go* was a consultant, Mike Hall-Taylor, the CEO of private sports consultancy firm HTC Sportsworld. According to their website (www.htcsportsworld.com) they are "global consultants in sport", with expertise in sponsorship, management, brand development, brand licensing, and strategic consultancy. Hall-Taylor's interests are listed as business strategy, development, investments, marketing, and sponsorship. Yet, nowhere on the website is there mention of HTC Sportsworld's experience or interest in obesity, education, or schools, and neither *Get Set Go* nor ActivePost were promoted on the website as clients or partners.

The *ActivePost Small Sticks In-School* programme (hereinafter *Small Sticks*) was designed by the national hockey organisation, Hockey New Zealand, and also received funding and support from ActivePost, as well as Fuji-Xerox, Ford, and New Zealand Community Trust – a 'pokie trust'[5] (for more details about pokie trusts in New Zealand and their connections to the gambling industry and charities, see Chapter 4). During my research at St Saviour's School, all students experienced four hockey sessions coached by Andrea, a representative hockey player from Auckland Hockey, whose training for the Small Sticks programme involved – in her words – a "very boring" "two-hour coaching seminar".

moveMprove was designed by GymSports New Zealand – the National Sports Organisation (NSO) for Men's and Women's Artistic Gymnastics, Rhythmic Gymnastics, Trampoline, and Aerobics, although it was also made possible by support from a number of key players, including Sport New Zealand (a Crown entity[6]), The Lion Foundation (another pokie trust), the New Zealand Olympic Committee, and local gymnastics clubs. According to the developers of the programme it was "a foundation skills programme, not a gymnastic programme" (GymSports New Zealand, 2006), although every *moveMprove* session I observed at St Saviour's School and Dudley School included numerous traditional gymnastics movements, such as forward rolls, jumping over a vault, and swinging on a horizontal bar. Locally endorsed gymnastics clubs would provide the school with equipment, as well as the coaches to instruct the students in foundation/gymnastics movement skills.

As I will explore in subsequent chapters, many physical activity and sports initiatives that target children tend to have a fairly weak connection to education. Yes, they may 'involve' children or schools through providing different events and coaching sessions, but they do not necessarily provide quality learning experiences that are underpinned by official curricula or taught by qualified teachers (see also Powell, 2015). When it comes to nutrition, however, there seems to be a stronger desire to explicitly 'teach' children about food, eating, and making healthy lifestyle choices through CSR programmes.

Nutrition education resources

The notion of education is employed by the food and drink industry (as well as other organisations and partners) as a key means to be seen as 'part of the solution' to childhood obesity. Take the EU Pledge as one example. This is, according the EU Pledge (2018a) website,

> a voluntary initiative by leading food and beverage companies to change the way they advertise to children … a response from industry leaders to calls made by the EU institutions for the food industry to use commercial communications to support parents in making the right diet and lifestyle choices for their children.

The 21 members of the EU Pledge include IFBA corporations (Nestlé, Ferrero, Kellogg's, Mondelēz International, Mars, PepsiCo, General Mills, The Coca-Cola Company, Unilever, and Danone), as well as McDonalds Europe, a number of corporate members of the European Snacks Association (e.g. Amica Chips, Intersnack, KiMs), and other leading food and drink companies, including Burger King and Scandinavian dairy giant Arla Foods. The pledge is also supported and endorsed by the World Federation of Advertisers.[7] The EU Pledge consists of two central commitments:

> No advertising of products to children under 12 years, except for products which fulfill common nutritional criteria. For the purpose of this initiative, "advertising to children under 12 years" means advertising to media audiences with a minimum of 35% of children under 12 years.
> No communication related to products in primary schools, except where specifically requested by, or agreed with, the school administration for educational purposes. (EU Pledge, 2018b)

Although at first glance it is not precisely clear what 'educational purposes' may include or exclude, the EU Pledge members provide the following footnote to explain their promise "not to engage in food or beverage product marketing communications to children in primary schools":

> Menus or displays for food and beverage products offered for sale, charitable donations or fundraising activities, public service messages, government subsidised/endorsed schemes, such as the EU School Milk Programme, and items provided to school administrators for education purposes or for their personal use are not covered.

> EU Pledge members commit to developing and publishing specific
> guidelines on permissible activities in schools which are undertaken
> as part of companies' corporate social responsibility programmes.
> (EU Pledge, 2018c)

Indeed, there are so many exceptions to their commitment, it is difficult
to fathom any aspect of schooling that is actually immune to their marketing communications, aside from an uninvited Ronald McDonald running through a classroom throwing free Happy Meal vouchers to children
(although if he shouted 'make healthy choices!' this would probably count as
an educational purpose).

To look at a more specific example of how corporations employ notions
of education to market their socially responsible, obesity-fighting activities,
we can examine the strategies of IFBA and EU Pledge member Danone,
which has also made a global commitment to educate 'future generations to
eat healthily'. Danone positions itself simultaneously as a socially responsible,
educational, health promotion organisation, with

> one of the major axes of its corporate responsibility to help people
> adopt healthy lifestyles and eating habits. Designing specific pro-
> grammes directed at children, in a context of rising childhood obe-
> sity, is a major factor in making this mission durable: the adults of
> tomorrow need to know better. (Danone, 2013)

Danone's endeavour to help children "adopt healthier eating habits" is based
on two key strategies: bringing "health through food to as many people as
possible" and to lead "a wide range of educational actions in the countries
in which it is located" (Danone, 2013). These socially responsible strategies
are supported by the Danone Institute, a network of 13 local institutes and
one international institute that "are non-profit organizations dedicated to
non-commercial activities" (Danone Institute International, 2015, para. 1).

One of the Danone's 'specific programmes directed at children' to teach
'the adults of tomorrow need to know better' is their United Kingdom *Eat
Like a Champ* programme: "Given the pressing social issue of poor nutrition and growing child obesity in the United Kingdom, Danone believe that
they have a role to play in promoting a healthy diet and lifestyle as part of
their corporate social responsibility agenda" (Danone, 2011). The *Eat Like a
Champ* programme is "a free, evidence-based healthy eating education programme aimed at primary school children", with the central aim "to **tackle
the growing issue of poor nutrition and obesity amongst children**
through six specially tailored lessons about healthy eating, hydration and staying active" and "to make healthy eating **exciting**, and to **inspire** children to
adopt the healthy choices of champions they admire" (Danone, 2011, bold in
original). To further promote the programme, Danone draws on notions of
expertise, as well as public health and public education policy, by stating that

the resources were produced "in collaboration with the **British Nutrition Foundation** to ensure that the lessons are of the highest possible standard", they are "up to date with the latest government guidelines, and complement primary school curricula throughout the UK", and have been "updated to reflect Public Health Englands' [sic] recent changes to the Eatwell Guide" (Danone, 2011, bold in original).

Danone's global CSR strategy and their UK-based initiative once again reinforces the central 'pillars' of corporate-led nutrition education programmes: dominant discourses of a childhood obesity as a growing crisis; the necessity for corporate philanthropy to intervene in children's schooling and lives; the need for globalisation of such programmes; and the requirement for children to be educated – "to know better" – in order to be able to make healthy lifestyle choices and not be fat (see also Powell, 2014a). They also illustrate the need for corporations to partner with trustworthy partners, such as the British Nutrition Foundation, to create their own 'not-for-profit' organisations (i.e. Danone Institutes), and to insert themselves into the public health (rather than public education) policy backdrop. Danone UK was also a partner for the Department of Health's *Public Health Responsibility Deal*, and the *Eat Like A Champ* programme currently claims to be "in line with the Change4Life campaign" (a public health social marketing campaign to reduce obesity) (Danone, 2011).

Another large-scale programme that focuses on providing healthy eating resources to teachers and students is *Energy Balance 101 (Healthy Schools, Healthy Kids)* in the United States (see Powell & Gard, 2014). This is a healthy lifestyles education resource for Grades K-5 (5–11-year-olds), part of the *Together Counts: We Thrive Together* initiative. *Together Counts* provides health tips for teachers, parents, and children, interactive web games, online pledges, and the *Energy Balance 101* curriculum, complete with detailed, prescriptive lesson plans. Officially, *Together Counts* and *Energy Balance 101* have been produced to assist families to

> make healthy decisions and establish healthy habits for life. The free wellness curriculum for grades Pre-K through five was developed in collaboration with Discovery Education, and has reached more than 47.9 million children since 2010 – that's half of all U.S. school children in grades K – 5. (Healthy Weight Commitment Foundation [HWCF] 2018a).

Although the involvement of the private sector is not as obvious as that of Danone, there is significant support by the food and drink industry in the creation and maintenance of these educational resources. *Together Counts* (and by proxy, *Energy Balance 101*) is funded and marketed by the HWCF, "a broad-based, not-for-profit organization whose mission is to help reduce obesity, especially childhood obesity, by encouraging positive and permanent lifestyle changes among school-aged children and their families" (HWCF,

2018b, para. 1). The HWCF promotes its work as developing and implementing "innovative and collaborative educational, marketplace and community
solutions with its coalition of 300 corporate and not-for-profit partners"
(HWCF, 2018b, para. 1). In fact, the foundation is so certain that it is having a
positive impact on children's health and fatness, they make the extraordinary
claim that "obesity rates among U.S. children aged 2–5 have plateaued and
receded. American families are getting the healthy lifestyle message – in part
thanks to the innovative work of the HWCF and its 300+ partners" (HWCF,
2018c, para. 2).

As the HWCF's website also shows, the organisation draws on familiar
discourses of obesity, education, and partnerships to be able to justify its philanthropic programmes that find their way into schools. Although the foundation makes the point that it is a 'not-for-profit' organisation, it certainly has
strong links to the for-profit food and drink industry. Indeed, it is governed
by key representatives of Big Food. In 2018, the HWCF's Board of Directors
included Molly Fogarty (Head of Corporate Affairs & Government Relations,
Nestlé), Dan Christenson (Senior Director Federal Government Relations,
PepsiCo), and Ryan Guthrie (Vice President of Government Relations, The
Coca-Cola Company), as well as Emeritus Board of Governors, such as Indra
Nooyi (CEO, PepsiCo), Ken Powell (CEO, General Mills), Paul Grimwood,
CEO, Nestlé USA), and Pamela Bailey (CEO, Grocery Manufacturers
Association) (see HWCF, 2018c). The boundaries between a for-profit indus-
try and not-for-profit organisations are blurry, to say the least.

It is a similar story in New Zealand – a messy mix of education resources
provided by multiple players that attempt to teach children about food, nutrition, physical activity, and making the 'right' healthy lifestyle choices. *Life
Education* is a good example. This externally provided health education programme is created and implemented by registered charity, Life Education
Trust (NZ), and 32 regional trusts, each of which is a separate registered
charity. The national organisation – Life Education Trust (NZ) – is currently sponsored and supported by a number of private sector organisations:
Mainfreight (freight company), Cigna (insurance); the Warehouse (household items), Apparel solutions (work clothing), Dove (toiletries, owned by
IFBA member Unilever), and ASG (education funds) (see Life Education,
2018a). The programme is delivered by registered teachers – and a giraffe
puppet called Harold – inside mobile classrooms to over 80% of primary
and intermediate school children in New Zealand (see www.lifeeducation.
org.nz). The promoted aim of *Life Education* is to 'educate' and 'empower'
children "to embrace positive choices for a healthy mind and body" (Life
Education, 2018b). Recently, *Life Education* partnered with *Garden To Table* to
launch a new programme called Empower, "a comprehensive and sustainable
programme to help tackle the biggest epidemic to threaten NZ children this
century – obesity" (see http://www.empowerkids.org.nz/).

There were two other nutrition education programmes of interest: *Iron
Brion* and *Be Healthy, Be Active*. *Iron Brion* was an educational programme

(and the name of the mascot) produced by Beef + Lamb New Zealand, a "farmer-owned, industry organisation representing New Zealand's sheep and beef farmers" with a desired vision of "profitable farmers, thriving farming communities, valued by all New Zealanders" (Beef + Lamb New Zealand, 2018). The widely promoted aim of *Iron Brion* was to "[support] educating young Kiwis about healthy eating and the role beef and lamb play in a healthy lifestyle" (New Zealand Beef and Lamb Marketing Bureau, n.d., p. 1). Programme highlights included the *Iron Brion BBQ Roadshow* (where Iron Brion would visit a school and teach students about the importance of consuming beef and lamb), teachers being provided with the *Iron Brion's hunt for gold resource kit* (with a series of prescriptive lesson plans), and students being given free 'healthy hamburgers'.

It is noteworthy that *Iron Brion* was an explicit component of New Zealand Beef + Lamb's marketing strategy, with education being one if its "*five main tactical areas of activity*" (Beef + Lamb New Zealand, 2008, p. 3). This was a strategy that New Zealand Beef + Lamb invested NZD\$429,500[8] in order to help reach its key performance indicator of increasing beef expenditure by 5% and lamb expenditure by 5%, to "protect beef and lamb's reputation, and continue to promote red meat's benefits to New Zealand consumers" (Beef + Lamb New Zealand, 2008, p. 3), and to ultimately "grow [consumer] demand for New Zealand beef and lamb on the domestic market via increased appreciation of the essential attributes of beef and lamb for health and wellbeing" (p. 16). The use of *Iron Brion* as a marketing tactic was further illustrated in the marketing report through Beef + Lamb New Zealand's (2008, p. 16) advice to their workforce to "continue to actively promote the show and its messages, within budgeting limits", "increase the number of shows to begin in the first term of the school year", "maintain media interest by inviting local politicians and mayors as guests" and to "aim for television coverage". The organisation's key performance indicator for this healthy lifestyles education programme was "at least 24 Iron Brion media articles" (Beef + Lamb New Zealand, 2008, p. 16). There was no mention of health or education outcomes for children.

Be Healthy, Be Active was a healthy lifestyles education programme funded and shaped by Nestlé New Zealand, in association with the New Zealand Nutrition Foundation and Millennium Institute of Sport & Health (now AUT Millennium). This programme was aimed at Year Seven and Year Eight (11–13-year-olds) children and included lesson plans, online interactive games, and other educational resources. It was one of the Nestlé's many CSR programmes, implemented under the broad banner of *Creating Shared Value*, whereby Nestlé claims to "work alongside partners to create shared value – contributing to society while ensuring the long-term success of our business" (Nestlé, n.d., para. 2). *Be Healthy, Be Active* in New Zealand was part of Nestlé's *Healthy Kids Global Programme*, an endeavour "to raise nutrition, health and wellness awareness of school-age children around the world ... to implement the scheme in all countries where we operate" and to "help children achieve and maintain a healthy body weight" (Nestlé, 2012, para. 1–2). Although this programme has recently been re-branded as *Nestlé for Healthier Kids*, its rationale, aims, and strategies have not significantly shifted:

> Today, more than 2 billion people in the world are overweight or obese and 800 million are malnourished. This calls for action.
>
> At Nestlé, we believe that by helping new generations eat and drink better and move more, we enhance quality of life and contribute to a healthier future. (Nestlé, 2018a, para. 1–2)

The targeting of schools through these types of healthy lifestyles programmes is achieved by positioning education as "a powerful tool for ensuring that children understand the value of nutrition and physical activity, and continue leading healthy lives as they get older" (Nestlé, 2012, para. 3), something that Nestlé New Zealand (2011, para. 4) argued would mean that "New Zealand as a whole will benefit from the programme, creating a happier, healthier nation". Nestle's school-based nutrition and physical activity programmes have been implemented in other countries across the Global South and Global North, including *Nutrir* in Brazil; a pilot *Nestlé Healthy Kids Programme* in Côte d'Ivoire; *Healthy Active Kids* in Australia; *Healthy Steps for Healthy Lives* in the United States; *Nestlé Healthy Kids Programme* in Nigeria; the *Good Nutrition Program* in Russia; the *Chinese Children's Nutrition & Health Education Program – Nestlé Healthy Kids Program*; *Healthy Kids Finland* programme; *Nestlé Healthy Kids-Ajyal Salima* programme in Lebanon; *Nestlé Abnaa Asehaa* programme in Egypt; *Nestlé UK Healthy Kids Network* programme in the United Kingdom, and many, many others (for a full list of case studies see Nestlé, 2018b, and for a critique of Nestlé's education programmes, see Powell, 2014b). The war on childhood obesity has resulted in an epidemic of healthy lifestyle education programmes that are shaped by, and for, corporations.

'Contrived' corporate philanthropy

For corporations to build a philanthropic image, their educational and healthy programmes must be seen *and* be profitable. As Kenway and Bullen (2001, p. 100) argued, "corporate public relations are increasingly designed to counteract poor reputations. Schools are a particularly good place for corporations to do this sort of ideological work and to establish a philanthropic image". In this way, the philanthropic efforts of the private sector to fight childhood obesity can be viewed as a type of "contrived philanthropy" (Attick, 2008, p. 170); a business strategy that attempts to divert public attention from less agreeable practices and shape people's image of the corporation, indeed an entire industry as trusted, socially responsible, and health promoting

(Powell, 2018). The conscious attempt by corporations to insert themselves into public education is a strategy to gain access to a 'captive audience' of children, and for corporations to benefit from the 'halo effect' of giving to schools (Molnar, 2005). This gifting of healthy lifestyles education programmes to schools is not driven solely (or at all) by altruism, but self-interest. In short, corporate philanthropy is part of an overall business strategy to look after the financial interests of shareholders, penetrate and retain their markets, and improve their bottom line (King, 2006).

Philanthropy is not the only tactic that the private sector uses to devise, fund, implement, and market their programmes. The corporate-influenced war on obesity includes a plethora of players, policies, and practices that help to re-position corporations as an acceptable, even preferable, 'part of the solution' to childhood obesity. Even though these attempts have been globalised, it is critical to examine how specific programmes are taken up in specific contexts – in this case, New Zealand – and how this works to re-shape children, teachers, and schools. The employment of 'partnerships' is critical to both.

Notes

1 Bruce Ross (2005) provides an excellent critical examination on the epidemiological use of BMI, as well as terms such as prevalence and incidence in obesity research.
2 At the time of writing (October 2018), the Kinder+Sport website (https://www.kinderplussport.com) claimed it had reached 28 countries and had 'moved' 4.4 million children.
3 Since *My Greatest Feat*, McDonald's in New Zealand decided to withdraw its sponsorship of educational resources in schools, including its longstanding relationship with the New Zealand Police's road safety programme.
4 Regional Sports Trusts (RSTs), such as Sport Auckland, receive funding from Sport New Zealand (a government-funded organisation), and "work across the physical activity, sport and recreation sector and have a wide range of duties including the organisation and distribution of funding and donations to regional sports organisations, schools, clubs, individuals and community groups and acting as a regional voice for the communities that they operate within" (Ministry of Health, 2018). There are approximately 17 RSTs across New Zealand.
5 'Pokie trusts' are charitable trusts that own and supply 'pokie' machines (also known as poker or electronic gaming machines) to pubs, clubs, and bars and use a percentage of their income to deliver 'grants' to a variety of community, education, and charity organisations.
6 In New Zealand, a Crown entity is an organisation that is part of the state sector and owned by the Crown, but is at 'arm's length' from government Ministers.
7 According to the World Federation of Advertisers (WFA) website (https://www.wfanet.org/), it "is the only global organisation representing the common interests of marketers. It brings together the biggest markets and marketers worldwide, representing roughly 90% of all the global marketing communications spend, almost US$ 900 billion annually".
8 Currency is in New Zealand dollars, unless stated otherwise.

References

Athletics New Zealand. (2013). *Get Set Go: Teachers manual*. Wellington: Author.

Athletics New Zealand. (2018). *Get Set Go*. Retrieved from http://athletics.org.nz/Get-Involved/As-a-School/Get-Set-Go

Attick, D. (2008). BusRadio: Music to a captive audience? In D. Boyles (Ed.), *The corporate assault on youth: Commercialism, exploitation, and the end of innocence* (pp. 158–173). New York: Peter Lang.

Ball, S. J. (2007). *Education plc: Understanding private sector participation in public sector education*. New York: Routledge.

Ball, S. J. (2012). *Global Education Inc.: New policy networks and the neoliberal imaginary*. Oxon, UK: Routledge.

Bazillier, R., & Vauday, J. (2009). *The greenwashing machine: Is CSR more than communication?* Retrieved from http://www.eea-esem.com/files/papers/EEA/2010/559/GW_45p.pdf

Beef + Lamb New Zealand. (2008). *Marketing plan 2008/2009*. Retrieved from www.beeflambnz.co.nz/documents/MarketingPlan_0809.pdf

Beef + Lamb New Zealand. (2018). *Company profile*. Retrieved from https://beeflambnz.com/about-blnz/company-profile

Blanding, M. (2010). *The coke machine: The dirty truth behind the world's favorite soft drink*. New York: Penguin.

Danone. (2011). *Eat like a champ: About us*. Retrieved from https://eatlikeachamp.co.uk/about/

Danone. (2013). *Educating future generations to eat healthily: Danone's commitment*. Retrieved from http://downtoearth.danone.com/2013/01/21/educating-future-generations-to-eat-healthily-danones-commitment

Danone Institute International. (2015). *Danone Institute: Nutrition for health*. Retrieved from https://www.danoneinstitute.org/danone-institute/nutrition-institute

Dinan-Thompson, M. (2009). Voices in health and physical education policy and practice in Australian States and Territories. In M. Dinan-Thompson (Ed.), *Health and physical education: Issues for curriculum in Australia and New Zealand* (pp. 38–59). South Melbourne, VIC: Oxford University Press.

Doane, D. (2005). The myth of CSR. *Stanford Social Innovation Review, 3*(3), 22–29.

Edwards, M. (2008). *Just another emperor? The myths and realities of philanthrocapitalism*. London: Demos and the Young Foundation.

EU Pledge. (2018a). *Home*. Retrieved from http://www.eu-pledge.eu

EU Pledge. (2018b). *The EU Pledge commitments*. Retrieved from http://www.eu-pledge.eu/content/eu-pledge-commitments

EU Pledge. (2018c). *Enhanced 2014 commitments*. Retrieved from http://www.eu-pledge.eu/content/enhanced-2014-commitments

Ferrero. (2017a). *United Kingdom*. Retrieved from https://www.kinderplussport.com/en/united-kingdom

Ferrero. (2017b). *Kinder + Sport: Introduction*. Retrieved from https://www.ferrero.co.uk/features/kinder-plus-sport-introduction

Ferrero. (2017c). *Project*. Retrieved from https://www.kinderplussport.com/en/project

Ferrero. (2017d). *Sweden*. Retrieved from https://www.kinderplussport.com/en/sweden

Gard, M. (2011). *The end of the obesity epidemic*. Oxon, UK: Routledge.

Grant, H. (2011). *MP Helen applauds school voucher scheme*. Retrieved from http://www.helengrant.org/news/local/mp-helen-applauds-school-voucher-scheme/44

Guthrie, D., Arum, R., Roksa, J., & Damaske, S. (2008). Giving to local schools: Corporate philanthropy, tax incentives, and the ecology of need. *Social Science Research, 37*(3), 856–873. doi:10.1016/j.ssresearch.2007.06.011.

GymSports New Zealand. (2006). *moveMprove.* Retrieved from http://www.gymsportsnz. com/page/moveMprove.html

Healthy Weight Commitment Foundation (HWCF). (2018a). *Programs: Creating programs to reduce obesity that are effective, sustainable and easy to replicate.* Retrieved from http://www. healthyweightcommit.org/programs/

Healthy Weight Commitment Foundation (HWCF). (2018b). *About HWCF: Engaging families, communities and schools to change the outlook of a generation.* Retrieved from http://www. healthyweightcommit.org/about/

Healthy Weight Commitment Foundation (HWCF). (2018c). *Impact: Galvanizing diverse stakeholders to focus on collective impact since 2009.* Retrieved from http://www.healthy-weightcommit.org/impact/

Heart Foundation. (2018). *Healthy fundraising ideas for schools – tool.* Retrieved from https:// www.heartfoundation.org.nz/resources/healthy-fundraising-ideas

Herrick, C. (2009). Shifting blame/selling health: Corporate social responsibility in the age of obesity. *Sociology of Health & Illness, 31*(1), 51–65. 10.1111/j.1467-9566.2008.01121.x

Hutt City Council. (n.d.). *Case study: The Football in Schools programme.* Retrieved from http://www.kiwisportfundamentals.co.nz/case-study—football-in-schools.html

International Food & Beverage Alliance (IFBA). (2011). *Executive summary for the 2009–2010 Progress report.* Retrieved from https://www.ifballiance.org/uploads/ ifbaResource/report/IFBA_Progress_Report_2009-2010_-_Executive_Summary.pdf

International Food & Beverage Alliance (IFBA). (2015). *2014 Progress report.* Retrieved from https://ifballiance.org/uploads/media/596393c962efc.pdf

J Sainsbury plc. (2017). *Live well for less: Annual report and financial statements 2017.* Retrieved from http://www.about.sainsburys.co.uk/~/media/Files/S/Sainsburys/pdf-downloads/ sainsburys-ar-2017-strategic-report

Kenway, J., & Bullen, E. (2001). *Consuming children: Education-entertainment-advertising.* Buckingham, UK: Open University Press.

King, S. (2006). *Pink Ribbons, Inc.: Breast cancer and the politics of philanthropy.* Minneapolis, MN: University of Minnesota Press.

Laufer, W. S. (2003). Social accountability and corporate greenwashing. *Journal of Business Ethics, 43*(3), 253–261.

Life Education. (2018a). *Supporters.* Retrieved from https://www.lifeeducation.org.nz/ supporters

Life Education. (2018b). *Our goals.* Retrieved from https://www.lifeeducation.org.nz/ourgoals

MacDonald, C. (2008). *Green Inc.: An environmental insider reveals how a good cause has gone bad.* Guilford, CT: The Lyons Press.

Ministry of Health. (2018). *Physical activity resources.* Retrieved from https://www. health.govt.nz/your-health/healthy-living/food-activity-and-sleep/physical-activity/ physical-activity-resources

Molnar, A. (2005). *School commercialism: From democratic ideal to market commodity.* New York: Routledge.

Molnar, A., & Boninger, F. (2015). *Sold out: How marketing in school threatens children's well-being and undermines their education.* Lanham, Maryland: Rowman & Littlefield.

Molnar, A., Boninger, F., Wilkinson, G., & Fogarty, J. (2008). *Schools inundated in a marketing-saturated world: The eleventh annual report on schoolhouse commercialism trends: 2007–2008.* Retrieved from http://nepc.colorado.edu/files/RS-CommTrends-FINAL2.pdf

Molnar, A., & Garcia, D. (2005). *Empty calories: Commercializing activities in America's schools: the eighth-annual report on schoolhouse commercialism trends 2004–2005.* Retrieved from https://eric.ed.gov/?id=ED508519

Nestlé. (2012). *Nestlé Healthy Kids Global Programme.* Retrieved from http://www.Nestlé.com/CSV/NUTRITION/HEALTHYKIDSPROGRAMME/Pages/HealthyKidsProgramme.aspx

Nestlé. (2018a). *Nestlé for Healthier Kids.* Retrieved from https://www.nestle.com/csv/global-initiatives/healthier-kids

Nestlé. (2018b). *Creating shared value in action.* Retrieved from https://www.nestle.com/csv/case-studies

Nestlé. (n.d.). *Nestlé in society.* Retrieved from https://www.nestle.co.nz/csv

Nestlé New Zealand. (2011). *Be Healthy, Be Active: Teachers' resource.* Wellington: Learning Media.

Nestlé Singapore. (n.d.). *CSV at Nestlé.* Retrieved from http://www.nestle.com.sg/csv/csv_at_nestle

New Zealand Beef and Lamb Marketing Bureau. (n.d.). *Iron Brion's hunt for gold resource kit.* New Zealand: New Zealand Beef and Lamb Marketing Bureau.

New Zealand Football. (n.d.). *ASB Football in Schools: Keeping our children active and healthy.* Retrieved from http://www.foxsportspulse.com/get_file.cgi?id=1981476

Newshub. (2017). *Chocolate fundraising faces chop by Government advisor.* Retrieved from https://www.newshub.co.nz/home/health/2017/04/chocolate-fundraising-faces-chop-by-government-advisor.html

Norris, T. (2011). *Consuming schools: Commercialism and the end of politics.* Toronto, Canada: University of Toronto Press.

Pedersen, E. H. (2006). Introduction: Corporate citizenship in developing countries – New partnership perspectives. In M. Huniche & E. R. Pedersen (Eds.), *Corporate citizenship in developing countries: New partnership perspectives* (pp. 7–28). Copenhagen: Copenhagen Business School Press.

Porter, M. E., & Kramer, M. (2002). The competitive advantage of corporate philanthropy. *Harvard Business Review, 80*(12), 56–68.

Porter, M. E., & Kramer, M. R. (2006). Strategy and society: The link between corporate social responsibility and competitive advantage. *Harvard Business Review, 84*(12), 78–92.

Powell, D. (2014a). Childhood obesity, corporate philanthropy and the creeping privatisation of health education. *Critical Public Health, 24*(2), 226–238. doi: 10.1080/09581596.2013.846465

Powell, D. (2014b). The corporatization of health education curricula: 'Part of the solution' to childhood obesity? In K. Fitzpatrick & R. Tinning (Eds.), *Health education: Critical perspectives* (pp. 142–156). Oxon, UK: Routledge.

Powell, D. (2015). Assembling the privatisation of physical education and the 'inexpert' teacher. *Sport, Education and Society, 20*(1), 73–88. doi: 10.1080/13573322.2014.941796

Powell, D. (2018). The 'will to give': Corporations, philanthropy and schools. *Journal of Education Policy, 34*(2), 195–214. doi: 10.1080/02680939.2018.1424940

Powell, D., & Gard, M. (2014). The governmentality of childhood obesity: Coca-Cola, corporations and schools. *Discourse: Studies in the Cultural Politics of Education, 36*(6), 854–867. doi: 10.1080/01596306.2014.905045

Richards, R., Darling, H., & Reeder, A. I. (2005). Sponsorship and fund-raising in New Zealand schools: Implications for health. *Australian and New Zealand Journal of Public Health, 29*(4), 331–336. doi: 10.1111/j.1467-842X.2005.tb00203.x

Robertson, D. (2007). *Tesco criticised over school vouchers.* Retrieved from https://www.thisismoney.co.uk/money/bills/article-1607548/Tesco-criticised-over-school-vouchers.html

Ross, B. (2005). Fat or fiction: Weighing the 'obesity epidemic. In M. Gard & J. Wright, *The obesity epidemic: Science, morality, and ideology* (pp. 86–106). Oxon, UK: Routledge.

Saltman, K. J., & Goodman, R. T. (2011). Rivers of Fire: BPAmaco's iMPACT on education. In K. J. Saltman & D. A. Gabbard (Eds.), *Education as enforcement: The militarization and corporatization of school* (pp. 36–56). New York: Routledge.

Scoop. (2010). *100,000 Kiwi kids stride towards FIFA World Cup*. Retrieved from http://www.scoop.co.nz/stories/CU1004/S00366/100000-kiwi-kids-stride-towards-fifa-world-cup.htm

Shamir, R. (2008). The age of responsibilization: On market-embedded morality. *Economy and Society, 37*(1), 1–19. doi: 10.1080/03085140701760833

Smithers, R. (2011). *Should we collect vouchers to fund equipment for schools?* Retrieved from https://www.theguardian.com/education/mortarboard/2011/feb/16/should-we-collect-school-vouchers

The Yummy Fruit Company. (2019). *School Sticker Promo*. Retrieved from https://www.yummyfruit.co.nz/schools/

The Yummy Fruit Company. (n.d.). *School Sticker Promo*. Retrieved from http://www.yummyfruit.co.nz/schoolstickerpromo

Tuggerah Lakes Secondary College. (n.d.). *Adidas School Fun-Run*. Retrieved from http://www.bvc.nsw.edu.au/sports.php?id=125

Utter, J., Scragg, R., Percival, T., & Beaglehole, R. (2009). School is back in New Zealand–and so is the junk food. *The New Zealand Medical Journal (Online), 122*(1290).

Vallentin, S., & Murillo, D. (2010). *CSR as governmentality*. Frederiksberg, Denmark: Copenhagen Business School Center for Corporate Social Responsibility.

Wiggins, A. (2017). *New Government health adviser hopes to end the sale of chocolate as a fundraiser in schools*. Retrieved from https://www.nzherald.co.nz/nz/news/article.cfm?c_id=1&objectid=11842060

4

'COMING TOGETHER'
TO SOLVE OBESITY

In 2012, Coca-Cola ran an advertisement calling for everyone to 'come together' to be part of the solution to obesity (see Powell, 2013). The advertisement began with the words: "For over 125 years we've been bring people together. Today, we'd like people to come together on something that concerns all of us – obesity. The long-term health of our families and our country is at stake" (Özüağ, 2013). This shared 'interest' in the shared 'problem' of childhood obesity has enabled alignments to be forged between corporations and schools, as well as an assortment of other private, public, and voluntary sector organisations. In this chapter I interrogate how partnerships are used as a key tactic – what Foucault (1984) may have described loosely as a technology of government – to bring together the interests of corporations, 'not-for-profits', the state, and schools, translating a collective ambition to shape children's bodies and behaviours into healthy lifestyles education programmes.

However, many of these organisations have contradictory interests and are somewhat strange bedfellows. This leads to moments when the various practices, policies, and rationales that shape and make healthy lifestyles education programmes are placed under increased tension. This is most evident when the profit-seeking interests of the private sector (i.e. public relations, policy-making, and advertising) contradict the education (and health) interests of schools, teachers, and principals. The ways in which disparate players come together to fight childhood obesity is complex and needs further in-depth examination to be able to understand how business strategies are used to re-invent corporations as healthy, educational, and altruistic.

Sharing an interest in childhood obesity

There are four central mechanisms that make it possible for institutions to align their shared interests in fighting childhood obesity: a shared interest based on an 'urgent need' to fix a problem (e.g. obesity, public relations); a shared interest in and agreement on who requires governing (e.g. children); a shared interest in solving the problem (e.g. using healthy lifestyles education programmes); and a shared interest in certain thoughts, actions, and bodies that need to be governed (e.g. children's choices of consumption) (see Powell & Gard, 2018).

The World Health Organization provides a useful example of how multiple stakeholders across all sectors of society are encouraged to share an interest in the global war against childhood obesity: "Curbing the childhood obesity epidemic requires sustained political commitment and the collaboration of many public and private stakeholders" (World Health Organization, 2018a, para. 3). Multisector partnerships are positioned by the World Health Organization as a key objective, "to mobilize these partners and engage them in implementing the Global Strategy on Diet, Physical Activity and Health", a strategy seen as "essential for sustained progress: it mobilizes the combined energy, resources and expertise of all global stakeholders involved" (World Health Organization, 2018a, para. 4–5).

It is obvious that the food and drink industry has chosen to 'mobilise' its 'combined energy, resources, and expertise' to act on concerns about childhood obesity, and obesity in general. This is by no means astonishing, considering the World Health Organization and other governmental organisations have singled out food and drink manufacturers and marketers (as well as those from the sporting goods industry) to play a greater role in promoting healthy lifestyles to children (see World Health Organization, 2010, 2018b, 2018c). What is far more startling, however, is the recent phenomenon of multinational food and drink corporations proactively forming business relationships with each other. We are now in a space where aggressive marketplace competitors – Pepsi vs Coca-Cola, McDonald's vs Burger King, Nestlé vs Mondelēz – have made a public and political stance to 'come together' to fight childhood obesity (Powell & Gard, 2018). In contemporary societies, the endeavour to shape certain kinds of citizens (in this case, the healthy, non-fat, responsible child-consumer) can only be achieved "through the actions of a whole range of other authorities, and through complex technologies, if they are to be able to intervene upon the conduct of persons" (Rose, 2000, p. 323).

The strategies of the International Food & Beverage Alliance (IFBA) demonstrate how food and beverage competitors use this 'multiple-authority' approach to their own advantage. It was in December 2008 when the IFBA member companies first promoted their shared interest in the problem of childhood obesity. The CEO's wrote and signed a letter to Dr Margaret Chan, then the Director-General of the World Health Organization, in which they outlined their *Global Commitment to Responsible Marketing and Advertising to Children*:

> Childhood obesity is a serious public health issue with no simple answer. Any effort to address it needs to be comprehensive in scope, with *active participation by all involved*. This includes the government, food and beverage industry, civil society, entertainment and media companies, schools and parents. (IFBA, 2008, p. 1, my emphasis)

All sectors of society have been called upon to be 'involved', including schools. As The Coca-Cola Company (2012, p. 2) also proclaimed in their document

Our Position on Obesity, "the collective efforts of everyone" are necessary to solve obesity. In the same way, IFBA member McDonald's maintained that they could not solve the problem of obesity without others taking a shared interest:

> There continues to be concern about obesity rates and related risks to human well-being among consumers, governments, NGOs, and health and nutrition experts .... We know we cannot address this problem alone, but we are committed to *being part of the solution.* (McDonald's, 2013, my emphasis)

By positioning themselves as 'part of the solution' – a phrase oft-repeated by the food and drink industry – the private sector is able to draw in other individuals and organisations. This helps to deflect criticism of the food and drink industry by shutting down debates that the industry is wholly responsible for childhood obesity. Possible discussions about political actions, such as regulatory and legislative actions to reduce obesity (e.g. 'sugar taxes', stricter controls on marketing to children), are subdued, attempting to shift the responsibility for children's (ill)health from corporations (and governments) to a problem that 'everyone' must take an interest in solving (Ken, 2014). To ensure that the connections between these corporations and other private sector players remain secure, the members of the IFBA ensure that their shared problem(s) also have a shared solution: to teach children to be more active, make better eating choices, and be less fat. The rhetoric of *partnership* is critical to ensuring that healthy lifestyles education programmes are inserted into schools and promoted to the public and policymakers alike.

An epidemic of obesity partnerships

A decade on from the IFBA's first letter to Dr Margaret Chan, the organisation published a report *Ten years of progress: 2008–2018 – working in partnership to improve global health*, in which they articulate how important it is for everyone to work collectively and form partnerships:

> Our work is global and based on the fundamental principle that the public health challenges we face today can only be solved through a whole-of-society approach and public-private partnerships.
>
> We have committed to do our part and working together, in collaboration with governments, the public health community and other stakeholders, we are delivering positive change.
>
> We have come a long way, but there is more to do. We will continue to leverage our global scale and lead our industry in efforts to improve global health.
>
> This report highlights our achievements and successful collaborations over the past ten years. (IFBA, 2018, p. 2)

In the section 'Working in partnership to improve global health', the IFBA provides a ten-year timeline demonstrating the different public-private partnerships that have made their attempts to 'improve global health' both possible and visible. These include supporting public health initiatives (e.g. *Change4Life* in the United Kingdom), working with government to reformulate products and packaging (e.g. *Soft Drinks Industry Sugar Reduction Commitment* in Europe, *Healthy Food Partnership* in Australia), and making pledges/commitments to government public health agencies (e.g. *Healthy Kids Industry Pledge* in New Zealand, *Public Health Responsibility Deal* in the United Kingdom) (for details, see IFBA, 2018, pp. 6–7).

Partnerships are certainly a vital technology for the Nestlé corporation. Janet Voûte, former Global Head of Public Affairs at Nestlé S.A. and current Chairperson of the Creating Shared Value Council, described Nestlé's role in childhood obesity prevention:

> ... we need a multi-sector response and Nestlé firmly believes industry has a vital role to play in this. We are convinced the best way to leverage our capabilities and expertise is by working in partnership with other organisations to help promote healthy nutrition and physical activity through community-based programmes. (Nestlé, 2012a, para. 7–9)

A search through Nestlé's *Creating Shared Value* case studies reveals how the company collaborates with multiple government education and health departments, universities, schools, and not-for-profit partners to ensure its global strategic philanthropy "create[s] value for our shareholders and our company" (Nestlé, 2018a, para. 1). The *Nestlé Healthy Kids-Ajyal Salima* in Lebanon provides an excellent case study of how these partnerships to fight childhood obesity work, with Nestlé describing how they "joined forces with the American University of Beirut to jointly roll out the *Nestlé Healthy Kids-Ajyal Salima* programme ... with the support of the Lebanese Ministry of Education" (Nestlé, 2018b, para. 1). One alarming impact of this Nestlé-led partnership with a government department and a university was that their healthy lifestyles education programme transformed from a corporatised initiative that schools *may* (or may not) use, to one they *must* use, as "the Lebanese Ministry of Education officially adopted the Nestlé Healthy Kids-Ajyal Salima programme into its mandatory Health Education Unit's curriculum in public schools in 2014" (Nestlé, 2018b, para. 10).

To reinforce an earlier point, those corporations that 'give', do so in order to receive. So, what is the return on investment for Nestlé and its shareholders? Well, Nestlé also spells out the 'value' of this philanthropic partnership on its website:

> The *Nestlé Healthy Kids-Ajyal Salima* programme establishes a global competitive advantage and demonstrates Nestlé's commitment to

address health issues globally. It also has a positive impact on Nestlé's reputation as a leading Nutrition, Health and Wellness company. (Nestlé, 2018b, para. 12)

Clearly, the value of healthy lifestyles education programmes for Nestlé is more than a 'warm fuzzy feeling' for its CEO and shareholders, but an essential element of their overall business strategy to be develop Nestlé's reputation, brand image, and competitive advantage.

It is worthy to reiterate that it is not only multinational food and drink corporations that have formed partnerships with one another. 'Anti-obesity' partnerships between all types of public, private, and voluntary sector organisations are noticeable in national contexts, such as Canada's *Companies Committed to Kids*, the *Partnership for a Healthier America* and *Healthy Weight Commitment Foundation* in the United States (see Powell, 2014), the *Healthier Australia Commitment*, and the former *Public Health Responsibility Deal* in the United Kingdom. When it comes to the global war on childhood obesity and the various programmes that target schools and beyond, partnerships are forming at 'epidemic' proportions, or what Huxham and Vangen (2000, p. 303) described as "partnershipitis".

An epidemic of healthy lifestyles education partnerships is also evident in New Zealand. There were 12 corporatised programmes that were (or had been) used by the three primary schools in my study (see Powell, 2015). These 12 programmes involved nearly 50 different partner organisations, including 25 private sector companies, 18 'not-for-profit' organisations, and 4 public-funded organisations. On top of that there were numerous other organisations and individuals that were *indirectly* involved in these programmes. As one example, the Life Education Trust – the charitable organisation that runs the programme nationwide – had (at the time of my research) a number of 'national sponsors': two 'pokie trusts' – The Lion Foundation and Pub Charity; two product brands – Just Juice (owned by Frucor) and Macleans (owned by GlaxoSmithKline); and five private sector corporations – ANZ (bank), AWF Group (temporary labour supplier), Konica Minolta (printing supplies), Mainfreight (freight), and The Warehouse (household items). The *Life Education* programme is also implemented through regional trusts that have additional regional partners. At Dudley School, for instance, *Life Education* was administered by a regional trust which partnered with an additional four large New Zealand-based corporations, four charitable trusts (all four were pokie trusts funded by proceeds from gaming machines), one non-gaming philanthropic trust, and a local 'Z' service station (formerly branded as Shell).[1]

When corporations form partnerships to position themselves as central warriors in the war on obesity, private sector companies are enabled to align *their* interests (including their philanthropic, financial, marketing, and policy-making interests) with organisations that shared similar interests. At the same time, these disparate organisations often have competing, even contradictory, aims. The tensions that manifest when profit-seeking corporations enter these new types of relationships must be resolved, otherwise the 'value' they hold for other organisations may be called into question. This seems to be especially evident when a "panoply of players" (Coveney, 2006, p. 208), including those very corporations blamed for childhood obesity, have been recruited to solve an urgent public health imperative.

Joining forces to fight fat in schools

As I described earlier, schools across the globe have been swiftly and often uncritically drawn into the 'obesity vortex'. New Zealand schools are, of course, no exception. Throughout my time in the three Auckland primary schools, teachers, principals, and external providers of programmes drew on crisis discourses of obesity, inactivity, and poor nutrition to argue that schools needed to do 'something' to be part of the solution to children's fat bodies and unhealthy lifestyles. For instance, in a conversation with *Life Education* teacher Marion, she criticised a school [not in my study] for selling 'junk food', which she linked to the children being fat and immobile:

> I can't believe [what] some tuck shops are still selling! Seriously? Are you kidding? Have you seen the size of your children? It's really sad when you sit in these classrooms, and you tell the children to sit down, and the children have to turn around to go on all fours before they can sit down on their bottom.

At St Saviour's School, Year Six/Seven classroom teacher Ms Ellie told me that they had an "obesity problem" at their school. This view was echoed by the principal, Mrs Sergeant, who also asked me for ideas on how to stop students eating potato chips at school (her main idea was to tell parents and children it was an issue of litter in the school grounds, rather than any health message). Miss Black, a first-year teacher with a Bachelor of Sport and Recreation,[2] shared her views about childhood obesity:

> I think that [the] childhood obesity problem is such a massive problem and is so multifaceted I suppose that it would be interesting to know if [these programmes] have much of an effect. I tend to think that [they] probably wouldn't have much of an effect … I think that whole childhood obesity problem is an entire society problem that goes far beyond schools.

Although Miss Black recognised that obesity was not something that could be solved by schools alone, at the same time she hoped that the programmes her students participated in – *Get Set Go, Life Education, moveMprove* – would make *some* difference; that "doing something" was at least "better than nothing".

These dominant obesity discourses were a significant way of forging alignments (Li, 2007) between corporations and schools. However, what really seemed to 'glue' the interests of different actors together was when healthy lifestyles education programmes were advertised or understood as being both healthy *and* educational (Powell & Gard, 2015). As Nestlé asserted:

> We believe that regular physical activity and establishing healthy eating habits help children achieve and maintain a healthy body weight. Education is therefore a powerful tool for ensuring that children understand the value of nutrition and physical activity, and continue leading healthy lives (Nestlé, 2012b, para. 2–3)

A number of organisations attempted to make connections between children's education and children's health. Life Education Trust (2011, p. 1), for instance, stated that its 'mission' is "To help give the young people of New Zealand, through positive health based education, the knowledge and skills to raise their awareness and to live a fulfilling and healthy life". Food industry representatives United Fresh New Zealand Inc. (hereinafter United Fresh) (United Fresh New Zealand Incorporated, n.d.-a, para. 2) claimed that its Fruit in Schools programme was "providing both health and education benefits and United Fresh strengthens these benefits by providing curriculum linked resources through the 5+ A Day Charitable Trust". *Iron Brion* was also promoted in a comparable way:

> As you know, a healthy eating programme is critical to the well-being of school-aged children. This resource kit provides you with activities to help promote healthy eating to your class, in particular the importance of iron in their daily lives .... The New Zealand Beef and Lamb Marketing Bureau firmly supports *educating young Kiwis about healthy eating* and the role beef and lamb play in a healthy lifestyle. We see both the Iron Brion Show and the Teacher Resource Kit as our contribution to the well-being of school-aged children, both now and in the future. (New Zealand Beef and Lamb Marketing Bureau, n.d., p. 1, my emphasis)

Advertising and marketing tactics, or what Miller and Rose (1997) referred to as *technologies of consumption*, open up opportunities for private sector players to combine their 'part of the solution' to obesity with broader business strategies that aim to increase public relations, consumption, and profit. The quote above provides a snapshot of how a marketing company that represented for-profit organisations (i.e. Beef + Lamb New Zealand Ltd, as well as the processors and retailers of New Zealand beef and lamb) attempted to 'sell' beef and lamb to children, teachers, and their families by promoting their resource and edutainment roadshow as a healthy lifestyles education programme.

The process of forming connections between concepts of health, education, obesity, and marketing is not always smooth. The strength of the relationships is made more fragile when the *commercial* purpose of a programme, especially one that employs obvious marketing and advertising strategies, appears to contradict and compete with the school's role as a site for education. For instance, Ms Ellie disagreed with Beef + Lamb New Zealand's claim that their mascot, Iron Brion, "captivates, entertains and informs" (New Zealand Beef and Lamb Marketing Bureau, n.d., p. 2). Ms Ellie told me that when Iron Brion and Beef + Lamb New Zealand-branded employees gave her students free hamburgers and other prizes:

MS ELLIE: I thought it was really ridiculous, but you know what, the kids absolutely loved it! And the intermediates [Year Seven and Eight students], who I thought would be lippy and disrespectful by not listening and fidgeting, were actually fantastic. And that was about the free food at the end.

DARREN: What was ridiculous?

MS ELLIE: They just leapt about did stupid jokes and ran into the crowd and got the kids to do silly things and gave away prizes and you know, low level humour I guess.

DARREN: So would you describe it as an educational programme?

MS ELLIE: No.

DARREN: How would you describe it?

MS ELLIE: Um, it was definitely promotional.

Far from being duped into believing that the *Iron Brion BBQ Roadshow* was primarily an educational endeavour, Ms Ellie recognised that Iron Brion and 'his' free hamburgers were aimed at improving public relations, the brand image of the industry, and their profit margins. This was a strategy she described as:

> unfortunately, a sign of the times ... a form of marketing that you have to filter very carefully for yourself, and for the children, the purpose behind it .... [it's] just a marketing thing that would be a tax incentive for them really! And they look like they are doing great things for the community, so it sort of ticks their ethical box around the board and I know that lots of companies, it's quite trendy to have an ethical side to your business and really there is a thin veil of disguise of what's actually, really going on.

However, rather than Ms Ellie's cynicism towards this form of "definitely promotional", non-educational, tax-friendly, marketing event placing so much stress on the connections between commercialism, education, and health that they fractured, tensions were resolved by Ms Ellie convincing herself that she needed to just "filter" the "purpose behind" these programmes. The term 'resolved' does not necessarily mean a definite, certain, or indeed permanent *solving* of a given tension, but can also be a means to deal with a tension in a temporary sense. For instance, Ms Ellie's 'filter' resulted in the desire of Beef + Lamb New Zealand (2008) to promote its marketing/health messages and products to children – to trickle through. The interests of an industry group were re-positioned as being relatively unimportant compared to children's and teacher's 'need' to receive free food, entertainment, and 'health education'. However, this is not to suggest that Ms Ellie's momentary 'acceptance' of Iron Brion completely disintegrated all tensions. Her personal objections to the *Iron Brion BBQ Roadshow* and her concern about and resistance to other forms of 'disguised' marketing to children remained.

The ability or willingness to critically interrogate the multiple purposes of a corporatised programme or resource (i.e. its profit-seeking, promotional, public relations, or branding purposes) was neither simple nor straightforward for the teachers or principals. For example, I asked Mrs Donna, a Year Two teacher at Dudley School, how she felt about corporations sponsoring and implementing school-based programmes like *Life Education*. She responded:

> To tell you the honest truth, things like that just don't worry me. I tend to throw a blind eye to a lot of things …. I've never worried about things like that. As long as someone is sponsoring them that's all that matters. And they're not using it as advertising to the kids, so I guess it doesn't matter. To tell the honest truth I had no idea who sponsored them because to me I don't care. It's about the education of the children that counts. It's always about the children being first, so I don't have a problem with it – although the gambling thing gets me, but because that's a different kettle of fish.

Even though Mrs Donna gave her students Macleans-branded gift bags (with Macleans-branded toothpaste, toothbrush, stickers, colouring-in pages, and links to a Macleans website and Smartphone app), and sent her students home with letters that carried healthy eating advice from Just Juice, Mrs Donna did not consider these as a form of "advertising to the kids" and instead "threw a blind eye" to the corporate influence on educational resources and programmes. In the end, Mrs Donna justified her idea that she did not "care" about corporate sponsorship by enlisting the idea that the only thing that "counts" was the education of her students.

The 'doing it for the good of the children' discourse was frequently used as a rationale for bringing programmes into schools. It acted as a means to 'trump' all other concerns, especially concerns about the educative value (or lack thereof) of obviously promotional programmes like *Iron Brion*, or clearly commercial strategies such as giving free products to children. For example, Mr Woodward, principal at Dudley School, acknowledged that the corporate interest in providing healthy lifestyles education programmes to schools was likely to have some degree of commercial intent. However, from his perspective, the bottom line was the benefit for students:

> Obviously [corporations are] going to make dough out of [school-based programmes] too, but if that's their prime purpose, well, we will see through it and wouldn't have them anyway. If it's only just for them, um, but if it's beneficial for kids, that's what it's got to be about, you know. Simple as that.

Mr Woodward justified his inclusion of corporate programmes in his school by bringing together two discourses: that his school's use of these programmes was 'beneficial for kids' and that his staff would 'see' – and be able to filter out – those programmes or companies whose "prime purpose" was to "make dough". However, as the earlier conversation with Mrs Donna demonstrated (as well as the fact that Mr Woodward had allowed McDonald's into his school to give out McDonald's-branded hats and balls[3]), it was difficult to tell what the "prime purpose" of the programmes was, especially when they were promoted as being 'all about' the health and education of students. The profit-seeking interests of organisations were rarely, if ever, perceived by the adults to be the "prime purpose" of corporations' desires to 'teach' children and schools.

Another significant tension was when an 'unhealthy' corporation (or product) partnered with or sponsored a 'healthy' educational activity. However, this tension was frequently alleviated when corporations, charities, and schools deemed it appropriate to endorse 'healthy' (or at least healthier) corporate products within a healthy lifestyles education programme. For example, Miss Black at St Saviour's School said: "I HATE fast food companies sponsoring anything to do with health, sports, fitness. Hate it. Any fast food is ridiculous. It's totally contradicting ... and they are so sneaky as well". She described corporations like Nike or Adidas as aligning better with the goals of a health education programme than McDonald's or Coca-Cola: "at least it has some alignment, you know". Although I pointed out to Miss Black that even though *Life Education* was sponsored by Just Juice (a product made by Frucor, the same company which makes Pepsi and 'V' energy drinks), she replied, "but still, it's not something that's unhealthy, so it's fine". Like Mr Woodward, for Miss Black the perceived 'healthiness' of the 'sponsor' – a branded fruit juice – appeared to obscure the "less healthy" products of a corporation, as well as the profit-seeking, public relations interests of the company that provided funding and 'nutritional advice' to the programme.

A so-called healthy (or even just 'more healthy') product acted not only as a buffer between the corporation, its public reputation, its products, and its programmes, but also as a way of connecting these elements. For example, I told

Miss Black how Adidas were organising 'fun runs' to help schools raise money in Australia, to which she replied:

MISS BLACK: That's good. Even Powerade – although I have issues with Powerade as well (laughs), anything, anything [other than McDonald's], that would be more aligned-
DARREN: -so would Powerade, Gatorade be a-
MISS BLACK: -that would be fine. I don't like the fact that people can think that Powerade is just a general juice drink that you would have if you are doing like half an hour or an hour of exercise and that's a good thing. Yeah. It's just a drink that you have instead of orange juice. I don't like that they have made it come across [to] have that image. It's sneaky. Yeah, but it would be surely be better than McDonald's.

Miss Black's comments demonstrated how teachers and external providers seemed to find themselves having to do one of two things: either choosing the lesser of two 'evils' (such as Powerade or Coca-Cola, Just Juice or Pepsi, McDonald's or New Zealand Beef + Lamb), or not having any sponsor – or healthy lifestyles education programme – at all. A third option – planning and teaching lessons without a sponsor or external provider – appeared, for the most part, to not be an option at all.

Partnerships, sponsorship, and 'healthy' branding worked as strategies to encourage teachers and principals to 'consume' the corporate solutions to childhood obesity. For instance, I asked Dudley School principal Mr Woodward if he would consider having a corporation like The Coca-Cola Company come to his school to deliver a health or physical education programme. He replied:

No, we won't do that ... we wouldn't want to be sponsored by Rothmans [cigarettes] which rugby used to be and athletics used to be a few years ago. But now tobacco companies don't really do that. But we wouldn't, I wouldn't want McDonald's sponsoring [school activities] really. Needs to be something that we can have moralistic views about.

Even though Mr Woodward stated clearly that he could not 'morally' use any activities that were sponsored by McDonald's or Coca-Cola (which he compared to a 'Big Tobacco' company) he regularly allowed, indeed extolled the virtues of, *Life Education* (funded at the time by beverage corporation Frucor, pharmaceutical multinational GlaxoSmithKline, two gaming/pokie trusts, and others) into his school to teach his students about health – and about corporate products. The fact that it was not Frucor or these other organisations and industries physically delivering *Life Education* appeared to help divert Mr Woodward's attention from who was funding and directing what was being taught to his students. I am not suggesting that Mr Woodward is a hypocrite. Rather, the nature of these partnerships appears to obscure and ameliorate concerns that people might have.

Life Education teacher Marion recognised the tensions that arose when a soft drink/fruit juice/energy drink company 'helped' *Life Education*:

> I am a bit of a fan of Frucor, even though juice is high in sugar – they do have a technology field there that tries to reduce these things like Just Juice Splash for example .... So, [Frucor] have a research team. They've also given us cards and we've developed cards together as a resource for schools for when we are doing health and things like that. It's based around nutrients, so they are very keen to help assist, even though they also sell other products (laughs) that we try and discourage ... Otherwise, any way that we can raise profile of both organisations to work together to build stronger communities is always important.

Although I could not be sure what Marion's private thoughts about this pro-gramme and partnership were, it does appear from this quote that she arrived at a kind of compromise by "smoothing out contradictions so that they seem superficial rather than fundamental" (Li, 2007, p. 265). The problem of high sugar drinks, those that *Life Education* aim to "discourage", is alleviated by the notion that their expert "technology field" and "research team" are trying "to reduce these things".

In addition, alignments between Frucor and *Life Education* are forged even stronger through the dual notions of partnership and social responsibility, or what Marion described as working "together to build stronger commu-nities". Potential tensions and weaknesses are transformed into a nexus of strength, as 'profiles are raised' for both organisations, which are then able to achieve their goals. As Marion argued:

> So you know, we [*Life Education*] want to lift our profile and if we can do that and look good at the same time, do it in the positive way – I know it's all part of marketing, all part of business ... depending on the ethos and interest of the company if there is a perfect fit, if there's a particular target that aligns with the business ... they get promotion and I think 'yay, happy to promote! Let's get scratched backs!'

Marion (as an individual) and the Life Education Trust (as an organisa-tion) obviously value their ability to 'get into bed' with corporate partners. However, Marion's use of the phrase "perfect fit" masks some of the imper-fections that exist when relationships are formed between two fundamentally dissimilar organisations. Tensions arise when there is a need to 'scratch each other's backs', especially when one of the partners may have more to gain or more to lose. When I asked for her thoughts about promoting sponsors' branded products during *Life Education* lessons, she replied:

> It's part of the promotion – that's what pays us. And I'm happy to do it if we can work it in and it's not too much of a stretch .... [It's]

a good opportunity to get the sponsor's product in without actually having to go out of my way to promote it. But yeah, definitely happy to promote. It's not always the favourite part of the job, but pays the bills. Better with than without.

Marion also rationalised the conspicuous commercialism within the *Life Education* programme by describing the corporate sponsorship as "better with than without"; that promoting Just Juice, Macleans toothpaste, and H2Go bottles of water to children was somehow less damaging than the alternative – not receiving sponsorship money. After all, Marion appeared to perceive the relationship as a 'win–win' situation. Both Frucor and *Life Education* profit (i.e. in terms of money, public relations, brand image, and ability to 'get into' schools) from their relationship by raising each other's "profiles", being seen to "work together to build stronger communities", and ensuring they are visible in schools and communities as providers of health, education, and healthy products.

Re-inventing the 'charitable' corporation in schools

Corporations are able to 'come together' and partner with schools through notions of charity, philanthropy, and corporate social responsibility. The philanthropic aims and ideals of different authorities and individuals, including schools, teachers, charities, external providers, and private companies, act in two broad, yet interconnected ways. The first is that philanthropy, in its broadest sense, acts as a congealing agent. Organisations and actors are brought together through their combined will to be altruistic; an ambition which helps to create, fund, shape, and implement school-based programmes and educational resources. The second is that notions of philanthropy help to re-invent the various authorities, particularly those representing the private sector, so that they are seen to be selfless, rather than self-interested, profiteering, or even unhealthy (Powell, 2018).

As described in the previous chapter, a significant technology used by the private sector to join discourses of philanthropy to the school-based war against childhood obesity is corporate social responsibility. In the New Zealand context, we witness many for-profit organisations drawing on discourses of 'social responsibility' or 'community' to ensure their programmes to fight obesity are actualised in schools, and promoted to politicians and the public. For example, McDonald's *My Greatest Feat* pedometer programme was part of its 'Community' programme, one area of their broader corporate responsibility strategy. On the McDonald's New Zealand website page 'Macca's® in the Community', it states: "We believe we've got a responsibility to give back to our local communities. Every year we help set up and support sporting, educational, charitable and environmental programmes designed to help a wide range of people and communities" (McDonald's Restaurants (NZ) Limited, 2018, para. 1).

New Zealand Post funded a number of physical activity programmes in schools, such as *Small Sticks* and *Get Set Go*, through *ActivePost*, a community wellness programme created as part of New Zealand Post's corporate responsibility strategy. Nestlé New Zealand's *Be Healthy, Be Active* was part of Nestlé S.A.'s *Healthy Kids Global Programme*. *Life Education* teacher Marion also told me about a promotion where she, other 'Life Educators' and 'Harold the Giraffe' made promotional appearances at local 'Z' petrol stations as part of Z's 'Good in the Hood' corporate social responsibility programme. Frucor's (2015, para. 1) investment in *Life Education* was part of its 'social responsibility' activities, a division of its broader 'community' programme: "As a company and as a team, we like to help others out whenever we can". Frucor's relationship with *Life Education* was publicised in a business-led corporate social responsibility report, *Do gooder and gooder: How doing good is good for business*. In this report, Frucor states that its "investment" in *Life Education* was based on its concern "at the growing level of obesity and inactivity amongst NZ children" (Robin Hood Foundation, n.d., p. 12).

A corporation's desire to be philanthropic, socially responsible, and 'do good' in the community acts in tension with the corporation's need to profit (Ball, 2012; Boyles, 2008; Molnar, 2005; Saltman, 2010). This tension is resolved, to a degree, by the fact that corporations are able to use their social responsibility/philanthropy programmes as a way to simultaneously improve their image and increase profit (Powell, 2018). Corporations clearly desire for a decent return on their investment in schools and public health. As Nestlé's former Vice President of Public Affairs, Niels Christiansen (2007, p. 40) explained, "we treat corporate social responsibility as a part of our overall brand strategy". The interest corporations such as Nestlé have in being socially responsible is not a 'pure' form of altruism, but intimately tied to building their brand image and business:

> There may not be one single definition of Corporate Social Responsibility that fits all companies and industries, but for a consumer goods company, building strong brands is the basis of a successful business, and how the public feels about a company relates directly to our brand equity. For this reason, consumer goods companies must build CSR into basic business strategy, as it is integral to the consumer perception necessary to build successful brands and long-term business. (Christiansen, 2007, p. 35)

The brand benefits of corporate social responsibility were made clearly visible in McDonald's implementation of the *My Greatest Feat* initiative. Although the stated aim of the programme was to get "children active, having fun, learning and involved" as "part of McDonald's ongoing commitment to the wellbeing of New Zealand children" (McDonald's, 2008, para. 1), the success of *My Greatest Feat* was not measured by children's physical activity or Body Mass Index (BMI), but the corporation's increased 'brand trust scores'. From a marketing perspective, this was seen to be the 'greatest feat' of all, given it was at a time where McDonald's were being blamed for childhood obesity (Powell, 2018). As Tribal DDB, one of the advertising companies responsible for marketing *My Greatest Feat*, argued: "McDonald's had been the whipping boy for everything big and bad about America and fast food. Brand trust scores were in decline. Correcting that would be no small feat" (Tribal DDB, 2009, para. 1). The advertisers then go on to explain how through the implementation of *My Greatest Feat* "which snowballed into the biggest physical activity programme ever undertaken in New Zealand .... McDonald's brand trust scores took a giant leap seeing increases up to 50%" (Tribal DDB, 2009, para. 3–5).

By using its own corporate social responsibility programme in conjunction with a partnership between the New Zealand Olympic Committee, a number of Olympic athletes, and at least three advertising agencies (DDB, Rapp, Tribal DDB, and Mango), McDonald's was able to attach its business strategies onto healthy lifestyles education programmes in schools. Astonishingly, this also helped to re-invent the multinational fast food company as not only trustworthy, but actually positive for children's health. Market research showed that following the *My Greatest Feat* programme, parents were far more positive towards the McDonald's brand. The parents' responses to the statement 'McDonalds is a company I can trust' increased by 33%, 'encourages active balanced lifestyles' increased by 50%, and 'has food I feel good about children eating' increased by 33%, "far exceeding the target of +5%" (International Post Corporation, n.d., p. 1–2).

Although some of the children I spoke to in my research where somewhat cynical about the reasons why McDonald's were wanting to promote pedometers in schools, others saw McDonald's as caring and healthy (see Powell, 2016). At Reynard Intermediate School I had a conversation with Year Seven boys Leroy and Sam about *My Greatest Feat*, and asked them if they thought McDonald's cared about children's health. Sam replied: "I think McDonald's probably does care a bit ... they have like Weight Watchers meals, so it shows they kind of care for health. But then again they mainly deal fast food ..."

McDonald's improved brand image extended outside the image of their food. Schools and external providers of healthy lifestyles education programmes also seemed more likely to accept McDonald's programmes when they were seen as socially responsible or charitable, and when philanthropy was seen as the 'prime purpose', rather than profit (Powell, 2018). For instance, *Life Education* teacher Marion was highly critical of McDonald's – their food, use of 'subliminal' advertising, restaurants being too close to schools, and impact on children's health – but still did not rule out the prospect of working with McDonald's:

DARREN: Would there be any corporations that you wouldn't want to work for or wouldn't want? Say if McDonald's

MARION: The government. We need more reliable funds than the government ... Charity is much more reliable. Um... McDonald's would be a hard one. I don't know that we would rule [McDonald's] out – no. I know Ronald McDonald House[4] hasn't ruled [them] out. At the end of the day funds is funds.

Here we see a rather curious phenomenon at play, whereby a significant tension – McDonald's providing health education to children in schools – was resolved by the 'charitable' act of giving and receiving. In this sense, a healthy lifestyles education programme is able to be strengthened by its connections to discourses of charity. Charity acts as a 'congealing agent' that brings organisations with disparate interests closer together. It also re-shapes a multinational fast-food restaurant company into something new; a philanthropic, healthy, and caring corporation (see Powell, 2018).

Private sector institutions were also able to re-invent themselves as altruistic and trustworthy by deliberately blending, if not dissolving, traditional demarcations between for-profit, 'not-for-profit', public, and voluntary sector organisations. This was certainly the case when the private sector helped to create or control charities or charitable trusts. The development of relationships between United Fresh and 5+ A Day Charitable Trust (and its *5+ A Day* education programme) is a useful illustration of how the blurring of boundaries works to re-invent private sector players and achieve their governmental ambitions.

United Fresh currently promotes itself as a *non-profit* organisation. Undermining United Fresh's non-profit status is that they represent "the New Zealand pan-produce industry", "work on behalf of members and the fresh fruit and vegetable industry", and connect "the fresh fruit and vegetable value chain by providing services and representation to industry" (United Fresh New Zealand Incorporated, n.d.-b). United Fresh is almost entirely funded by donations from its corporate members, which include the likes of The Yummy Fruit Company Limited (which promote an incentive scheme in primary schools), T&G Global (Turners and Growers), and New Zealand's two largest supermarket chains, Countdown and Foodstuffs. In short, *non-profit* United Fresh is funded by a number of wealthy *for-profit* companies. In its advertising to corporate members (that pay up to NZD$6,000 plus GST to be members of United Fresh and to use the 5+ A Day logo, see United Fresh New Zealand Incorporated, n.d.-c), part of United Fresh's core business is interacting with stakeholders, including government (i.e. Ministry of Health), industry, non-governmental organisations (such as The Heart Foundation), public health agencies, media, the public, and international organisations. As United Fresh New Zealand Incorporated (2014, p. 3) confidently tells its current and future members: "We are in touch with every group that impacts your bottom line".

Schools are one group that is considered to have an 'impact' on corporate members' profit, and thus are targeted by the fruit and vegetable industry. In fact, United Fresh New Zealand Incorporated (2014, p. 2) state that their *Fruit in Schools* contracts (a programme with the explicit purpose of providing free fruit to children in low socio-economic areas) will help members achieve "market access" to schools and government. United Fresh describes the benefits of their *5+ A Day* programme to its members as follows:

> In 2007, United Fresh set up The 5+ A Day Charitable Trust with New Zealand's children as its beneficiaries. The Trust focuses on increasing consumption through education, communication, partnerships, marketing, promotion and sponsorship. (United Fresh New Zealand Incorporated, 2014, p. 2)

We see here how the 5+ A Day Charitable Trust is designed as a vehicle to bring together children, schools, and business. It is also a charity that uses business strategies – partnerships, sponsorships, promotion, marketing – as technologies of consumption. Children are positioned as 'beneficiaries' of 5+ A Day's and United Fresh's charitable giving (presumably by learning that they needed to eat more fruit and vegetables), masking the profit-seeking intent of the industry to shape children as consumers.

A significant reason that these two 'not-for-profit' organisations are so well aligned is that 5+ A Day was *created* by United Fresh and is *governed* by United Fresh. On the New Zealand charities registry, the 'entity structure' of the 5+ A Day Charitable Trust states:

> The 5 + A Day Charitable Trust was established in May 2007 by United Fresh New Zealand Incorporated (United Fresh). The trustees of the 5 + A Day Charitable Trust are currently the executive members of United Fresh, 2 independent trustees and its independent President. The trustees oversee the strategic direction of the 5 + A Day Charitable Trust. (New Zealand Government, n.d.)

Every one of United Fresh's executive committee is a trustee on the board of 5+ A Day Charitable Trust, including United Fresh president and Brand Development Manager for MG Marketing, Jerry Prendergast (see New Zealand Government, n.d.; United Fresh New Zealand Incorporated, n.d.-d). One 'independent' trustee is David Smith: former president of United Fresh, co-founder and director of multinational Freshmax Group ("one of the largest fresh produce marketing and distribution operations in the Southern Hemisphere", see www.freshmax.group), and also director of Freshmax NZ Limited – a paid member of United Fresh.

By 'breaching and blending' the divisions between for-profit and not-for-profit, educational and charitable 'motives' (Ball, 2012), the interests of the fruit and vegetable industry in New Zealand are obscured. For example, when I suggested that charities were influenced by corporate funding, Miss Black observed: "I mean The Heart Foundation and 5+ A Day are non-profit organisations aren't they? So that's different". The 'difference' is that when boundaries between private and 'charitable' organisations are not just blurred, but dissolved, it makes it difficult to know "what not-for-profit means" (Ball, 2012, p. 89) and impossible to tell where business ends and charity begins. An entire 'for-profit' industry has been re-imagined as healthy, philanthropic, and educational. It is not the only one.

Gambling with health

It was not the official intention of all partners of school-based healthy life-styles education programmes to actually be 'part of the solution' to childhood obesity. Some organisations, such as 'pokie trusts', were accidently drawn in by the broader policy environment and the ambitions of various organisations to shape regulations, schools, and consumers (see Powell, 2018).

Every year pokie trusts (also called gaming trusts, gambling trusts, and gaming machine societies) deliver tens of millions of dollars of 'grants' to a variety of community, education, and charity organisations (see www.lionfoundation.org.nz). A number of the programmes that aim to teach children to eat better, be more active, live healthier lives, and not be fat also receive pokie funding. For example, in 2012 *Small Sticks* received funding from the New Zealand Community Trust (see New Zealand Community Trust, 2012). The Lion Foundation grants funds to the Life Education Trust and to GymSports New Zealand for the *moveMprove* programme, while Pub Charity and The Southern Trust also help to fund the *Life Education* programme.

Pokie trusts are legally defined not-for-profit "organisations that own and operate gaming machines and make grants to non-profit community organisations" (Department of Internal Affairs, 2017a, para. 9). These trusts are *corporate societies*[5] that have the status of a charitable trust (as defined by the Charitable Trusts Act 1957) and "*must* distribute all money generated by pokie machines to *authorised purposes*, except for money paid out as prizes, operating expenses for venues and the trusts themselves, and taxes and levies paid to the government" (Problem Gambling Foundation, 2014, p. 2, my emphases). Although the trusts own the pokie machines, they have a legislated and regulated obligation to pay a certain percentage (at time of writing, a minimum of 40%) of expenditure back to 'the community' (for a description of how the 'pokie trust machine' works, see Problem Gambling Foundation, 2014). This money did not have to, nor did it always, end up back in the same community from where it was taken from (see Auckland Council, 2014).

There are four authorised purposes for pokie trusts to raise funds:

- a charitable purpose;
- a non–commercial purpose that is beneficial to the whole or a section of the community;
- promoting, controlling, and conducting race meetings under the Racing Act 2003, including the payment of stakes; and
- Classes 1–3 gambling can also raise money for an electioneering purpose (Department of Internal Affairs, 2017b, para. 2).

However, the 'authorised purpose' for a pokie trust is different from a charitable purpose. Although the purpose *can* be for charity, it does not *have* to be (Powell, 2018). In New Zealand legislation, charity is defined as:

> helping people in need in the community. Typical recipients of charitable grants are the needy, for example, poor, sick, disabled or elderly people. Grants to further public health, religion and education may also be charitable. (Department of Internal Affairs, 2017b, para. 4)

Pokie trusts take advantage of a lack of government funding to schools and other organisations that aim to promote health (e.g. Life Education Trust) or 'education' (e.g. GymSports New Zealand) by promoting themselves and their grants as charitable. Pub Charity, for example, is not a registered charity under the Charities Act 2005. However, what does or does not count as charity is often contested. A number of organisations and their 'charitable' programmes do not always fall neatly within the law that stipulates "nobody should make a direct commercial profit from any authorised purpose grant" (Department of Internal Affairs, 2017b, para. 2).

The pokie trusts were seen by adults and children in the three schools as providing funding for schools and 'other' charities, as well as being charitable themselves. Pokie trusts were able to be re-invented when the trusts (and the recipients of the grants) successfully joined together discourses of charitable giving (i.e. grants) *and* 'doing good' in the community (Powell, 2018). For instance, The Lion Foundation (2018, para. 1–2) makes the grand claim: "Since 1988 we have returned over $850 million back to the community, supporting thousands of good causes all around New Zealand …. In fact, there are few Kiwis whose lives have not been touched by a Lion Foundation grant".

Although pokie trusts are legally required to give a pre-determined percentage of their gambling profits back to communities, they promote their grants and organisations as being altruistic. As Epperson (2013, p. 90) argues:

> The gambling industry in New Zealand, especially pokie machines, has also had some clever advertising successes in associating gambling with charity. The industry has a statutory obligation to return some of the money lost in pokie machines to the public, and they have seized this as an opportunity to link themselves vehemently to the notion of philanthropy.

The gift of grants from pokie trusts acts as a central strategy for organisations to achieve their multiple goals, especially those wanting to insert themselves into schools and influence children's education. The Lion Foundation (n.d., para. 1), for instance, promotes its funding of the Life Education Trust:

> The Trust delivers health-based education to give young people the knowledge and skills to live a fulfilling and healthy life. Funding

from The Lion Foundation ensures the Trust's national office is adequately resourced and able to provide all teaching resources and support free of charge.

This above quote demonstrates how the philanthropic gifting to health education/promotion charities results in the enactment of a healthy lifestyles education programme in schools. The former Chief Executive of the Life Education Trust, Peter Cox, was quoted on The Lion Foundation's (n.d., para. 2) website as stating:

This Lion Foundation funding removes the administrative and resourcing headaches that our regional trusts would otherwise face, allowing them to focus on what matters – delivering life changing programmes to the country's children.

In *Pokie proceeds: building strong communities*, a booklet published by the New Zealand Government's Department of Internal Affairs (n.d.), *Life Education* is promoted as a case study of how pokie trust funding 'works' for charities, schools, and children. Life Education Trust CEO, John O'Connell, is quoted in this document as follows:

Our organisation is very dependent on gaming funds. They're a core part of our income stream and without them we just couldn't run our programmes nationwide .... Being a child and growing up is not easy. We help children understand their own identity – that it is OK to be different – and we help build their resilience. Bullying, cyber-safety and obesity are all challenges for children today and mental health and wellbeing is so important to how a child responds to these challenges. (Department of Internal Affairs, n.d., p. 5)

The funding from pokie trusts is articulated as an absolute necessity for charities. It was perceived by external providers as a secure source of money that ensured the operation, if not survival of the charity, sporting body, or healthy lifestyles education programme. In the New Zealand context, funding from gambling and the gambling industry is now a significant strategy that helps charities 'get into schools' and attempt to shape children's health knowledge, behaviours, and identities.

There was, however, a significant tension when schools and other healthy lifestyles education organisations sought grants from pokie trusts. During my time in schools (in particular St Saviour's School), children, teachers, and principals consistently excoriated the gaming industry and their pub-based machines for their harmful impact on the health and well-being of children, families, and the wider community. Amy, an 11-year-old Pākehā girl in Ms Ellie's class, described how her mother had been an "alcoholic" and "pokie addict" since Amy was only one year of age. On a number of occasions,

Amy's mother had spent lengthy periods away from her family while in "rehab". Amy's classmate and good friend, Mary, an 11-year-old Samoan student, told me that her aunty and uncle "were addicted to pokies" and had to leave their children (Mary's cousins) to live with Mary and her family because they could not support them anymore. Mrs Sergeant and Ms Ellie were highly critical of pokies and talked fervently about their opposition to receiving grants from pokie trusts. Despite this, Ms Ellie and Mrs Sergeant regularly utilised programmes and resources that were either directly or indirectly the result of pokie trust grants, such as *moveMprove* and *Life Education* (see also Powell, 2018).

My discussions with teachers and principals about pokie trust grants demonstrated how the relationships between gambling, marketing, philanthropy, health, and education formed a difficult tension for underfunded schools. These tensions were resolved, however, when potential gatekeepers dismissed their concerns as irrelevant and trivial compared with the opportunity for students to participate in an externally provided 'health' programme:

MRS SERGEANT: We've had parents in the past who have had problems with gambling – I can't cope with [pokie trusts]. It's tricky because I don't go to them for money – I just go to the ASB [bank] and places like that – because I just loathe and detest those pokies with an absolute vengeance to be honest.

DARREN: The majority of the programmes, like *moveMprove*, are funded through–

MRS SERGEANT: I know, I know. And that's okay as long as I don't have to deal directly with them. And it's a tiny little, pathetic little tantrum that I'm throwing. I would *never ever* say to move and improve [sic] that you're not coming in here because you've got pokie money, because what am I'm doing? I'm satisfying some ridiculous little tantrum that I'm having, and then compromising all our little children who need to have the basics of athletics. And they're not overtly influencing children through those programmes, unlike the Ronald McDonald thing [*My Greatest Feat*] – which is quite insidious. (Mrs Sergeant's emphasis)

Even though the pokie industry and their ever-present gambling machines were seen by children and adults as inherently harmful, the funding of healthy lifestyles education programmes was understood as profoundly harmless. A substantial tension was diffused by discourses of charity joining programmes in a way that acted as a shield between the interests of pokie trusts and the potential dangers they held for children and their families. Political questions about the (un)ethical place of pokies in society (and pokie money in schools) were re-articulated as matters of technique; as an issue of the best place or programme to spend the money, rather than whether the money should be taken from the community in the first place, or from trusts at all. The possibility to challenge the legitimacy of the pokie industry and the inequities it propagates was shut down. Possible resistance was translated into possible acceptance – and possible funding. The idea that schools needed to provide children, particularly children 'in need', with charity was an important element that helped to persuade principals and teachers to sanction multiple charitable and philanthropic institutions to enter their schools and shape schooling (Powell, 2018).

Philanthropy, partnerships, and the role of schools

The war on childhood obesity is an almost perfect example of a multiple-authority approach to modern government, where an array of techniques and tactics are used to shape the conducts of people 'at a distance'. The school-based solutions to childhood obesity and unhealthy lifestyles were made possible through a number of policies, partnerships, sponsorships, pieces of legislation, charitable donations, philanthropic gifts, and corporate social responsibility programmes that encouraged corporations, charities, industry groups, state agencies, pokie trusts, and schools to 'work together'. Given the disparate, even opposing interests, within this messy mix of authorities and actors, clear tensions arose, especially when an industry or company with a reputation problem (such as the pokie industry or McDonald's) aligned themselves with schools and notions of health. These tensions were often resolved through the notion that these cross-sector relationships and resultant 'health' programmes were essentially a 'win–win' situation for everybody involved, especially 'for the kids'. As Miller and Rose (2008, p. 34) argued, for disparate parties to align they must first convince each other "that their interests are consonant, that each can solve their difficulties or achieve their ends by joining forces or working along the same lines". Healthy lifestyles education programmes have become useful means for organisations to achieve contradictory ends.

The implementation of healthy lifestyles education programmes was not forced upon naïve or unsuspecting teachers, and principals in primary schools. Multiple technologies were employed in the programmes and resources to encourage children to 'consume' products (for further discussion, see Chapter 7), tactics that were also used to 'conduct the conducts' of teachers, principals, and external providers. Teachers and principals were convinced to endorse an array of products, brand images, and (not)for-profit players based on their understanding that the children *needed* these free gifts (whether free food or free healthy lifestyles education), and were mobilised to become more than 'just' educators, but also consumers and givers of charity and philanthropy.

Corporations (and their products) were able to be seen as healthy, caring, philanthropic, and socially responsible while also improving their brand image and bottom line. Charities received much needed funding to continue to implement their various health/education programmes in schools. Industries, such as the pokie industry and the fruit and vegetable industry, re-invented their business strategies as charitable. The state continued its 'hand's off' approach to funding solutions to 'wicked' social problems, such as obesity and poverty (see Levin, Cashore, Bernstein, & Auld, 2012, for a discussion on wicked problems). And schools, teachers, and principals were gifted a plethora of free programmes that would help inform children about obesity and (un) healthy lifestyles, as well as teach their students about the 'philanthropic' and 'healthy' organisations that made these programmes possible.

These philanthropic partnerships in the name of fighting childhood obesity are not harmless. They work to shape the thoughts, actions, and identities of those actually teaching children in schools about health in ways that neatly align with private sector players' less altruistic interests: branding, public relations strategies, avoidance of stricter regulations and legislation, and of course, profit.

Notes

1 I have withheld the names of this particular regional Life Education Trust and its partners in order to protect the confidentiality of participants.
2 The Bachelor of Sport and Recreation degree from AUT (Auckland University of Technology) aimed to provide graduates with expertise in sport, recreation, and fitness, where students can major in areas such as sport coaching, exercise science, and health and physical education.
3 Since the *My Greatest Feat* initiative, McDonald's has committed to stop sending Ronald McDonald into New Zealand schools.
4 Ronald McDonald House is a McDonald's charity that provides support (including accommodation) for families of children admitted to a state hospital.
5 Under the Gambling Act 2003, a corporate society is a society that is incorporated as a board under the Charitable Trusts Act 1957.
6 In New Zealand, Pākehā is a common Māori word to describe immigrants to Aotearoa/New Zealand of European decent.

References

Auckland Council. (2014). *Gambling working party – New regulations for the distribution of class 4 (pokie) gambling grants to communities.* Retrieved from https://s3.amazonaws.com/s3.documentcloud.org/documents/1272921/pokies-report-full.pdf

Ball, S. J. (2012). *Global Education Inc.: New policy networks and the neoliberal imaginary.* Oxon, UK: Routledge.

Beef + Lamb New Zealand. (2008). *Marketing plan 2008/2009.* Retrieved from www.beeflambnz.co.nz/documents/MarketingPlan_0809.pdf

Boyles, D. R. (2008). *The corporate assault on youth: Commercialism, exploitation, and the end of innocence.* New York: Peter Lang.

Christiansen, N. (2007). *Defining corporate social responsibility: Creating shared value for shareholders and societies.* Paper presented at the CSR Plus: Strategies that enrich the poor and build corporate brands, London, UK.

Coveney, J. (2006). *Food, morals and meaning: The pleasure and anxiety of eating* (2nd edition). Abingdon, Oxon: Routledge.

Department of Internal Affairs. (2017a). *Funding for community groups.* Retrieved from http://www.dia.govt.nz/diawebsite.nsf/wpg_URL/Services-Casino-and-Non-Casino-Gaming-Funding-For-Community-Groups?OpenDocument

Department of Internal Affairs. (2017b). *Authorised purpose guidelines for societies and clubs.* Retrieved from http://www.dia.govt.nz/diawebsite.nsf/wpg_URL/Services-Casino-and-Non-Casino-Gaming-Authorised-Purpose-Guidelines-for-Societies-and-Clubs?OpenDocument

Department of Internal Affairs. (n.d.). *Pokie proceeds: Building strong communities.* Retrieved from http://www.dia.govt.nz/diawebsite.nsf/wpg_URL/Services-Casino-and-Non-Casino-Gaming-Funding-For-Community-Groups?OpenDocument

Epperson, S. (2013). *Lessons from the tobacco industry: What problem gambling services can learn and next steps for public health.* Retrieved from http://www.pha.org.nz/documents/PHANZ_2013_conference_proceedings.pdf#page=99

Foucault, M. (1984). Space, knowledge, and power: Interview with Paul Rabinow. In P. Rabinow (Ed.), *The Foucault reader* (pp. 239–256). New York: Pantheon.

Frucor. (2015). *Community.* Retrieved from http://www.frucor.co.nz/index.php/social_responsibility/community/

Huxham, C., & Vangen, S. (2000). What makes partnerships work? In S. Osbourne (Ed.), *Public-private partnerships: Theory and practice in international perspectives* (pp. 293–310). London: Routledge.

International Food & Beverage Alliance (IFBA). (2008). *Re: Global commitment to responsible marketing and advertising to children.* Retrieved from https://www.ifballiance.org/sites/default/files/Letter%20to%20Dr%20%20Chan%2012%2018%2008.pdf

International Food & Beverage Alliance (IFBA). (2018). *The International Food & Beverage Alliance ten-year progress report.* Retrieved from https://ifballiance.org/ten-year-progress-report

International Post Corporation. (n.d.). *Direct mail case study: My Greatest Feat.* Retrieved from http://www.ipc.be/~/media/Documents/PUBLIC/Markets/Case_Studies/Best%20Practice%20-%20McDonalds%20-%20My%20Greatest%20Feat%201.ashx

Ken, I. (2014). A healthy bottom line: Obese children, a pacified public, and corporate legitimacy. *Social Currents, 1*(2), 130–148. doi: 10.1177/2329496514524927

Levin, K., Cashore, B., Bernstein, S., & Auld, G. (2012). Overcoming the tragedy of super wicked problems: Constraining our future selves to ameliorate global climate change. *Policy Sciences, 45*(2), 123–152. doi: 10.1007/s11077-012-9151-0.

Li, T. M. (2007). Practices of assemblage and community forest management. *Economy and Society, 36,* 263–293. doi: 10.1080/03085140701254308

Life Education Trust. (2011). *Teacher's resource.* Retrieved from http://www.lifeeducation.org.nz/site/lifeedutrust/files/teaching_resources/Intro%20to%20Life%20Education.pdf

McDonald's. (2008). *My Greatest Feat: A national programme for primary school students.* Retrieved from http://awards.iwihost.com/mygreatestfeat/

McDonald's. (2013). *Nutrition and well-being: Offering customers quality, choice and nutrition.* Retrieved from http://www.aboutmcdonalds.com/mcd/sustainability/our_focus_areas/nutrition_and_well_being.html

McDonald's Restaurants (NZ) Limited. (2018). *Macca's® in the Community.* Retrieved from https://mcdonalds.co.nz/learn/responsibility/maccas-community

Miller, P., & Rose, N. (1997). Mobilizing the consumer: Assembling the subject of consumption. *Theory, Culture and Society, 14*(1), 1–36. doi: 10.1177/026327697014001001

Miller, P., & Rose, N. (2008). *Governing the present.* Cambridge, England: Polity.

Molnar, A. (2005). *School commercialism: From democratic ideal to market commodity.* New York: Routledge.

Nestlé. (2012a). *Nestlé joins call for more community-based programmes to prevent childhood obesity.* Retrieved from http://www.nestle.com/media/newsandfeatures/global-obesity-forum

Nestlé. (2012b). *Nestlé Healthy Kids Global Programme.* Retrieved from http://www. Nestlé.com/CSV/NUTRITION/HEALTHYKIDSPROGRAMME/Pages/ HealthyKidsProgramme.aspx

Nestlé. (2018a). *Creating shared value in action.* Retrieved from https://www.nestle.com/csv/ case-studies

Nestlé. (2018b). *Nestlé Healthy Kids Programme – location: Lebanon.* Retrieved from https:// www.nestle.com/csv/case-studies/allcasestudies/nutrition-healthy-kids-lebanon

New Zealand Beef and Lamb Marketing Bureau. (n.d.). *Iron Brion's hunt for gold resource kit.* New Zealand: New Zealand Beef and Lamb Marketing Bureau.

New Zealand Community Trust. (2012). *New Zealand Community Trust annual report 2011/2012.* Retrieved from http://www.nzct.org.nz/assets/pdf/NZCT-2012-Annual-Report-FINAL.pdf

New Zealand Government. (n.d.). *Charity summary.* Retrieved from https://www.register. charities.govt.nz/Charity/CC10745

Özüağ, E. (2013, January 15). *Coca Cola coming together.* [Video file]. Retrieved from https:// www.youtube.com/watch?v=SKi2A76YJlc

Powell, D. (2013). *Coca-Cola part of the solution to obesity? Yeah right!* Retrieved from https:// theconversation.com/coca-cola-part-of-the-solution-to-obesity-yeah-right-11662

Powell, D. (2014). Childhood obesity, corporate philanthropy and the creeping privatisation of health education. *Critical Public Health, 24*(2), 226–238. doi: 10.1080/ 09581596.2013.846465

Powell, D. (2015). *'Part of the solution'?: Charities, corporate philanthropy and healthy lifestyles education in New Zealand primary schools.* (Doctoral dissertation, Charles Sturt University, Bathurst, Australia). Retrieved from https://researchoutput.csu.edu.au/files/9316089/80326

Powell, D. (2016). Governing the (un)healthy child-consumer in the age of the childhood obesity crisis. *Sport, Education and Society, 23*(4), 297–310. doi:10.1080/13573322. 016.1192530

Powell, D. (2018). The 'will to give': Corporations, philanthropy and schools. *Journal of Education Policy, 34*(2), 195–214. doi: 10.1080/02680939.2018.1424940

Powell, D., & Gard, M. (2015). The governmentality of childhood obesity: Coca-Cola, corporations and schools. *Discourse: Studies in the Cultural Politics of Education, 36*(6), 854–867. doi: 10.1080/01596306.2014.905045

Powell, D., & Gard, M. (2018). Schools, corporations and promotion of physical activity to fight obesity. In J. Piggin, L. Mansfield, & M. Weed (Eds.), *Routledge handbook of physical activity and sport policy* (pp. 383–395). Oxon, UK: Routledge.

Problem Gambling Foundation. (2014). *Class 4 gambling: 'The pokies'.* Retrieved from http:// pgfnz.org.nz/wp-content/uploads/2014/06/FS13-Class-4-Gambling.pdf

Robin Hood Foundation. (n.d.). *Do gooder and gooder: How doing good is good for business.* Retrieved from http://www.robinhood.org.nz/Files/dogooders2_mr.pdf

Rose, N. (2000). Government and control. *British Journal of Criminology, 40,* 321–339.

Saltman, K. J. (2010). *The gift of education: Public education and venture philanthropy.* New York: Palgrave MacMillan.

The Coca-Cola Company. (2012). *Position on obesity: Including well-being facts.* Retrieved from http://assets.coca-colacompany.com/9b/62/c661da674cc690db3ccad9195639/obesity-position-statement.pdf

The Lion Foundation. (2018). *About us.* Retrieved from http://www.lionfoundation.org. nz/about/

The Lion Foundation. (n.d.). *Life Education Trust.* Retrieved from http://www.lionfoundation. org.nz/helped/grant-features/7016251/life-education-trust/

Tribal DDB. (2009). *My Greatest Feat.* Retrieved from http://www.tribalddb.co.nz/tribalog/?paged=64

United Fresh New Zealand Incorporated. (2014). *Our mission: To provide valuable, relevant services to our members and represent them in good faith on pan-industry issues.* Retrieved from http://www.unitedfresh.co.nz/unitedfresh/assets/PDFs/United%20Fresh%20Profile%20June%202014.pdf

United Fresh New Zealand Incorporated. (n.d.-a). *Fruit in schools.* Retrieved from http://www.unitedfresh.co.nz/services/fruit-in-schools

United Fresh New Zealand Incorporated. (n.d.-b). *About us: Our structure.* Retrieved from https://www.unitedfresh.co.nz/about-us

United Fresh New Zealand Incorporated. (n.d.-c). *Membership application form.* Retrieved from https://www.unitedfresh.co.nz/membership/membership-application

United Fresh New Zealand Incorporated. (n.d.-d). *About us: Executive committee.* Retrieved from https://www.unitedfresh.co.nz/about-us/executive-committee

World Health Organization. (2010). *Global strategy on diet, physical activity and health: Set of recommendations on the marketing of foods and non-alcoholic beverages to children.* Retrieved from http://www.who.int/dietphysicalactivity/publications/recsmarketing/en/

World Health Organization. (2018a). *Global strategy on diet, physical activity and health: What can be done to fight the childhood obesity epidemic?* Retrieved from https://www.who.int/dietphysicalactivity/childhood_what_can_be_done/en/

World Health Organization. (2018b). *Global strategy on diet, physical activity and health: The role of the private sector.* Retrieved from http://www.who.int/dietphysicalactivity/childhood_private_sector/en/index.html

World Health Organization. (2018c). *Global strategy on diet, physical activity and health: Marketing of foods and non-alcoholic beverages to children.* Retrieved from http://www.who.int/dietphysicalactivity

5

THE NEW 'EXPERTS'
IN CHILDREN'S HEALTH
AND EDUCATION

Although an analysis of the individual organisations, people, and other elements that make up healthy lifestyles education programmes provides us with a deeper understanding of how disparate parties have aligned their interests in fighting obesity, there also needs to be a critical examination of the practices that bring these elements together and make them 'stick'. This chapter describes how healthy lifestyles education programmes are constituted by paying close attention to the means by which outsourcing these programmes to external providers has been re-imagined by teachers and principals as natural and necessary – a 'perfect' practice. It is a practice, however, that results in some unpredictable outcomes that could be considered 'dangerous' for classroom teachers and students alike. Here I aim to shed light on how different organisations and actors attempt to improve children's bodies and behaviours through shaping teachers' desires, routines, and beliefs about health and physical education (HPE). My focus here is on how two complementary subjects – the *inexpert classroom teacher* and the *expert external provider* – shaped teachers and principals, and even further encouraged the use of corporate-friendly 'solutions' to childhood obesity. To do this I look at dimensions of healthy lifestyles education programmes that are integral to influencing primary school teachers and the teaching of HPE: discourses of sport and healthy lifestyles, tactics of privatisation and outsourcing, government policies and funding, specific school-based programmes and resources, and the shaping of (in)expert teachers.

The 'problem' of inexpert classroom teachers

To be able to introduce any intervention, such as a corporate and/or charitable solution to obesity, a specific situation or moment in which conduct is conceived as a 'problem' must first be identified (Miller & Rose, 2008). A common theme that emerged from my research was that classroom teachers' conduct was problematised by teachers, principals, and external providers in terms of a lack of expertise to be able to teach their own students. This perceived problem of inexpert classroom teachers was not related to their teaching in a broad sense (i.e. their knowledge, skills, and dispositions to successfully plan, teach, and assess English or maths, give appropriate pastoral care, or demonstrate leadership), but rather their inexpertise to teach HPE. Teachers and external providers frequently talked about generalist classroom teachers[1] in deficit terms: their inability to 'teach' sports (e.g. hockey, athletics, gymnastics), technical sports skills (e.g. performing a forward roll, hitting a hockey ball, sprinting), and 'facts' about health (see Powell, 2015).

In stark contrast, external providers were consistently positioned and promoted (by themselves and others) as HPE 'experts'. St Saviour's School classroom teacher Miss Black, for example, stated that a key benefit of using external providers was that "there's definitely a level of expertise that comes with [outside] teachers". The external providers certainly understood that they were the HPE 'experts' and teachers were not. For example, *Small Sticks* coach and representative hockey player Andrea stated that the main reason teachers used her, alongside other external providers, was for "that specialist and expert knowledge". Similarly, Jonie, the *Get Set Go* facilitator from Sport Auckland, thought she was recruited into schools because the teachers and principals "thought that I was like, maybe, I was really good in that area [of PE]. So I am important, because I am a professional in that area". While the external providers of *Get Set Go* and *Small Sticks* were seen as professionals and experts in particular sports, they were not necessarily experts in the type of HPE articulated in *The New Zealand curriculum* (Ministry of Education, 2007), nor were they even qualified or registered teachers. Instead, notions of (in)expertise were underpinned by dominant discourses of physical education (PE) that conflated the practice of teaching PE with coaching sports skills (Powell, 2015).

Coaching sport as quality physical education

Teachers, principals, and external providers frequently talked about the PE component of HPE in ways that favoured the technical elements of sport, principally being able to 'teach' children to perform sports-related 'skills' (e.g. doing a forward roll, kicking a soccer ball). For instance, during a conversation with Year Two teacher Miss Black, she told me that "*moveMprove* was great because [the coaches] knew exactly which skills they wanted [the children] to learn and they focused on that". In another discussion with Mr Spurlock, a Year Seven and Eight classroom teacher at Dudley School with school-wide leadership responsibilities for PE, he too drew on a narrow view of PE as simply teaching and learning 'skills':

> I see PE, in the end, more about teaching skills. And you can teach the same skill in Year Seven and Eight to a kid in Year Two or Three. I mean, it just depends on how much they take it on board – dumb it down a bit more for Year Two and Three.

A number of the programmes brought into these schools focused on developing skills associated with a particular sport. The *Small Sticks* programme focused entirely on hockey skills such as passing, dribbling, and shooting a hockey ball with a hockey stick. The *ASB Football in Schools* programme stated that all "learning takes place using the sport of football" (New Zealand Football, n.d., p. 1), while *moveMprove* and *Get Set Go* were described as 'fundamental movement skills' programmes. These were not so much focused on a specific sport *per se*, but centred on children being taught sports-*related* skills. For instance, the *Get Set Go* programme (a partnership between *ActivePost* and Athletics New Zealand) did not claim to coach specific athletics events (e.g. long jump, shot put), but focused on teaching children basic sports skills (Athletics New Zealand, 2012). These 'fundamental' skills included developing spatial awareness, balancing on one foot, sprinting, and throwing a ball overhand. The developers of *moveMprove* seemed at pains to state it was "developed as a foundation skills programme, *not* a gymnastic programme" (GymSports New Zealand, 2006, my emphasis). However, every *moveMprove* session I observed at St Saviour's School and Dudley School included numerous traditional gymnastics movements, such as forward rolls, jumping over a vault, and swinging on a horizontal bar. During my time at these two schools, *moveMprove* was most commonly referred to by teachers and students as 'Gymnastics', was sometimes called "move and improve" (which Mrs Sergeant thought was an athletics programme), and on very rare occasions called *moveMprove*. I never heard *moveMprove* or *Get Set Go* described by the adults or children as a 'fundamental' or 'foundation' skills programme.

Whether or not the children were taught sport-specific skills or fundamental movement skills, the point is that programmes were taught by the 'expert' external providers as part of the school's curricula PE programme. During my six months at St Saviour's School *every* PE lesson for Ms Ellie's and Miss Black's classes were programmes delivered by an external provider: *moveMprove*, *Get Set Go*, *ASB Football in Schools*, and *Small Sticks*. Every programme was conducted during curriculum time, as opposed to before school, during lunchtime, or after school as extra-curricular activities. And all four programmes were both promoted and perceived as being PE. For example, the brochure advertising the *ASB Football in Schools* initiative stated:

> The football literacy programme entails 2 × 5 week blocks of football curriculum *delivered in school time as part of a typical physical education class* .... We believe that the ASB Football in Schools programme and *our football expertise*, partnered with your schools (sic) educational prowess, will increase the opportunity for our children to have more meaningful learning experiences. (New Zealand Football, n.d., p. 1, my emphases)

The discursive connection between sport and PE meant that the coaches of *Small Sticks, moveMprove, Get Set Go,* and *ASB Football in Schools* were viewed by the teachers, principals, and themselves as experts in hockey, football, athletics, or fundamental movement skills – and as experts in PE. Conversely, the classroom teachers positioned themselves as inexpert because they did not think they had the necessary knowledge or skills to teach PE (as sport) *in relation to* the specialist 'expert' football/gymnastic/Sport Auckland/hockey coaches. There is a critical contradiction that did not seem to be picked up by teachers or external providers. The teachers brought in external providers because they were inexpert in coaching sports skills. However, the external providers did not claim to be teaching sports skills. Rather, they were providing PE or fundamental movement skills. In other words, the external providers were not officially offering what the teachers said they needed — experts to teach sports skills.

moveMprove promoted the idea that they were the experts — and teachers were not — by publishing in the *Educator's guide* (GymSports New Zealand, n.d.-a, para. 3) the following testimonial from a Year One teacher:

> I found the extra skills and strategies that the experts taught the children were done so much better than I could have done it. E.g., how they handled the children who were scared to do forward rolls, or ensuring safe rolls/landings.

At Dudley School I had a conversation with Mrs Donna in her classroom, where she described the benefits of using the local gymnastics coaches. She too compared the 'experts' to her own abilities and confidence:

> *I think it was better for the children* because they had someone actually promoting the warm-up side of it first — getting them to use their body parts and stretch before they went into the activity. When we do it it's straight into the activity and we rotate around, whereas with this one they rotate around but they don't get to every activity. I think that was great. *And it was less stress on us. Because we often, I often, worry about teaching them the right move,* whether they're going to hurt themselves. And some of the equipment they have, we don't have, so we can't get them to do things like the 'lift and holding themselves' [horizontal bar activity] you know? I think that was really good. *It was much better than us.* (my emphases)

Ms Ellie, the school-wide leader of PE at St Saviour's School and the classroom teacher for Year Six/Seven, explained to me that the advantage of using external providers for PE was that the coaches were better at teaching specific sports and sports skills:

> Well, we have an expert to teach. It's a focus on that particular sport, and they can break down the skills probably better than [the teacher] .... And a lot of the teachers don't have the skills nowadays, or the time to prepare what they should do, like in the old days they used to.

Ms Ellie's understanding of the "better" outsourced expert was intimately connected to the idea that the coaches were better at teaching a "particular sport", even though the same external providers claimed they *were not* teaching particular sports, but broader 'movement skills'. The dominant discourse of PE as sport, as well as her own perceptions of the inexpert classroom teacher who lacked the time, skills, and motivation to "break down" specific sports skills for their students, meant that coaches were now invaluable to the classroom teachers and their curricula PE programmes – especially when "teachers don't know anything about hockey" or other sports.

Small Sticks coach Andrea agreed with Ms Ellie. She thought that teachers were specialists in maths and literacy, but lacked the expert knowledge to be able to teach hockey and lacked the confidence to teach PE in general. I asked Andrea why teachers utilised external providers like herself. She replied:

> It's more for expertise ... I know this sounds bad but [teachers are] afraid to teach or get it wrong or to get that expert information ... Like the teachers could easily do what I do, but for me I can sort of tweak it, you know? I know the ins and outs of hockey. And it's fun for them to just sit back and watch ... Especially because with primary teaching, a lot of them specialise in maths and English ... that's why a lot of them leave [the classes during hockey lessons], because they don't feel comfortable with physical education, you know. It is hard.

Andrea, Ms Ellie, and a number of other teachers and external providers seemed to be oblivious to significant slippage in the terminology used to describe PE/sport, teaching/coaching, expertise/specialists. The external providers and their partners drew on discourses of PE and fundamental movement skills that masked self-interests, such as promoting 'their' sport. At the same time, by re-imagining curricula PE (i.e. a form of PE informed by *The New Zealand curriculum*) in ways that aligned closely with sport *and* the aims of sporting authorities, a number of organisations were able to have their presence in schools endorsed by teachers and principals. In doing so, the practice of outsourcing PE teaching to the experts was legitimised and normalised (also see Dyson, Cowan, Gordon, Powell, & Shulruf, 2018).

The teachers I interviewed re-worked 'old' discourses construing PE as primarily about "sports" and "sports skills" (Ms Ellie) in ways that helped divert attention from the fact that they were not willing or able to teach PE, a compulsory Essential Learning Area of *The New Zealand curriculum*. Further, by re-imagining the field of PE, schools were able to effectively hand over the teaching of this curriculum area to outside experts with little or no knowledge of *The New Zealand curriculum*, its suggested 'effective pedagogies', or even the students they were teaching. The ways in which outsourcing was seen as ideal and necessary was not achieved by external organisations 'forcing' schools to change their practices. It was made possible by broader education policies (and funding arrangements) that helped to simultaneously realise the ambitions of multi-sector organisations and direct the conducts of teachers, schools, external providers, and the state.

The sportification of PE in primary schools

The availability of Kiwisport funding was a significant shift in government policy that reproduced the 'PE as sport' discourse and made it possible, if not inevitable, for teachers to outsource their PE programmes the 'experts' (Powell, 2015). In both full primary schools, St Saviour's School and Dudley School, their provision of 'PE' learning experiences was dominated by external organisations (and their coaches/instructors) funded by the state through Kiwisport. A newsletter was even sent to the parents of students at St Saviour's School that read: "This year we are on the Kiwisport contract where expert coaches come and teach our children skills". Notions of expertise, outsourcing, Kiwisport, and PE as coaching sports skills were neatly brought together and promoted as a normal, if not valuable, teaching practice.

Kiwisport was an \$82 million[2] initiative launched in August 2009 by erstwhile Prime Minister John Key (2009, para. 27) with an expressed aim to "increase the opportunities for young Kiwis to get involved in sport. The Government wants to see more Kiwi kids participating in sport so that they get the health and lifestyle benefits of better physical fitness". The main three aims of Kiwisport were clearly laid out by the Ministry of Education (n.d., para. 2):

- Increase the number of school-aged children participating in organised sport.
- Increase the availability and accessibility of sport opportunities for all school-aged children.
- Support children in developing skills that will enable them to participate effectively in sport.

The National-led coalition government developed a new policy and funding regime for schools to access a range of sport-related coaching programmes. The funding of Kiwisport – and the subsequent outsourcing of primary school PE to Kiwisport providers – was achieved through two means. First, primary schools were able to apply for their share of \$24 million of Direct Funding allocated to primary schools – to a maximum of \$13.11 per student, per year. This funding was provided through the Ministry of Education (although the money was provided by the Ministers of Health, Education, and Sport & Recreation) and was allocated through the school's operational grant payment.[3] According to Key (2009, para. 21), schools will

> have the flexibility and the freedom to apply the money to address their specific needs to help ensure more children play sport. The

reporting requirements for this funding will not be onerous and bureaucratic, but will hold schools to account that they are using the funds to promote sport.

As demonstrated in the above quote, the official rationale for Kiwisport funding is underpinned by neoliberal canons: the autonomy of primary schools, 'small government' accountability, and freedom of choice. It is a funding regime built on notions of efficiency through its lack of "onerous" bureaucracy, but at the same time stresses the importance of accountability for the self-governing school. Dudley School principal Mr Woodward contradicted Key's claim that Kiwisport funding was easy and efficient, telling me in a conversation that he had to submit a lot of paperwork "to justify how Kiwisport was done". While rhetorically schools are given "the flexibility and freedom" to "decide how to best use this funding to encourage more children into organised sport" (Key, 2009, para. 28), their decisions are constrained by a number of rules and provisions. For example, transport does not receive Kiwisport funding, although Mr Woodward told me that he managed to use his Kiwisport funds to pay for the buses that took his students to a local gymnastics club, adding that the Kiwisport funders "don't need to know that!"

Schools are also required to spend their money on the 'right' providers (those authorised by Regional Sports Trusts, such as Sport Auckland) in a way that achieves the specific aims of Kiwisport. In other words, teachers are not able to use the Kiwisport funding to meet the *learning needs of their students* in terms of meeting the learning outcomes and achievement objectives of PE as defined in *The New Zealand curriculum*. As the policy states, schools can only use "the money to address their specific needs to help ensure more children play sport" (Key, 2009, para. 21). Yet again, principals, politicians, the Prime Minister, and teachers agreed that these Kiwisport programmes were about getting students to play sport. The external providers, however, continued to claim that they were more than that. They wanted to be seen as educators – physical educators.

The other way that Kiwisport is funded is through the $37 million 'Regional Partnership Fund'. The 17 Regional Sports Trusts (including Sport Auckland) across New Zealand receive a bulk fund based on the number of children in their region. Each Regional Sports Trust is then responsible and accountable for administering and allocating the contestable funds to projects that they believe will help attain the goals of Kiwisport (although the final 'signing off' of funds is made by Sport New Zealand). Between 2010 and 2012 Sport Auckland distributed $2,359.000 to community sports organisations and their programmes via its Regional Partnership Fund (Sport Auckland, n.d.). These programmes included a number of healthy lifestyles education/fundamental movement skill programmes that were implemented as curricula PE in primary schools. *moveMprove* at St Saviour's School was made possible through Tri-Star Gymnastics (a local gymnastics club) receiving $71,250 of Kiwisport funding from Round 1 and another

$66,528 from Round 2. Auckland Football was allocated $52,500 to help implement the *ASB Football in School's* programme. Auckland Hockey was awarded $65,635 to bring the *Small Sticks* programme into primary schools (Sport Auckland, 2012). In short, clubs and sports organisations received funding via Sport Auckland, then brought their coaches into the primary schools to lead a given programme.

Kiwisport played a vital role in the creation and implementation of healthy lifestyle programmes. The state provided funding and access to organisations that schools were financially encouraged to outsource their PE programmes. However, by governing teachers and schools to use these external experts and programmes, Kiwisport also acted as a discursive connection between sport and PE, resulting in a 'Kiwisportification' of PE in New Zealand primary schools (Powell, 2015).

The dominant discourse of 'PE is the same as coaching sports skills' was reproduced because all of the Kiwisport funded programmes – *moveMprove*, *ASB Football in Schools*, *Small Sticks*, and *Get Set Go* – took place in curricula PE time. In addition, these four programmes were funded, devised, and implemented by sporting organisations and their sports coaches: GymSports New Zealand, Tri-Star Gymnastics Club, and Counties Gymnastics Club; New Zealand Football and Auckland Football Federation New Zealand; Hockey New Zealand and Auckland Hockey; Athletics New Zealand and Sport Auckland. The principals, teachers, and children I talked to described and understood these outsourced programmes as 'sport'. The children were regularly taught to develop their performance of specific hockey, athletics, gymnastics, and/or football skills. Yet the Kiwisport-funded providers repeatedly drew on the language of PE and fundamental movement skills (such as running, throwing, and jumping), rather than specific sports or sports skills. Ultimately, these externally provided programmes and associated resources were devised by sports organisations whose funding was dependent upon achieving the goals of Kiwisport, not the aims and vision of *The New Zealand curriculum*. However, they were also programmes that were understood as having a role to play in making children healthier, more active, and less fat.

Learning sports skills will lead to healthy, active lifestyles

Although the overwhelming emphasis in Kiwisport and the programmes associated with it was on developing children's sporting ability and participation, this was discursively associated in policy and programme documentation – and in the discussions I had with the teachers, principals, children, and external providers – with obesity and healthy lifestyles. I was frequently told by adults in schools that playing sport and learning sports skills would lead to children being active, getting fitter, living healthy lifestyles, and being less fat – both now and for the rest of their lives.

A number of external providers and their corporate partners described the Kiwisport-funded and externally provided programmes as though they were some kind of 'gateway drug', a form of physical activity that would 'push' children into a lifelong physical activity habit and prevent obesity. For example, the rationale for the *ASB Football in Schools* programme was underpinned by taken-for-granted assumptions that "kiwi kids" have serious problems with obesity, physical inactivity, fitness, confidence, and socialisation; problems that would be solved through learning how to play football:

> With physical activity levels among kids on the slide, and obesity on the rise, it is critical to get kiwi kids back on track. The benefits of physical activity through sports such as football are that children have better physical fitness, are given the chance to be part of a team, and development of physical skills can lead to greater self-confidence and self-esteem. The latter can flow on to other aspects of their life and have a positive impact on their relationships with peers. (Hutt City Council, n.d., para. 3)

The *moveMprove* programme also gathered together various ideas that children's movement skills were problematic and needed 'fixing', stating that: New Zealand children were deficient in their movement skills; *moveMprove* would improve children's skills; developing these skills would make children healthier ("stay well") and more active, "enjoying physical activity for life" (GymSports New Zealand, n.d.-b, p. 2). GymSports New Zealand (2006, para. 6) justified their programme on the basis that:

> kiwi kids between the ages of 3 and 10 years are lacking important movement skills required for participation in sport, recreation and lifelong health and well-being. Therefore, *moveMprove* has been developed as a foundation skills programme, not a gymnastic programme. It provides children with the opportunity to experience and participate in movement that will assist development in skills required to play all type of sports and recreational activities.

To strengthen the connections between these 'truths', GymSports New Zealand used their *Educator's guide* (provided free to teachers) to claim that "children who do not master fundamental movement patterns" (those that children who participate in *moveMprove* are required to rehearse) "often reject participation in physical activity as part of their lifestyle", while those "children who have well developed fundamental movement patterns" "are likely to maintain an active and healthy lifestyle" (GymSports New Zealand, n.d.-a). In fact, GymSports New Zealand (n.d.-b, p. 2) claimed that "an expected result [of *moveMprove*] is that children will be healthier, happier, with improved academic abilities". No further evidence was provided on how *moveMprove* will actually achieve these expectations.

GymSports New Zealand's rhetoric renders the multifaceted dimensions of children's health, well-being, lifestyles, sport participation, physical activity, skills, movement, education, and futures as *anti-political* (see Li, 2007). Political questions around the complex determinants of children's health, such as the impact that poverty had on the 'lifestyles' of students at St Saviour's School, are re-posed as matters of technique. The 'problems' of fatness, inactivity, and ill health are re-imagined as being 'solvable' and 'improvable' through children participating in a series of six 45-minute sessions. *moveMprove* is not the only programme to make these claims and connections.

Get Set Go was (and continues to be) marketed as "a new and exciting initiative to help our Kiwi Kids develop the skills they need so that they can choose and enjoy being more active through play and sport" (Athletics New Zealand, 2012, p. i). It was rationalised as a programme that focuses on developing children's fundamental movement skills, because these children "have been shown to have greater participation levels in physical activity experiences, both throughout later schooling and in adult life" (p. 5). To connect the dots between the development of fundamental movement skills and physical health and well-being benefits, the teacher's manual draws on the Ministry of Education's guidelines for sustainable physical activity in school communities. In the introduction to the *Get Set Go* resource, Brian Roche, Chief Executive of New Zealand Post, justifies his organisation's partnership with this programme by stating that learning fundamental movement skills

> can help young people to develop a love of sport and recreation that leads to lifelong participation. To achieve this, young people must learn fundamental movement skills .... We owe it to our children to help them grow into healthy and confident adults – Get Set Go will help them achieve that. (Athletics New Zealand, 2012, p. 2)

Roche's conviction that children *need* these programmes, and that learning sports/fundamental movement skills at school *will* lead to children being healthier, fitter, thinner, and more active was echoed by teachers, principals, and external providers. For example, I asked Andrea, who had coached *Small Sticks* and other Kiwisport-funded programmes in primary schools, if she thought these programmes had a part to play in fighting childhood obesity:

> Oh yeah, seriously. Physical activity full stop will keep [children] away from obesity ... look now (points out the window at the children on the courts) – they are playing hockey out there. They are running around, and just like, being active and things like that ... I think that running around is the best way of fighting obesity. That and food. I agree that Kiwisport is helping 'cause you are introducing [sports] to them, like Year Ones, at such a young age.

In another example, Sport Auckland employee and *Get Set Go* facilitator Jonie described how she, along with the primary school teachers she worked with, felt the need for children to be taught fundamental movement skills to address the sedentary, protected nature of contemporary children's lives; children Jonie had described as "wrapped in cotton wool" and "a lot lazier" than previous generations:

JONIE: So that's why I keep saying to [teachers] how important it is to teach these fundamentals, because it's not a natural progression [for children] as much as what it would have been 30 years ago.

DARREN: What do you think the link is between learning fundamental movement skills and encouraging the children to be more active or making more active choices?

JONIE: What is the link?

DARREN: Yeah, how do you think *Get Set Go* encourages children to be more active?

JONIE: Well, we always discuss the sessions about 'where can you practice your activities?' and 'instead of when you go to the toilets today, instead of running to the toilet, or walking, why don't you skip or do this or try different things?' Trying to make sure there is a home link … I guess those fundamentals there are easily taught. Like, it's not like 'we are going to play cricket, we have to play cricket in this place'. It's incorporating [fundamental movement skills] into everyday life.

Jonie and Andrea, as well as a number of other teachers and principals, were apparently mobilised to implement these healthy lifestyles education programmes by the unquestionable 'truth' that they would lead to children living healthier lifestyles, being more active, and less likely to be fat. By attaching dominant obesity and physical (in)activity discourses to these healthy lifestyles/sports programmes, the point and purpose of PE was re-imagined. This also demonstrates a practice that Li (2007) describes as rendering technical, an over-simplistic set of relations which asserts that the *problem* (in this case, inexpert teachers and unhealthy children) + *intervention* (external providers and their 'PE' programmes and resources) = *beneficial result* (sporty, healthy, non–obese children).

St Saviour's beginning teacher, Miss Black, also held out some hope that her students' health and physical activity would benefit from the *Kiwisport-funded 'PE' programmes*:

DARREN: These different programmes – especially *Get Set Go, moveMprove, Kiwisport, Small Sticks* hockey – do you think that they will have or have had an effect on the children's health or physical activity?

MISS BLACK: I think so. I mean, they are so little and you know, there's a lot to happen between now and adulthood. I mean, you just never know. I'd like to think yes, it has a positive effect (laughs). That's what I'd like to think!

> It's helping them to have positive attitudes towards physical activity and you know, surely them doing something rather than not doing any physical activity, surely that's got to be beneficial? Surely it's going to help? I do think so (laughs). But who knows, I haven't done any research on it (laughs).

Even though Miss Black held on to her belief that these programmes would "surely" help her students be healthy and physically active, both for now and in the future, there was an element of doubt. This hesitation was based on her knowledge that "there's a lot to happen between now and adulthood"; that there were *other* influences on children's ability to be (in)active than just externally provided 'sports' programmes.

Despite their scepticism of the alleged health benefits of these sports-related programmes for their students, teachers continued to tell me that these various programmes and resources were also a valuable part of their students' education. The programmes were valued because of the combined strength of the 'PE as sports' and 'sports will lead to healthier lifestyles' discourses, where the best people to teach children were not teachers, but the expert sports coaches. However, the shaping of the teachers' investments in these programmes was not achieved through the mere presence of external providers and Kiwisport funding, but through other government education policies that made the corporatisation of education possible and preferable.

The role of National Standards

The teachers in my research were not necessarily cultural or political 'dupes' who were unwilling or unable to engage in, understand, or resist the politics of educational reform. A common topic of conversation in the staffrooms at all three schools (aside from food, dieting, and children's behaviour) was the politics of education, in particular the impact of what teachers referred to as the Global Education Reform Movement (GERM) (see Sahlberg, 2011). At St Saviour's School, for instance, circular placards reading "Fight the GERM" were displayed on the wall of the staffroom – signs that New Zealand Education Institute (NZEI) teachers' union had distributed to members during meetings, debates, and protests about the reform of education within New Zealand.

There were a number of so-called GERM reforms that particularly raised teachers' and principals' ire: the prospect of performance pay for 'expert' teachers and principals in the 'Investing in Educational Success' scheme; increased class sizes; the botched outsourcing of payroll services to Australian company Novopay; school closures and mergers following the Canterbury earthquake; public-private partnerships for the construction, maintenance, and management of school buildings; league tables that compared and ranked primary schools against each other; and the controversial legislation that allows the introduction of charter or 'partnership' schools. However, the reform that by far received the most criticism and condemnation by the teachers and principals was the introduction of National Standards for reading, writing, and maths (for an excellent critique of National Standards, see Thrupp, 2018).

National Standards were a key neoliberal reform of education in New Zealand, designed to 'raise achievement' by giving "teachers, children, parents, families and whānau [extended family group] a clear idea of where children are at in reading, writing and maths, and what they have to do next in their learning" (Ministry of Education, 2010). Following the passing of the *Education (National Standards) Amendment Act 2008*, all public (i.e. state) primary and intermediate (and some secondary) schools were required to assess all children in years one to eight (aged 5–13) as being 'at', 'above', 'below', or 'well below' benchmarked standards in reading, writing, and maths. Schools were also required to report each child's progress at least twice a year to parents *and* to the Ministry of Education in the areas of reading, writing, and maths.[4] National Standards were used in schools from 2010 and results were publicly available from 2012, including the publication of a school league table by news website *Stuff*.[5]

Rather than seeing the implementation of this new assessment and reporting regime as advantageous to teaching and learning, teachers and principals viewed National Standards as burdensome, restrictive, unnecessary, and producing a renewed emphasis on reading, writing, and mathematics at the expense of other areas of the curriculum. For instance, when I talked to Mr Woodward, the principal of Dudley School, about why HPE seemed to be a curriculum area targeted by external providers, he replied:

> I mean if you listen to the government, the Ministry, [we] would only be doing reading, writing and maths. Nothing else matters. So physed doesn't matter, art doesn't matter, technology doesn't matter. It's just those three. If they'd left it as it was, and they concentrated on getting kids to school and eating properly and getting here … instead of trying to change everything. National Standards – stupid, the crap [the Ministry of Education] are doing.

The prioritisation of teaching in reading, writing, and maths was described as the main reason why HPE and 'other' Essential Learning Areas (i.e. the arts, social sciences, languages, technology, and science) were relegated to the status of "don't matter" subjects. As Evans and Davies (2014, p. 3) argued, "subjects not considered 'core' (i.e. transparently, economically productive) have tended to become vulnerable luxuries and their teachers insecure in their responses to such pressures". Mrs Donna, for instance, said that although she loved "playing games and that …. PE is not my first priority. My first priority is maths and literacy".

The prioritisation of actual in-class teaching and learning in reading, writing, and maths was not the only factor that restricted teachers' ability or motivation to teach HPE. Teachers and principals recognised that the National Standards policy impacted teachers' workloads which needed to reflect the new priorities, whether they agreed with National Standards or not. As Ms Ellie explained:

> Everything is on the backburner other than reading, writing or maths. And the sad thing is … the arts curriculum is where our children are really successful and you can actually teach reading and writing through those areas, but the money has dried up. We did an African dance thing – we got some funding and the learning out of that was amazing – but all of a sudden there's no money for that. There's only money … to get to that [National] Standard, and to pull into line schools that don't conform really … and it's definitely a huge issue, because we want whole citizens.

As Ministry of Education and school funding concentrated on reading, writing, and maths, more time was required for teachers to plan, teach, assess, and think about these three areas. Consequently, as less money was spent on HPE and other non-National Standard subjects, the time to focus on those areas also diminished. *Life Education* teacher Marion also noted that National Standards and the de-prioritisation of HPE meant that some schools were choosing not to make use of the *Life Education* programme:

> One big thing at the moment that's coming through is the National Standards. So [schools] are struggling to meet the National Standards and therefore are choosing to look at Life [Education] as a sort of extra thing, rather than getting the most value out of it.

It was made clear by teachers, principals, and external providers that the emphasis on National Standards had a negative impact on children, both in terms of their learning in those non-priority subjects, as well as a loss of rich and varied learning experiences in general. The curriculum had been narrowed and teaching intensified.

A shift in teaching priorities meant that teachers were less willing to give time to plan and teach HPE, and less able to access professional development (PD) opportunities. For instance, Ms Ellie told me that teachers used external providers in HPE because "a lot of the teachers don't have the skills nowadays, or the time to prepare what they should do, like in the old days they used to … because of the constraints of the curriculum and the National Standards". When I asked Ms Ellie to explain this link between National Standards and a lack of skills to teach HPE, she responded that there was

> definitely not enough training in health and PE and not a lot of experts that come in [for professional development]. I mean we have the e-learning person come in for the digital classroom and we definitely have a lot of Ministry [of Education] input in [reading, writing and maths]. I guess the money's been directed into other areas because of that. Yeah, it is a concern.

As Ms Ellie pointed out, it was more than just the introduction of National Standards and attached professional support, funding, and resources that forced teachers to place more emphasis on these learning areas. The government acted in a deliberate way to de-prioritise HPE and 'other' subjects by removing *all* funding and advisory support for primary school teachers in these subjects (see Patterson, 2010).

Professional (under)development of teachers

Prior to the introduction of National Standards, all state schools across New Zealand were able to access a Ministry of Education advisory service – School Support Services (SSS) – which provided experienced, specialist subject advisors in all curriculum areas, including HPE. These advisors assisted schools and staff for an extended length of time and provided a variety of services, such as developing school-specific planning, assessment, policies, mentoring, resources, and appropriate pedagogies. In August 2009 (the same month that the $82 million Kiwisport initiative was announced), schools learnt that this PD support service was to be cut in all areas except Information Communication Technology (ICT), literacy and mathematics (McKay, personal communication, 30 April 2014).[6]

The prioritisation of reading, writing, and maths in the National-led government's education reforms coincided with the implementation of PD policies that would de-skill and de-professionalise teachers. It also occurred at the same time as new funding mechanisms were made available to schools so they could outsource their teaching to external experts. This facilitated the process of teachers and principals positioning Kiwisport coaches as experts in teaching PE, and *Life Education* teachers like Marion (as well as the police officers who took the *DARE*[7] and *Keeping Ourselves Safe* programmes) as experts in health education. The withdrawal of funding and support to develop teachers' professional capabilities to teach HPE acted as a key technology that shaped how teachers understood HPE and how they perceived themselves as inexpert teachers.

The teachers also pointed to the inadequacy of their initial teacher education to prepare them for teaching HPE in a primary school. For example, beginning teacher Miss Black was unimpressed with the "limited" preparation to teach HPE she received during her postgraduate diploma at the University of Auckland:

> We had one week for PE and health combined, so that was, we must have had five two-hour sessions, something like that for health *and* PE, which was a bit of a joke really! We had to write some ridiculous essay on what is health and PE – a wordy, unpractical assignment that to me is not teaching me the skills to be able to be successful in teaching PE and health, at all. I think that had I not done a Bachelor of Sport and Recreation as my undergraduate degree I would be a lot

less equipped to actually teach PE and health ... if I didn't have that background knowledge and experience, PE wouldn't be something that I would want to teach or like to teach. It would be something I would avoid, I think. Which it's not. I like teaching PE (laughs).

Although Miss Black 'liked' teaching PE, held an undergraduate degree in sport, and a postgraduate qualification in primary school teaching, she still felt that it was best to use outside sport coaches (who were *not* qualified teachers) to teach her students PE. These coaches included Jonie who had completed the same undergraduate degree as Miss Black, but had no teacher education qualification.

Teachers at Dudley School had differing ideas as to how much PD they had received and with what effect. Mrs Donna was sure that she had participated in "heaps" of PD for HPE over the past seven years, but could not recall who conducted these PD opportunities, or what the content was. When I specifically asked Mrs Donna about her PD for health education, she responded that the *Life Education* "bus" came to Dudley School "and we usually get them at the end of the year, for like a week and they teach the kids health and that ... We haven't actually had any actual PD on it, so, but I think you don't need any PD on things like that". Mrs Donna's colleague, Mrs Constansa, said she could not recall having participated in *any* PD for health education or PE. I asked her if this was a problem, to which she smiled and replied: "Nothing's changed in the past ten years, has it?" Mr Spurlock, the leader of PE at Dudley School, recalled participating in four PD experiences. Three of these were one-off, sport-specific coaching courses: one run by a private company (for tennis), and two provided by a Regional Sports Trust (cricket and rugby). The other 'professional development' experience, in Mr Spurlock's view, was for health education:

> I haven't done many health courses .... It's been a bit strange. I suppose the Life Ed woman [Marion] came in – she [took] a staff meeting. I suppose you could call that PD. Um, it doesn't really spring to mind for health. And I suppose that could be part of the reason why health isn't done a lot at [Dudley School], because you just don't have the expertise, or the PD on it, to get that expertise.

I shared with Mr Spurlock my worry that most of these external providers, whether teaching students or providing PD, were not qualified or experienced teachers and therefore may not have the required 'expert' knowledge to teach the New Zealand curriculum (for a similar discussion, see Petrie, Penney, & Fellows, 2014). However, Mr Spurlock appeared to be unconcerned:

> I haven't opened my curriculum document to PE and health for a long time. I think you know, um, [PE] is more based on modified games and we teach specific skills. I couldn't tell you how that

linked in with an achievement objective and the curriculum though. I couldn't tell you what one of the achievement objectives for Level Four is at the moment. I see PE, in the end, more about teaching skills. And you can teach the same skill in Year Seven and Eight to a kid in Year Two or Three. I mean, it just depends on how much they take it on board – dumb it down a bit more for Year Two and Three. For health, yeah, um, again I have no idea what achievement objectives there are …. I was living overseas when the new curriculum documents came through so when I started teaching back here again I had to ring the Ministry [of Education] and say 'can I have a new curriculum document please, because I have no idea what it is'. And I got one, had a browse through and that's about it … it's sitting up there (points to a top shelf).

The intimate and unproblematic linking of PE with coaching sports skills meant that Mr Spurlock and his colleagues did not feel the need to seek PE PD opportunities that drew on holistic, child-centred, developmentally appropriate, socio-critical versions of PE as advocated in *The New Zealand curriculum*. Instead, they either sought training in coaching sports (as did Mr Spurlock), or more commonly, were convinced that outsourcing their PE teaching would *also* 'teach the teachers'. In other words, the outsourcing of PE lessons to external providers was rationalised as being the normal way for children to learn sports skills and/or be healthier *and* a means for teachers to develop their professional capacity to teach PE. In this way, the boundaries between outsourcing PE and outsourcing PD were increasingly blurred, often becoming one-and-the-same. This blurring was less evident for the field of health education, but only because teaching health education, outsourcing health education, and being developed professionally in health education were positioned by teachers as being unimportant – certainly in comparison with other curriculum areas.

Seeing the outsourcing of HPE as a form of PD was not 'imagined' by the teachers. The corporate and their charitable partners promoted the idea that the external providers of programmes for children (e.g. a local gymnastics coach, Regional Sports Trust employee) were also expert providers of PD for the inexpert classroom teachers. For instance, the *ASB Football in Schools* drew together taken-for-granted notions of 'PE as sport', 'sport leading to healthy, active lifestyles', the external 'expert' sports coach, and the 'inexpert' classroom teacher, with tactics of outsourcing and PD:

> The concept of the football literacy programme is to *help teachers deliver football as part of physical education* …. In simple terms it *provides teachers with the tools to build competence and confidence* to bring football, the world's most popular game, alive during class time.
>
> When your school adopts the ASB Football in Schools programme you will receive educational resources, consisting of session plans and

associated global and specific learning intentions, Let's Play activity cards and *human resources to train and mentor staff*/volunteers facilitated by one of our seven regional federations.

Schools are a natural breeding ground for unstructured play and New Zealand Football is aiming to capitalise on this by *providing parents, teachers and players with the expertise and tools* to get the ball rolling.

The ASB Football in Schools approach offers our children new opportunities to get active through football. At the same time it presents volunteer parents and *teachers with the tools to create and deliver simple programmes* that will encourage their children to become more active in the school setting. (New Zealand Football, n.d., p. 1, my emphases)

Again, the complex problem of inexpert teachers was solved by rendering the problem technical. Outsourcing a simple, corporate-funded football programme was assumed to have a 'beneficial result': 'trained' and 'mentored' teachers (and children) who would become football and PE experts.

Several outsourced HPE programmes claimed to provide PD opportunities for classroom teachers. For example, New Zealand Post (2012, para. 4) promoted the benefits of its *Small Sticks* programme as including "the teacher being trained, a minimum of four coaching session (sic) in school time with an accredited coach, a resource kit for schools to use after the programme is finished". The *moveMprove* programme 'expected' and 'encouraged' teachers "to be present during the session to work alongside the coaches and to assist the children with the activities" – an opportunity for teachers to "develop and further their understanding of movement learning" (GymSports New Zealand, 2006, para. 11).

Get Set Go also offered "teacher & coach professional development" (New Zealand Post, n.d., para. 3) with the aim to "support teachers, coaches and parents in the assessment, planning and development of foundation skills", as well as "to increase teachers, coaches and parents understanding of the critical importance of fundamental movement skills, play and positive movement experiences for children" (Athletics New Zealand, n.d., p. 4). At St Saviour's School this support and PD took the form of an after-school staffroom session, led by Jonie and one other Sport Auckland employee, for the benefit of Miss Black and the Year One teacher. Then, for each *Get Set Go* session Jonie led the lesson with Miss Black's students, with the aim of increasing Miss Black's involvement in each lesson as the sessions went on "so at least once in the term you try and get the teacher to deliver a session with some of the kids" (Jonie). I asked Jonie how teachers responded to taking 'control' of their own classes for *Get Set Go*:

JONIE: We found some teachers didn't like to plan and do a session, and would say 'I don't want to do it'. And I'd go: 'Well you have to, like, how are you going to be able to teach a session when we leave?'

DARREN: Why do you think that is? Why do you think some teachers

JONIE: I don't know. I think workloads [are] a huge thing for them, and a lot of the schools I worked in last year – workloads and other priorities – it's huge. But the programme isn't about someone just coming and delivering it ... I think that's what [teachers] kind of don't understand fully when they get involved. And we say 'look, I want you to take a game next week. You have to come up with a game and in a couple of weeks' time, I want you to do a whole session'. And that's when, maybe their confidence, their time management, planning, being creative ... it might be hard.

During a conversation at St Saviour's School, *Small Sticks* coach Andrea told me that:

> I have had teachers who have walked off. They've just dropped their class off and then walked off and they are like 'Oh yeah, here you go, thanks'. And then some teachers get involved completely where they play. And then some just watch and observe. I just think the ones who dropped them off are completely useless (laughs). The ones who observe, they can learn something from it ... and some have asked for the actual [resource] sheets .... But some just like see it as an hour off. So I don't mind, you know I've taught [in schools before], so I don't mind having a class myself, but I do mind for [the students] that their teacher's looking lazy and just goes have a cup of tea. [The teachers are] not learning anything.

Despite the various claims made by teachers, principals, external providers, and outside organisations that these programmes would enable teachers to learn from the experts, it was clearly evident that not all teachers were willing or able to be fully supported in their PD. And even those teachers who 'watched and learned' from the expert-led lessons (the ever-present pedagogy of the external provider) still preferred using an external organisation and their affiliated coaches to teach HPE for them.

'I think it's perfect': resolving tensions

Teachers, principals, and external providers were persuaded that the outsourcing of HPE to external providers was best practice. This was not achieved by teachers' indifference to the value of HPE, or by being "useless" or "lazy", or being tricked into outsourcing HPE programmes by for-profit corporations and their 'not-for-profit' counterparts. Rather, it was created through a complex and messy assemblage of a range of policies and practice. To make the government of children and teachers possible, however, the brittle connections between notions of inexpertise, Kiwisport, National Standards, professional (under)development, outsourcing, and discourses of healthy lifestyles, HPE, and sport were made more robust by those with governmental ambitions. This necessitated a relentless resolving of tensions and careful management of both successes and failures by various organisations and actors, including sporting organisations, corporate sponsors, and schools. To understand how healthy lifestyles education programmes (in their broadest sense) 'work', requires an interrogation of *how* tensions are resolved, *how* the failure of these governmental programmes to provide expert HPE or PD are transformed into a success, and *how* teachers' critiques of (or resistance to) the healthy lifestyles education programmes are contained (see Powell, 2015).

As outlined earlier, the outsourced HPE programmes were promoted by the external providers as beneficial to students' learning *and* teachers' teaching. However, what external providers 'promised' in terms of PD for teachers, what I observed in the schools, and how these teachers understood and experienced these HPE-PD sessions contained a number of tensions, failures, and contradictions. *Small Sticks*, for example, was promoted as a programme that would 'train' the teacher through the four hockey sessions that the children received. Yet the four sessions I observed at St Saviour's School contained no formal 'training' with the teachers and neither Ms Ellie nor Miss Black utilised the "resource kit for schools to use after the programme is finished" (New Zealand Post, 2012, para. 5). Despite the apparent failure of the programme to provide the 'training' it promised, and its failure to support or enthuse the teachers to continue coaching hockey to their students, Ms Ellie managed this failure by arguing that there were

> *lots of things that I got out of [Small Sticks] by watching* that can actually transfer to lots of other sports. Like [Andrea] played 'Rob the nest', which is like a Kiwidex thing and I've played it with tennis balls and for a warm-up and with running. And you can see now how you can transfer that to other sports. So there is some professional development. (my emphasis)

This particular pedagogy for teacher PD – learning "by watching" from the sideline – frequently resolved the tension between what might be considered 'quality' or 'effective' PD in other curriculum areas and what was provided (or claimed to be provided) by external organisations. When I asked Mrs Donna how she felt about these outside authorities taking her students for HPE, she replied:

> Doesn't worry me one bit. Because I'm *watching them and learning too,* because I always take on board what they are doing and sometimes it's nice [to have providers] who are focused on one thing. I mean as school teachers we've got to focus on reading, writing, maths, health, PE, science, and it's like sometimes our brains are braindead, and you do get into a rut and teach the same thing again and again and again. *And then you see someone else with another idea* and you think 'that's so cool'. (my emphases)

There was another notable contradiction: teachers perceived the externally provided programmes as a PD opportunity, yet once the external providers had left the school, the same teachers continued to prefer – and rely on – external experts to teach PE for them. One way that teachers managed this particular contradiction was by describing the outsourcing of HPE as PD, and that by watching the experts teach their students they had been 'inspired' to take an HPE lesson in the future. This is an important contradiction, given that following the various PD programmes, teachers continued to rely on the external experts to teach for them (Powell, 2015). For example, when I asked Mrs Donna how she felt about using external providers to teach her students, she replied:

> *I think it's perfect.* I personally think it should happen more often ....
> PE – it's not my sort of passion. If I can miss out PE I will miss out
> PE! (laughs). Because me, I am art. I love to do art. I would sacrifice
> PE to do art ... if someone is coming in [for PE] I would say 'yes'.
> I can go out, I can watch, I can learn from it. I will probably use it
> again. But I don't have to think about 'Oh my god, what I going to
> do with the kids for PE today? What game am I going to do that I
> haven't done?' Or 'how am I going to teach them that without get-
> ting stressed out because they are not listening?' (my emphasis)

Mrs Donna's belief that outsourcing PE to the experts was a "perfect" practice successfully obscured the fact that these programmes had failed to develop her skills, confidence, or expertise to teach her own students a compulsory subject. Teachers were implicated in resolving tensions and managing contradictions that ensured the *status quo* remained strong. The consequences of this were that the place of healthy lifestyles education programmes and providers prevailed, while the absence of PD was explained away and mitigated as a non-issue. The failure of the programmes to deliver HPE in line with the national curriculum was made invisible.

In a number of the lessons I observed across the three schools, both those conducted by teachers in the classroom and external providers in the gym or on the sports field, there was another palpable tension. The practices and pedagogies offered by various external providers often contrasted with what teachers and principals discussed or demonstrated as 'best practice' in teaching non-HPE subject areas (particularly priority subjects like reading, writing, and maths). This contrast was made especially visible in the situations where classroom teachers drew on their knowledge of students (e.g. students' learning needs, (dis)abilities, levels of confidence, family situations, lives) to plan and deliver learning experiences, while external providers often struggled in lessons due to their lack of *knowledge of the children* they were teaching. As Petrie and colleagues (2014, p. 31) also argued, in the New Zealand context few outside providers of HPE "appear to have knowledge of learners or learning, education settings, curriculum or pedagogy".

The failure of the external providers to know the students in their class was, at times, dangerous. For example, in St Saviour's Year Six/Seven students' second *Small Sticks* session, Andrea instructed the students to play a game called 'Minefield', where they needed to dribble hockey balls around cones placed inside a ten by ten metre square. If their hockey ball touched one of the 'mines' (cones) their leg would be "blown off" and they would have to hop on one leg and dribble for the rest of the game. One of the students looked at me with a confused look on his face, as if asking 'What am I meant to do?' He only had one leg.

The external providers' reliance on pre-planned, pre-packaged resources and lessons also demonstrated the assumption that there was no need for the external providers to know the students. The consequences of this were evident one day at St Saviour's School. Ms Ellie's Year Six/Seven class and Miss Black's Year One/Two students participated in separate, yet almost identical *moveMprove* sessions. This was just one of a number of externally provided lessons where a 'one-size-fits-all' strategy failed to meet the wide-ranging needs of the children, not only in terms of educational needs, but also their physical, emotional, language, spiritual, social, cultural, and behavioural needs (see Powell, 2015).

The external providers did not have an in-depth understanding of the children's abilities, skills, interests, or knowledge. There were a number of moments I observed in *moveMprove* when individual students were unable to perform the 'right' skill in the 'right' way (e.g. six-year-old Asatasi at St Saviour's School could not bunny-hop over the bench). At other times, children thought *moveMprove* was "easy" (Chardonnay, six-years-old) and "boring" (Anita, six-years-old). Following one *moveMprove* session at Dudley School, I had a conversation with two of Mrs Donna's students, Anita and Chardonnay, at an outdoor table beside their classroom:

DARREN: Where there any [*moveMprove*] activities that were too easy?
CHARDONNAY: All of them were easy!
DARREN: What about you Anita, were they all easy as well?
ANITA: All easy.
DARREN: Would you want for some of [the activities] to be a little bit harder?
ANITA: Yeah!
CHARDONNAY: Make it more challenging. I like things challenging.
DARREN: Me too.
ANITA: Me too.
DARREN: How could you make things more challenging?
ANITA: Handstands without the wall.
CHARDONNAY: I would put monkey bars up [higher so] people [would not] use any stairs and make it really hard.

Whether *moveMprove* was too easy or too hard, students' experiences contradicted claims made in the 'Why the movement pattern approach?' section of the *Educator's guide* (GymSports New Zealand's, n.d.-a, para. 4–5) that the programme promoted "a learner-centred approach" through "flexible delivery models", where the expert coaches would "add variety and to continually challenge children" by "adapt[ing] equipment to suit the activity".

Tensions were also unmistakeable when the outside experts failed to provide quality learning experiences. Teachers and principals resolved this tension through the belief that it was better for the students to be taught by someone with a 'new face' and a 'new voice', rather than 'just' the classroom teacher. The discourse of the 'fresh' external provider giving children a break from their 'stale' classroom teachers allowed the teachers and principals to ignore the limitations of outsourcing. Miss Black explained:

> I think it's good for the kids to have a break from the classroom teacher. Because the same person all the time – it's good for consistency and they need that – but also I think it is really beneficial to have someone fresh. It adds a bit of interest, so they're not just listening to the same voice all the time, the same person all the time. And you know, other teachers bring other skills as well and teach things in different ways. It gets the kids, sometimes I guess, out of their comfort zone.

This quote provides an example of how a teacher manages the tension between quality teaching and the (in)expertise of the external provider. As Miss Black stated, children needed to have a 'consistent' classroom teacher, but also needed a new teacher with a new voice. Both principals I talked with recognised this significant tension: bringing in external providers when they already employed qualified and experienced primary school teachers. When I talked with Mr Woodward inside his office at Dudley School, he also explained the advantage of bringing in external providers in terms of the appeal of novelty: "another option for kids apart from the teacher – the same teacher all the time". However, as he said this he paused and added: "Although we have great staff, great teachers. But I think it's an outside agency that gives a lift to the programme". Mrs Sergeant, principal of St Saviour's, agreed:

> I mean it's like when you listen to any old, crap record going on and on and on, you know? You just switch off. I think teachers here bend over backwards to make sure what they're presenting to children is engaging and you know, hugely grabbing and effective. But having someone come in is brilliant! Because it's a new face, and a new voice and a new approach. And we can't beat variety! Come on, it's brilliant! Kids love it! …. I think part of it is having somebody different telling them these things rather than just their teacher …. it's just a change, and they're not having them all the time, and it's something to look forward to … they like variety, they need it.

Mr Woodward and Mrs Sergeant clearly valued their "great", "engaging", and "effective" educators. However, it seemed as though these teachers' faces, voices, and approaches were still no match for external sports coaches who did not know the students, were not experienced, qualified, or registered teachers, appeared to have limited knowledge and understanding of the New Zealand curriculum, and implemented 'one-size-fits-all' programmes that were not tailored to the students' needs.

Although the idea that external providers gave students quality learning experiences that the classroom teacher could not was ubiquitous, some teachers, principals, and students recognised moments when external providers failed to meet the specific needs of students. However, these failures were glossed over as insignificant. For instance, Ms Ellie told me:

> Even the one sport that didn't have great coaches, the children still loved it. I guess it's a different voice that's harping on to them. They make them quite fun activities, especially with the Kiwisport sports.

Similarly, Mrs Sergeant noted that not all coaches had the appropriate pedagogical knowledge and experience to successfully teach her students:

> I think the only disadvantage, and its minor, and it doesn't happen very often because mostly the people who come in, they know their stuff, that's the only thing they focus on, they generally have the weight of a big organisation behind them, occasionally say for Sport Auckland we may get a new coach who's a little bit nervous about the children or maybe doesn't quite understand how they learn best – and that takes a long time to know that! So, on occasion that happens, but the advantages hugely outweigh the disadvantages.

Although there were obvious points of tension and moments of failure that made the healthy lifestyles education programmes vulnerable, these were presented "as the outcome of rectifiable deficiencies" (Li, 2007, p. 265). The failure of outsourced coaches/teachers to adequately understand how children "learn best" was passed off as a superficial, "minor" "disadvantage". For Mrs Sergeant, the advantages of external providers – a "new face, and a new voice and a new approach" – outweighed the disadvantages; disadvantages which included external providers not differentiating a lesson to meet the varied needs of her students, not knowing students' names, whether or not they spoke English, or only had one leg (Powell, 2015).

My point here is not to criticise individual external providers for failing to teach curriculum-based HPE, nor is it to 'bash' teachers or principals for a lack of resistance when dealing with external providers. Rather, my intent is to problematise the ease by which tensions were successfully resolved. Although maintaining connections between elements is a difficult and complex task, the 'triumph of "the neoliberal imaginary"' (Ball, 2012, p. 2) was well illustrated by the fact that teachers relied on external providers to teach HPE to their students, and even re-imagined the outsourcing of HPE as natural, normal, and in the words of Mrs Donna, "perfect".

De-valuing and de-professionalising teachers

Teachers were, by and large, seen by students as lacking the appropriate content and pedagogical knowledge *in comparison to* the expert sport coaches and health education providers. During a chat with Reynard Intermediate School students in the final month of their academic year, I asked them if Miss Knight (school-wide leader of HPE) or Mrs Pederson (their classroom teacher) had ever taught them about health:

BRODIE: We were supposed to – with Miss Knight.

NIAMH: But we didn't do it.

BALJIT: Part of having Miss Knight was for health and sport, but we haven't talked about the health side yet.

DARREN: Would you want your teachers to do more health education?

ALL: (laugh)

EMMA: No. (laughs)

BRODIE: Not really.

DARREN: Is there anyone who would want Miss Knight or Mrs Pederson? (long pause) Why not?

EMMA: First of all, what they know is probably just information, and they may be wrong. And it's just not that interesting to know.

Aside from three sessions with *Life Education*, this group of Year Seven girls had not been taught "the health side yet" by their classroom teacher or the HPE specialist for an entire year. And they did not perceive this as a problem. There was a sense that they did not see the value of health education as a learning area (one deemed 'essential' in the curriculum). As Emma said, "it's just not that interesting to know". Furthermore, the students did not perceive any value in either Miss Knight or Mrs Pederson trying to teach them about health. When I asked these girls why the school brought in a teacher (and a puppet) from outside the school to teach them about health, Emma replied: "Because they probably just do it all the time, so they probably know more". The expertise, knowledge, and experience of the *Life Education* teacher and Harold the Giraffe seemed to outdo that of their experienced Reynard Intermediate School teachers.

At Dudley School I talked one-to-one with Caitlyn, a five-year-old Pākehā girl, about her classroom teacher – Mrs Constansa. Caitlyn described Mrs Constansa as a "fun" teacher, who also "picks me up [from school] every day". I asked Caitlyn if Mrs Constansa ever taught her about health. She replied, "only when we had *Life Education* books". I then asked Caitlyn:

DARREN: Why do you think they bring the *Life Education* van into school ... and have Harold come in, instead of Mrs Constansa teaching you?

CAITLYN: She probably doesn't know that stuff.

It was a similar case at St Saviour's School when I had a conversation with a group of Year Seven boys in the staffroom. I asked them why so many external providers taught them HPE, "but not your class teacher":

CARLOS: Because they're more professional. That's what they do. That's what they're there for. It's their job and they know more about it.
AFU: I think it's because they're professionals.
DARREN: What do you mean 'they're professionals'?
DJ: I think they come and teach us because they know a lot more information than the teachers. Also because-

It was at this point that DJ noticed that Miss Black was in the staffroom (doing reading assessments with a Year One student). He whispered to Afu, who responded, "You can say it aloud". DJ looked at Miss Black, then back to Afu and said "Nah". Miss Black kindly interjected: "You guys can say whatever you like". DJ picked up my digital voice recorder and whispered something into it. Then he leaned back over to Afu, cupped his hands around Afu ear and whispered again. Afu then passed 'the whisper' on around the group until it reached the final student, Hone. Hone looked at me, and forgetting he was supposed to whisper the message, said aloud: "He thinks that teachers are lazy!". This was the same message that DJ had whispered into the voice recorder. So I asked DJ what he meant by "teachers are lazy", to which he responded:

> sometimes they just don't bother. Like on Fridays in Term Two and Term One we're meant to have sports, but Miss (Ms Ellie) said, that we need to stay inside and do our work. Sometimes they're lazy 'cos they just need to do their work – they've got a lot of stuff to do.

While DJ recognised that teachers like Ms Ellie were under pressure and had "a lot of stuff to do", by outsourcing HPE to external experts, these same teachers – who worked long hours and repeatedly went out of their way to meet the personal and learning needs of students – were seen by their own students as 'lazy' and lacking the appropriate knowledge and professionalism to be able teach HPE effectively, or even to be able to teach HPE at all. For the relationship between teachers and the students, this is an unpredictable and dangerous outcome. Unfortunately, as I will shed light on in the next two chapters, this is not the only aspect of healthy lifestyles education programmes that may do more harm than good.

By defining both the problem (inexpert teachers; non–sporty, inactive, unhealthy, potentially 'obese' children) and the solution (external providers), a range of public, private, and voluntary sector organisations and actors have been able to re-draw and re-define the boundaries of the HPE field. The purpose of HPE, what quality teaching looks like, and who is fit to teach HPE have been re-worked in ways that align with external organisation's own expertise, interests, and governmental ambitions. I am not arguing that all corporations, state agencies, charities, and sporting organisations have a hidden agenda to de-professionalise, de-skill, and de-value classroom teachers. However, there are a number of instances when these multi-sector organisations attempt to use their programmes, partnerships, and expert status to contain sociopolitical challenges and govern others towards largely selfish ends. The philanthropised resources and pedagogies that target children are essential techniques to achieve this.

Notes

1 In New Zealand, the majority of primary school teachers are required to teach all curriculum areas.
2 Currency is in New Zealand dollars, unless stated otherwise.
3 According to the Ministry of Education (2014, para. 1–2): "Operational funding is the money a board of trustees receives from the Government to implement the goals of the school's charter, and for the running of the school. Operational funding does not include funding for the salaries of entitlement teachers, property, or large capital items. These are paid for separately".
4 Independent schools (i.e. private schools), integrated schools (i.e. Catholic, Montessori, Anglican, and Presbyterian schools of 'special character'), and partnership (i.e. charter) schools were not required to report National Standards to the Ministry of Education or parents. There were only a handful of state schools that initially refused to provide National Standards data to the Ministry of Education.
5 Shortly following the election of a Labour-led coalition government in December 2017, the Ministry of Education (2017) announced that National Standards would be removed as a mandatory requirement for primary schools.
6 At first, schools were not informed directly by the Ministry of Education about these cuts to professional development. Rather, the Ministry of Education published these reforms on their website, which was then picked up by different media sources and a teachers' union, which then raised schools' awareness.
7 DARE (Drug Abuse Resistance Education) started as a drug abuse prevention programme in the United States and was 'imported' into New Zealand in the 1990s. In New Zealand schools, the DARE programme was designed and implemented by a partnership between the now-defunct DARE Foundation of New Zealand and the New Zealand Police. At Saviour's School, a police education officer took the Year Seven and Eight students for a DARE lesson on how to 'just say no' to drugs. Keeping Ourselves Safe is a child protection programme designed by the New Zealand Police that focuses on teaching children about relationships and abuse.

References

Athletics New Zealand. (2012). *Get Set Go: Teachers manual*. Retrieved from https://www.zeus-sport.com/Athletics/Resource.aspx?ID=15789

Athletics New Zealand. (n.d.). *Get Set Go: Fundamental movement skills for kiwi kids information booklet*. Retrieved from http://www.athletics-oceania.com/fileadmin/user_upload/RDC/Kids_Athletics/Kids_Athletics_-_Get_Set_Go.pdf

Ball, S. J. (2012). *Global Education Inc.: New policy networks and the neoliberal imaginary*. Oxon, UK: Routledge.

Dyson, B., Cowan, J., Gordon, B., Powell, D., & Shulruf, B. (2018). Physical education in Aotearoa New Zealand primary schools: Teachers' perceptions and policy implications. *European Physical Education Review, 24*(4), 467–486. doi: 10.1177/1356336X17698083

Evans, J., & Davies, B. (2014). Physical education PLC: Neoliberalism, curriculum and governance. New directions for PESP research. *Sport, Education and Society, 19*(7) 869–884. doi: 10.1080/13573322.2013.850072

GymSports New Zealand. (2006). *moveMprove*. Retrieved from http://www.gymsportsnz.com/page/moveMprove.html

GymSports New Zealand. (n.d.-a). *Educator's guide*. Retrieved from http://www.gymsportsnz.com/files/mMp_EducatorsA5_v9_HR.pdf

GymSports New Zealand. (n.d.-b). *MoveMprove flyer*. Retrieved from http://www.gymsportsnz.com/files/mMp_Flyer_Generic.pdf

Hutt City Council. (n.d.). *Case study: The football in schools programme*. Retrieved from http://www.kiwisportfundamentals.co.nz/case-study—football-in-schools.html

Key, J. (2009). *Kiwisport initiative good for young people*. Retrieved from http://johnkey.co.nz/archives/782-Kiwisport-initiative-good-for-young-people.html

Li, T. M. (2007). Practices of assemblage and community forest management. *Economy and Society, 36*, 263–293. doi: 10.1080/03085140701254308

Miller, P., & Rose, N. (2008). *Governing the present*. Cambridge, England: Polity.

Ministry of Education. (n.d.). *Kiwisport*. Retrieved from http://www.minedu.govt.nz/NZEducation/EducationPolicies/Schools/SchoolOperations/Resourcing/OperationalFunding/Kiwisport.aspx

Ministry of Education. (2007). *The New Zealand curriculum*. Wellington, New Zealand: Learning Media.

Ministry of Education. (2010). *About National Standards*. Retrieved from http://www.minedu.govt.nz/Parents/YourChild/ProgressAndAchievement/NationalStandards/Introduction.aspx

Ministry of Education. (2014). *Introduction to operational funding*. Retrieved from http://www.minedu.govt.nz/NZEducation/EducationPolicies/Schools/SchoolOperations/Resourcing/ResourcingHandbook/Chapter1/IntroductionOperationalFunding.aspx

Ministry of Education. (2017). *National Standards removed*. Retrieved from https://education.govt.nz/news/national-standards-removed/

New Zealand Football. (n.d.). *ASB Football in Schools: Keeping our children active and healthy*. Retrieved from http://www.foxsportspulse.com/get_file.cgi?id=1981476

New Zealand Post. (2012). *Small Sticks*. Retrieved from http://www.activepost.co.nz/programmes/small-sticks/

Patterson, G. (2010). Haere ra primary PE advisors. *Journal of Physical Education New Zealand, 53*, 12–14.

Petrie, K., Penney, D., & Fellows, S. (2014). Health and physical education in Aotearoa New Zealand: An open market and open doors? *Asia-Pacific Journal of Health, Sport and Physical Education, 5*(1), 19–38. doi: 10.1080/18377122.2014.867791

Powell, D. (2015). Assembling the privatisation of physical education and the 'inexpert' teacher. *Sport, Education and Society, 20*(1), 73–88. doi: 10.1080/13573322.2014.941796

Sahlberg, P. (2011). The fourth way of Finland. *Journal of Educational Change, 12*(2), 173–185.

Sport Auckland. (2012). *Kiwisport: Community report – April 2012*. Retrieved from http://www.sportsground.co.nz/files/site/222/08/Pdf/130219163838EGYOGQNE.pdf

Sport Auckland. (n.d.). Kiwisport. Retrieved from http://www.sportsground.co.nz/sportauckland/85225/5

Thrupp, M. (2018). *The search for better educational standards: A cautionary tale*. Cham, Switzerland: Springer.

6

LEARNING ABOUT HEALTH, FATNESS, AND 'GOOD' CHOICES

A central focus of my research for this book was to interrogate how the corporate 'part of the solution' to childhood obesity connected with people; how they were actually enacted, experienced, understood, and felt by children and adults in primary schools. There were two interconnected elements integral to my analysis: the *resources* funded, devised, produced, and distributed with the assistance of corporations; and the *pedagogies* employed by teachers, corporate mascots, and external providers to teach children to be healthier and less fat. In order to critically examine these elements, I looked at aspects of resources and pedagogies that coincided with the kinds of neoliberal ideas about health and conduct that have considerable currency both politically and popularly: 'informing' students about good lifestyle choices; illustrating the bad consequences for those who do not heed the healthy advice; and, attempting to re-place the responsibility and blame for children's health and fatness onto children themselves.

Being informed about 'healthy lifestyle choices'

Corporations and charities position the education of children as an almost certain route for children to live healthier lives. The corporate-influenced healthy lifestyles education resources, along with their suggested pedagogies, tend to be based on the rationale that 'giving' children knowledge about fatness, physical activity, and food *will* make children have healthier habits and healthier body weights for life. The *Be Healthy, Be Active* resource in New Zealand, for instance, reinforced Nestlé's global obesity goals by aiming "to support students to develop healthy eating habits that contribute towards maintaining a healthy body weight" (Nestlé New Zealand, 2011, p. 14). To be able to successfully 'improve' children's (un)healthy habits requires more than just teaching children about health *per se*. The emphasis of the resources (and the pedagogies employed to achieve the aims of the resources) is on increasing children's knowledge and awareness of what *choices* they should make:

> We all want to be healthy and live full and balanced lives. Kiwis have
> never been busier or been faced with as many choices of what to eat,

what activities to engage in, and what values to use to guide their actions. Helping children to understand these choices and providing them with the knowledge and skills to make good decisions has become increasingly important. (Nestlé New Zealand, 2011, p. 1)

The notion of *informed choice* is a dominant feature of these healthy lifestyles education resources. The *Iron Brion* programme promoted the idea that "the food choices made by individuals and families affect all aspects of their life. Food and nutrition education enables students to make *informed choices* about food and the choices that will contribute to their own well-being" (New Zealand Beef and Lamb Marketing Bureau, n.d., p. 5, my emphasis). Likewise, *5+ A Day* (5+ A Day Charitable Trust, 2011, p. 2, my emphasis) states its intention to teach students "to engage in a range of learning experiences which encourage children to make *informed choices* for healthy lifestyle practices".

Life Education Trust (2018) promotes itself as "a charity that educates and empowers children to make healthy choices so they can live full and healthy lives". The writers of the *Life Education's 'Warrant of Fitness'* workbook stated that they "hope that all the things you have learned will help you make some excellent choices for your growing body" (Life Education Trust, n.d.-a, p. 5). Students were also told how important being 'informed' is to be able to make the right (i.e. healthy) choices: "To make great choices we need to be informed. When we are thinking about food choices, we need to be informed about what is in the food we eat" (Life Education Trust, n.d.-a, p. 15). Dudley School teacher Mr Spurlock agreed that this was the right approach to teach his students about health: "Like I said, [health] is more about choices that kids make. And [*Life Education*] does teach kids 'this is what will happen if you eat these foods continuously'".

The notion of informed choice rearranged the point and purpose of the health education by being securely fastened to the concept of healthy life-styles. For instance, Nestlé New Zealand (2011, p. 32, my emphasis) explic-itly connected health, choices, and life by providing students and teachers with a glossary of key words, one of which defines 'lifestyle' as "the way a person *chooses* to live, especially in relation to his or her diet or physical activ-ity". As a new type of healthy lifestyles education – a healthy lifestyles *choices* education – these corporatised resources and pedagogies represent specific attempts not only to shape children's thoughts and actions around health, but how they live their lives. In another example, Module Four of *Be Healthy, Be Active* stated:

there are many factors that affect students' lifestyle choices, and not all of them are in their control. Students need to understand that gradually building the skills and practices that contribute to a healthy lifestyle *will help them throughout their lives.* People who have a healthy lifestyle have more skills, and they can cope better with life's challenges. (Nestlé New Zealand, 2011, p. 26, my emphasis)

The *5+ A Day* resources promote the need for children and their families to change their lives in ways that align with the interests of the fruit and vegetable industry:

> Whether we are growing fruit and vegetables, eating them, or looking at fresh produce advertisements, 5+ A Day really can be *part of our everyday lives*. This resource aims to help *make 5+ A Day a way of life* for children and their families. (5+ A Day Charitable Trust, 2011, p. 4, my emphases)

This connection between children's lives and private sector interests was similar to the *Iron Brion* programme which stated its rationale as follows:

> The New Zealand Beef and Lamb Marketing Bureau firmly supports educating young Kiwis about healthy eating and *the role beef and lamb play in a healthy lifestyle*. We see both the Iron Brion Show and the Teacher Resource Kit as our contribution to the well-being of school-aged children, *both now and in the future*. (New Zealand Beef and Lamb Marketing Bureau, n.d., p. 1, my emphases)

Some resources and lesson plans invoked the idea that a healthy lifestyles education was critical for children's health, but at the same time articulated the resources in ways that were beneficial to corporate interests (e.g. to increase people's meat or vegetable consumption). There was also an assumption reproduced across a number of the resources that by teaching children how to make 'educated' choices, children would continue to make these choices 'both now and in the future'. The cover of the *'Warrant of Fitness'* (WOF) workbook produced by the Life Education Trust (n.d.-a), for instance, features illustrations of children wearing badges that read: 'WOF For Life'. When I talked to educator Marion, she told me that the "big aim" of *Life Education* was "encouraging [children] to make better choices for their future … I can't target what [their choices] are now because it's out of their control, as well as ours". However, as Leahy (2009) noted, the idea that by 'knowing' about health (or obesity, fatness, or physical activity) children *will* change their behaviour and make 'good' choices is widely disputed.

Learning to make good choices (and what bad things happen if you do not)

The corporate-produced resources and suggested pedagogies reinforced a healthy lifestyle message that resulted in some tensions around the neoliberal concept of 'freedom of choice'. This was particularly the case when the choices that children were told to make were restricted to those that aligned with corporate interests (e.g. *Iron Brion* promoting New Zealand beef and lamb) or 'official' recommendations (e.g. to eat five or more fruit and/or vegetables every day). A common strategy was to inform children about which choices were the 'right' ones to make (i.e. healthy, energy-balanced ones), and which 'wrong' choices (i.e. unhealthy, obesity-causing, lazy) they needed to avoid or abstain from.

Making right choices was positioned as a secure and stable route for children to lead the right lifestyles, display the right conduct and possess the right (i.e. healthy, non-fat, active) bodies. For example, the *'Warrant of Fitness'* workbook emphasised that "with the right attitude, activity and appetite we might just get there in style" (Life Education Trust, n.d.-a, p. 7). In one of the 'read and response' cards in the *Be Healthy, Be Active* resource – 'Building a healthy body' – the good/right choices were clearly expressed:

> How do you build a healthy body? It's simple: When you *eat the right foods*, you give your body what it needs to grow strong and healthy. *What are good food choices?* They are foods that have lots of nutrients – carbohydrates, proteins, fats, vitamins, and minerals. (Nestlé New Zealand, n.d.-b, p. 9, my emphases)

There are a number of pedagogical devices employed to teach children the difference between 'right and wrong' or 'good and bad' choices. One such device is the ever-present food pyramid (and food pyramid-type illustrations). The *Iron Brion* resource included a "My healthy food pyramid" (New Zealand Beef and Lamb Marketing Bureau, n.d., p. 18), with 'fats and sugar' at the top, "meats and alternatives" and "milk and milk products" in the middle, and bread, cereals, fruit and vegetables at the base. Alongside the pyramid were lessons and suggested learning activities, such as making a food pyramid with cut-out magazine photographs or examining copies of a food pyramid poster made by The Heart Foundation. The intention of these activities was for students to be able to "classify a variety of foods using the healthy food pyramid and identify foods rich in iron" and "explain which categories of the Food Pyramid they currently select from and how they may make changes" (p. 16). As this last learning intention illuminates, the need to teach children about food choices does not stop at just *informing* children which were good or bad, right or wrong, but comes with an expectation that the children need to act, "make changes", alter their conduct, and improve their health, based on this information.

Life Education's 'Warrant of Fitness' workbook included two versions of a food pyramid. One showed the "recommended fuel for a healthy body", with treats at the top (accompanied by a picture of hot chips, sweets, and a fizzy drink), "Milk and milk products" and meat, eggs, fish, nuts, dried peas, and beans in the middle, and fruit, vegetables, bread, cereals, rice and pasta at the base (alongside a bottle of H2Go water) (Life Education Trust, n.d.-a, p. 9). On the following page, the same food pyramid was reproduced, but this time with added information about the 'good' or 'bad' ingredients of each of these food groups and how much you should eat per day. Here we see a noteworthy contradiction. At the top of the page, the text stated:

> Remember that a healthy diet is about what we eat and how much we eat. Don't get hung up on thinking about foods as fattening or bad. Labelling food as bad isn't the way to go ... just get interested in healthy options instead. (p. 10)

Although students were told not to think about food in a negative way, at the same time they were informed to "be careful" (Life Education Trust, n.d.-a, p. 7) and to avoid consuming 'treats' – "sugary, fatty, salty food that we simply don't need every day" (p. 11). Curiously (and hopefully by mistake) the 'treats' section of the food pyramid included alcohol as a treat for children "to eat in small amounts occasionally" (p. 10). The *Life Education* resources also stated that the 'other' foods (those at the bottom of the pyramid) are inherently good: "It is almost impossible to over eat on a variety of fruit and vegetables which means they are the best snacks!!" (p. 11).

In *Be Healthy, Be Active* students were expected to learn about healthy choices by using a 'food plate':

> The Interactive Food Plate is a visual way of exploring food groups and *discovering sensible choices* for a balanced diet – and it's fun and engaging! .... The interactivity is designed to allow you and your students to explore the many aspects of a balanced diet and *wise food selection*. The plate links to a number of activities in the modules, but it can be used at any time when focusing on the *importance of sensible eating* and how it helps people to feel good and stay healthy. (Nestlé New Zealand, 2011, p. 2, my emphases)

For the online version of the *Interactive Food Plate*, students and teachers were also informed that "the food plate is a great way to learn about different foods and making good food choices to ensure you are having a balanced diet ... Learn about how much you need to drink and the best choices" (Nestlé, n.d.-a, para. 4–5). The decisions that students were required to make in order to "feel good and stay healthy" and be a healthy body weight, stressed the importance of making "sensible choices" through "wise food selection" and "sensible eating". Of course, this value-laden articulation of choice intimates that if you do not make the suggested choices, you will not just be unhealthy, but foolish.

Games are another key pedagogical device used to teach children to make the right choices in a 'fun' way and to demonstrate what 'bad' things happen if you make the wrong choices. Nestlé New Zealand (2011, p. 3) provided several "fun and informative" web-based games to teach "students the value of healthy eating and how this relates to exercise". These games also demonstrated to players the consequences of making good/bad or right/wrong choices. For example, *The Fuel Up Challenge* (Nestlé, n.d.-a, para. 1–2) was promoted as a

> fun and interactive game [that] helps you learn the benefits of healthy eating and how this can affect sporting performance. The Fuel Up Challenge lets you choose 3 foods and see how either Josh or Jess perform. They can swim, run or skateboard and depending on the foods you have chosen for them, they will either get a good time or need to perform better next time round.

The game included a section with unattributed, unreferenced quotations to give 'hints' to students and to enable them to play this game successfully (e.g. "Fruit and vegetables are always great choices") (Nestlé, n.d.-b). To begin the game, students were required to select either Josh or Jessica as their character, then pick an activity – either swimming, skateboarding, or running. At that point they needed to choose three food items to "fuel up" from a choice of eight pictures: a bowl of unbranded cereal, five sweets, a meat pie with tomato sauce, a kiwifruit, five potato chips, a banana, a glass of water, and an unbranded red and white can of "fizzy drink". After making their selection, the player then clicked 'start' and their character performed the chosen activity. For example, if a student selected swimming as their activity and made only 'good' food choices (e.g. cereal, water, and a banana), their character would swim the 50-metre length in 30 seconds and receive the following praise and information at the end of the activity: "Excellent! And remember, you will always perform better when you have had a drink of water or milk". However, if a player chose the 'wrong' foods (e.g. a pie, chips, and soft drink) it took the character (with an exhausted, sad expression) 60 seconds to swim the same distance with the advice: "Oh no, you ran out of energy. Next time go for low fat choices without too much sugar". Although the *Be Healthy, Be Active* resource and *The Fuel Up Challenge* drew on the language of choice, students' 'freedom' to choose was restricted to predetermined 'good' choices – those that are low in fat and sugar, yet also high in energy.

Teaching children about 'good' versus 'bad' choices was made even more overt in the *Health eDash* interactive web-game:

> a free, web-based game promoting healthy eating with activity. Students control the Benny Bolt character to run through a landscape that's filled with a variety of foods. Benny has more bounce when he makes healthier choices, and can run faster and for longer. (Nestlé, n.d.-a, para. 8)

The aim of the game was to "try and collect as many good foods as you can and avoid the bad foods. Good foods will boost your energy and help you run further. Bad foods will reduce your energy and means you can't run as far" (Nestlé, n.d.-c). Once a student began the game, they needed to make good choices rather than bad ones, which assisted them to run as far as possible. If Benny Bolt jumped up and chose 'good food', such as an orange, milk, or kiwifruit, a voice shouted out words of encouragement such as "Awesome!", "Eureka!", "Nice!" or "Boo-yah!". However, if Benny chose 'bad foods' – pies, soft drinks, or potato chips – the same voice shouted admonishments like "Uh oh!", "Oh no!", or "Oh man!". These 'voices from above' are an example of what Leahy (2009, 2012) described as affective pedagogies; a strategy to connect young people's emotions to their good/bad choices. Sadness and disappointment were attached to unhealthy, 'junk food' choices, while feelings of happiness and success were tied to those choices deemed healthy, or 'correct'.

The concepts of energy and energy balance are frequently taught to students as a way of 'informing their choices' and demonstrating the consequences of good and bad choices. For instance, in Nestlé's *The Fuel Up Challenge*, Year Seven and Eight students were informed that a sugary soft drink had *less energy* than water (which has zero calories). Although portrayed as a 'scientific concept', the notion of energy is often taught in a way that reflects the moral values attributed to good/healthy food and bad/junk food, more than actual energy measurements.

Misleading information about energy was also given to the Year One students at Dudley School through *Life Education's* '*Harold's Picnic*' unit. Although the "key message" for this unit was for children to learn that "we need lots of different foods all through the day to have lots of energy" (Life Education Trust, 2011a, p. 1), fruit and vegetables were constantly promoted as the best source to get energy. Dudley School Year One student Caitlyn was well-versed in *Life Education's* 'facts' about fruit and vegetables giving "you heaps of energy" and "sweet stuff" making you "slow down". Following Caitlyn's '*Harold's Picnic*' lessons, I asked her:

DARREN: Finish this sentence for me: We need to eat a variety of foods because…
CAITLYN: It is healthy for you.
DARREN: Why is it healthy for you?
CAITLYN: Because they give you heaps of energy.
DARREN: And why do you need energy?
CAITLYN: So you can do stuff.
DARREN: What things do you need to keep your body healthy and happy?
CAITLYN: Sleep.
DARREN: Anything else?
CAITLYN: Fruit and vegetables. You need to clean it.
DARREN: What did you learn from '*Harold's Picnic*'?
CAITLYN: That you have to eat healthy stuff.
DARREN: What's healthy stuff?
CAITLYN: Apples and tinned tomatoes and bananas.
DARREN: Why is that stuff healthy?

CAITLYN: Because it's fruit and vegetables.

DARREN: What's some unhealthy stuff that you learnt about?

CAITLYN: Chocolate and cupcakes and sugar.

DARREN: Why are sugar and chocolate and cupcakes unhealthy?

CAITLYN: Because they have sweet stuff in it.

DARREN: What's wrong with sweet stuff? Sweet stuff is tasty!

CAITLYN: Yes, but it's not good for your body.

DARREN: What will happen if you eat sweet stuff?

CAITLYN: Bugs will poo on your teeth.

DARREN: Anything else if you just eat sweet stuff?

CAITLYN: And you won't have that much energy … It will slow down.

There were other games that Caitlyn and her classmates played to help them learn the difference between good and bad choices, as well as reinforce the idea that fruit and vegetables were *the key* to good health. One afternoon, Caitlyn and her Year One classmates were allowed to independently complete activities in their '*Harold's Picnic*' workbook. One game in this workbook was for the children to finish a simple maze with the instruction: "Help Harold find his way through the maze by eating all the healthy food only" (Life Education Trust, n.d.-b, p. 4). However, when a child chose to go down the 'wrong' road (e.g. a road with a can of 'Fizz', an ice-cream, or a single sweet) they ended up at a dead-end and failed the task. The ability of an individual to choose to be healthy was re-imagined by the resources and pedagogies to be as simple as playing a game: all you need to do to be healthy is choose the 'right' food and avoid the 'wrong' food.

It was not only informing children about energy *sources* that saturated the healthy lifestyles education programmes, but energy *balance* also. When Marion led a staff meeting at Dudley School to inform the teachers about the *Life Education* units she would be teaching (the same meeting that Mr Spurlock described as professional development), Marion told the staff that the '*Warrant of Fitness*' unit was about energy balance: "We are looking at how much energy we need to burn to balance energy in with energy out". On hearing this, the teacher in charge of health education shouted "Good!", to which another teacher half-heartedly joked: "Is that for the teachers as well?".

The unit outline for '*Warrant of Fitness*' (Life Education Trust, 2011b, p. 2) stated that "successful learning" will result in "children demonstrating an understanding of the energy in–energy out relationship". However, not all students felt like they had 'successfully' learnt (or been taught) about health or energy, as Dudley School Year Seven boy Eton explained:

ETON: Well, they [Marion and Harold] kept on saying, well, they were telling the truth, but they're telling the obvious truth … I don't think they did a whole bunch of research … Like, it was nice information, but it wasn't the information that I thought they'd give. It was information everyone knows about.

DARREN: So you didn't feel like you learnt anything new?

ETON: No, not really.

DARREN: What would have you liked to be told more about?

ETON: Like, they told us how long it would take to walk off your food, but I'd like to know how long it would take to run off your food and sprint off your food .... I don't think they should be like hard-out scientists, but I don't think they should just repeat themselves every time I go there ... In this term they kept repeating like, 'you are what you eat' so you should eat healthy, and that's practically the main message, and she just kept on saying that.

DARREN: Do you feel like you've had this sort of message again and again?

ETON: It kind of got annoying after a while, but you had to put up with it.

Eton also bemoaned the repetitive nature of the 'you are what you eat' message, something that he (and other students) felt like they were exposed to every time *Life Education* came to Dudley School. In addition, both Eton and his friend Brian attributed the failure of *Life Education* to teach them effectively or in detail to an over-emphasis on what they perceived as irrelevant games. For instance, they told me about an activity when Marion asked them to explain what fast food they would buy with $10 and why:

DARREN: What did you learn from that?

ETON: I'm not sure. I think it was just to make up some time, because she didn't really go into detail, like I said before. I feel like it was a fun, little game–

BRIAN: –yeah.

DARREN: So it was more about the fun?

ETON: Yeah.

BRIAN: She would play games every session.

Having fun, playing games, and being entertained (or 'edutained') were frequently promoted as positive pedagogies to teach children to make healthy lifestyle choices. At the same time, more negative pedagogical devices were used to emphasise the bad things that would happen if you made the 'wrong' choices and had the 'wrong' size body.

Bad pedagogies: fear, disgust, the 'abject other', and silence

There are a number of *biopedagogies of health* used by teachers, corporations, and charities to try and convince children that certain choices will lead to fat/thin, healthy/unhealthy, good/bad bodies (also see McDermott, 2012; Powell & Fitzpatrick, 2015; Wright & Harwood, 2009). The term biopedagogies denotes the bringing together of the notion of pedagogy with Foucault's (1978) concept of biopower: the diverse tactics used by disciplinary institutions to control individuals and populations – the 'power over life'. In this sense, biopedagogies can be understood as the diverse spaces where dominant discourses of health and obesity work (e.g. schools, homes, shops, websites), but critically how these sites "have the power to teach, to engage 'learners' in meaning making practices that they use to make sense of their world and their selves and thereby influence how they act upon themselves and others" (Wright, 2009, p. 7). In the context of a childhood obesity 'crisis', these pedagogical devices are "directed towards inciting, and building the capacity of, young people to behave in particular ways that align with contemporary governmental imperatives around weight and the body" (Leahy, 2009, p. 173). However, some of the biopedagogies that aim to teach children about 'bad' choices and 'bad' consequences are potentially problematic and dangerous. This is especially the case when emotions, such as fear and disgust, are recruited in order to invoke in children "a bodily response" (Leahy, 2009, p. 179) to notions of fatness, laziness, junk food, ill health, or things "that poo on your teeth" when you eat sugar.

During 'Harold's Picnic' at Dudley School, the Year One children were informed about the risks of sugar. In one moment, Life Education teacher Marion told the five-year-old students that when you ate sugary food, like soft drinks (but not Just Juice), "germs poo on your teeth". The students responded with a collective "Eeeeuuuwwwww!!!" and turned to each other with looks of disgust on their faces. A number of biopedagogical devices were used in this Life Education lesson to 'teach' children about unhealthy teeth, the effect of sugar on their health, and a brand of toothpaste. Notions of fear and disgust were harnessed to make children fear those "bugs" that "will poo on your teeth" (Caitlyn). The employment of fear and disgust to teach children about health appeared to be in stark contrast with one of the central planks of the Life Education philosophy, displayed on the inside of the mobile classroom's door:

> Life Education does not necessarily work on changing children's behaviour, it works on changing desires. Rather than frightening children with various forms of scare tactics, the Life Education philosophy focuses on creating a sensitivity to values which lead to an understanding and appreciation of human life. This enables the child to make decisions about any negative influences that might impede the development of their fullest potential.

Telling a five-year-old that "germs poo on your teeth" appears to contradict Life Education's mission to not frighten children and give them an "appreciation of human life" and "values". However, there is also a tension here. Life Education's aim to change children's "desires", yet not change their behaviour, conflicts with their interest in enabling children "to make decisions about any negative influences". Shaping children's decision-making is an attempt to change certain behaviours. What Life Education attempts to do is shape children's desires, as well as their thoughts and identities. Furthermore, the use of 'disgusting pedagogies' (Leahy, 2009) is stealthily connected to technologies of consumption. At the conclusion of the lesson the children were given free gift-bags by *Life Education* partner and toothpaste-brand Macleans (manufactured and marketed by GlaxoSmithKline). Mrs Constansa's students took the Macleans bags back to their classroom and unpacked the contents. Inside was a tube of Macleans-branded toothpaste, a toothbrush, stickers, colouring-in pages and a brochure promoting the Macleans website and a Smartphone app. In other words, after being taught that germs defecated on their teeth, the children were provided with a branded solution – Macleans toothpaste and toothbrushes.

Healthy lifestyles education programmes and providers ensured that children were informed about the 'negatives' of health – those unhealthy desires, decisions, and bodies that needed to be avoided. In the Year One's *'Harold's Picnic'* lesson at Dudley School, the students were shown a *Life Education* 'traffic light' system for classifying food groups in terms of which food to eat 'most' (green light), 'some of' (amber light), and only 'now and then' (red light). Fruit and vegetables, as well as bread, pasta, and rice, received a 'green light'. Eggs, meat, and fish were classified as 'amber light'. Sugar, salt, and fat (interestingly, three types of 'food' that are ingredients of most food, rather than something children would eat by itself) were deemed to be 'red light' food.

Next to the category 'fruit and vegetables', Marion displayed drawings of different fruits and vegetables. Next to the word 'bread', Marion produced a photograph of loaves of bread and continued to use such illustrations for each food group – until she arrived at 'salt, sugar, and fat'. For these 'red light' foods, Marion chose to show a grotesque caricature – a cartoon picture – of a fat man running along a street, a hamburger in one hand, a soft drink in the other, with his fat belly overhanging his shorts and protruding from beneath his shirt. Displaying pictures of salt or sugar or fat was deemed to be an insufficient, or at least ineffective, illustration to teach children about the alleged dangers of these foods. Rather, the young children needed to be shown the 'disgusting' consequences of consuming these 'treats': being fat.

A number of students I talked to, from five-year-olds in Mrs Constansa's class to twelve-year-olds in Mr Spurlock's class, talked about fatness in ways that reflected their disgust of fat people, their fear of becoming fat, their desire to eat and exercise in the 'right' way, and to achieve the 'right', non-fat body. In a conversation at Dudley School, Anita and Chardonnay (both six-year-old girls) talked with me about the idea that "if girls have huge muscles, we will look ugly!". So I asked them:

DARREN: What sort of body would make a girl not ugly?
CHARDONNAY: Eating healthy foods, getting skinny. Sometimes girls want to get skinny. I do!
ANITA: I don't want to be fat. I will look ugly!

CHARDONNAY: So you will be skinny.
DARREN: So you both want to be skinny?
ANITA: Yes.
CHARDONNAY: I want to be as skinny as a stick.
DARREN: Why?
CHARDONNAY: So I can lie on the ground and someone can pick me up.
ANITA: My little sister loves me. She's a bit fatter than me.
DARREN: And does that make any difference that she's a bit fatter than you?
ANITA: Yeah, 'cause meat makes people fat and makes poos smelly.
CHARDONNAY: My mum only gives me one candy a day.
DARREN: Why one candy?
CHARDONNAY: If I have ten [pieces of] candy a day I might get fat.
DARREN: Why don't you want to be fat?
CHARDONNAY: Because then I'll be as fat as a ball!
ANITA: As fat as a fat man!

Anita and Chardonnay made similar judgements on certain bodies, with "fat" or muscular bodies seen as "ugly" (especially for women), and skinny as "healthy". They knew that other girls wanted to get skinny, that they personally wanted to get "skinny" and that eating healthy foods, avoiding candy, and doing exercise (e.g. dancing) was a secure route to skinniness. This conversation was also a pertinent reminder that the pedagogies which shaped these Year Two girl's ideas about fatness, self, and others, had not only been the formal pedagogies of school and *Life Education*, but home and beyond too (for further discussion on pedagogies of skinniness and fatness, see Powell, 2010; Powell & Fitzpatrick, 2015).

Fear is a powerful pedagogical strategy to shape children's conduct – their desires and decisions. This is particularly so when disgust of the "unhealthy, abject other" is fused to children's fear of becoming the fat and unhealthy 'other' (Leahy, 2009, p. 179). As Leahy (2012, p. 188) also argued, while the "abject other functions as a potent warning mechanism within health education pedagogical assemblages ... disgust is central to its production". Fear and disgust of the 'abject' and unhealthy, fat 'other' are harnessed as a means to ensure children understood the consequences of their choices or decisions, both for now and in the future (see also Burrows & Wright, 2007). In another example, Mr Spurlock's Year Seven/Eight class participated in three *Life Education* lessons that constituted the '*Warrant of Fitness*' unit. In one lesson, *Life Education* teacher Marion taught the students about body image. On the inside wall of the mobile classroom, Marion displayed photographs of two famous people: former New Zealand Prime Minister, the late David Lange, and former Australian model, Elle 'The Body' Macpherson. The students were asked to describe the two people. This was followed by a discussion where the main point was "not to judge a book by its cover ... we are all special and unique" (Marion). Marion pointed out to the students that "just because [Macpherson] is skinny doesn't mean she is healthy, but just because she is beautiful doesn't make her stupid". Then Marion proceeded to tell the class that David Lange "died of obesity-related illness and he was fat his whole life, he was overweight his whole life, and he was picked on because of that". By connecting David Lange's fatness with his death (which was incorrect, as he died from complications relating to amyloidosis, a rare and incurable blood plasma disorder), Marion attempted to convince students of the risks associated with becoming the 'unhealthy other'. She tried to mobilise multiple fears – fear of fatness, dying, and being "picked on" – to coerce students into changing their 'unhealthy' thoughts, actions, and bodies.

For some students, the fear of fatness, being teased about being fat, and not having friends because they were fat, was a cause of anxiety. During one conversation with Eton, he told me that people teased him because he was fat. The relationship between being teased and being fat was so certain in Eton's mind that he was confused and somewhat angry that there was someone else in his class who was "bigger than me ... but he doesn't get mocked as much as I do". The prospect of social exclusion was accepted by children as a 'normal' consequence of being fat. As six-year-olds Anita and Chardonnay show, the solution to this particular problem was easy: fat people just needed to lose weight.

CHARDONNAY: If you were fat and your friends were skinny, and they didn't like your fat–

ANITA: You'd have to dance [does a little dance move].

CHARDONNAY: The person who was fat would have to do some exercising to burn all the fat out.

DARREN: Would that help them have more friends?

CHARDONNAY: Yeah. The friends that the person had when he was fat, he'd get his friends back again?

DARREN: Why do you think that you'd get more friends if–

CHARDONNAY: You'd get skinny? Because they might think you look better.

The solution to this type of marginalisation was based on two interconnected ideas: that people who were *excluded* needed to change their bodies and behaviours, and that the solution to fatness was ultimately one of individual responsibility – they "would have to do some exercising". Furthermore, we see how fatness is not directly connected to ill health, but the need to "look better".

Demonstrating the consequences of 'bad' lifestyle choices did not always require the invention of an unhealthy fat man or woman. In another *'Warrant of Fitness'* lesson, biopedagogies of disgust were used in conjunction with an 'abject other', who this time was not human, but an animated pig. Dudley School Year Seven and Year Eight students were required to watch 'Life TV', a cartoon news-style programme featuring two central characters. The antagonist was Ham Trotter, described by Eton as a "fat pig" who was "eating burgers all the time". The other character was Henrietta

Hen, described by Eton's classmate Helen as a "skinny bird" who was the "expert" on matters of health, at one stage taking away Ham Trotter's car in order to "to make him walk". *Life Education* teacher Marion described this lesson to me:

> So we have our video clip of a couple of cartoon characters, Ham Trotter and Henrietta Bird. And they are presenters on Life TV and they are talking to us through a series of clips that we are watching about how to care for the body. And Ham Trotter – being stereotyped as a big pig, right – so he gets obese, can't stop eating, rah rah. She, being a 'skinny stringbean' as she calls herself. Right, so she's seen as the Professor – Henrietta Bird. I'm just [studying] sociology at the moment, so my head is like (laughs) 'oh, this is terrible stuff' (laughs).

Although Marion had previously told me one of the aims of *Life Education* was to challenge stereotypes (such as stereotyping Elle Macpherson as 'stupid' because she was beautiful), the *Life Education* resource writers deliberately created a stereotype of an "obese" individual (albeit a pig) who was fat because they "can't stop eating". On the other hand, the smart individual was positioned as someone who was educated ("the Professor"), who could tell fat people (or pigs) what to do (e.g. not to use their car), what to eat (e.g. healthy fruit and vegetables, not hamburgers), and what to look like (e.g. to be skinny and not be fat).

I asked Brian and Eton what the central message of Ham Trotter's and Henrietta Bird's Life TV 'news story' was. They replied:

ETON: The pig was like, huge and the hen was like, skinny as, and she was always saying 'eat healthy', but he was saying 'bigger the better'.

BRIAN: He was like, saying eat healthy, but he just [ate] hamburgers and things.

DARREN: Do you think that's fair to fat pigs or fat people that they are portrayed in that way, to be eating junk food all the time, because surely there's some people-

ETON: No, it's their choice isn't it?

DARREN: It's their choice to be fat or to eat?

ETON: Well, to eat, but it's their choice to go to McDonald's every day of [their] life.

Eton was, in his own words, "chubby", but admitted he did not eat McDonald's or other 'junk food' on a daily basis, and said he scootered or bicycled almost every day with his dogs. However, through the invention of the stereotyped, gluttonous "fat pig", the subjectivity of Eton and fat 'others' was bound to healthist discourses that conflated health with 'bad', immoral, consumptive choices. In a research conversation with Eton, James, and Brian, the three

Year Seven boys started to argue about whether MILO,[1] and separate ingredients in MILO (e.g. chocolate, cocoa, sugar, water) were healthy:

DARREN: Is chocolate healthy?
ETON: No, I learnt that the hard way.
DARREN: What do you mean you learnt that the hard way?
ETON: I ate too much of it.
DARREN: And what did it do to you?
ETON: It turned me fat! [Eton, James, Brian, and Darren laugh] I turned chubby in like a week.
DARREN: And what's wrong with being fat?
ETON: It's irritating. People mocking you all the time.
DARREN: Is that what happened?
ETON: Yeah. I don't eat chocolate anymore.

In the end, Eton blamed himself for his fatness and for being mocked "all the time". It was Eton who had to change, rather than those who teased him needing to make changes to their own attitudes, biases, and behaviours.

Five-year-old Leon, a student in Mrs Constansa's class, also knew that to be healthy (as well as fit and strong) you needed to "eat healthy things", "exercise", and not be fat. Following the 'Harold's Picnic' lesson, I sat outside Leon's classroom with him and asked what he learned from Life Education:

LEON: To eat healthy things. You can only eat treats sometimes and you can eat ice-creams a little bit and you eat sandwiches every day and breakfast and morning tea. And you need healthy things, otherwise you won't get strong and run for pretty long.
DARREN: Why do you need to eat healthy things?
LEON: So you can get fit, strong, and you can run for a long time.
DARREN: What does being fit mean?
LEON: I think it means you are being strong.
DARREN: What happens if you don't eat healthy things?
LEON: Um, you might, if you eat heaps of not healthy things, I think you get fat!
DARREN: What happens if you get fat?
LEON: I don't know.
DARREN: Why are fat people fat and skinny people skinny?
LEON: If you [are] doing exercise you are skinny, and if you aren't you might get fat.

I am not suggesting that Life Education was the main or only activity that shaped children's understanding of health, fatness, and self. As Harwood (2009, p. 21) reminds us, biopedagogies are not a straightforward, linear process of passing knowledge onto students, but rather complex "practices that impart knowledge writ large, occurring at multiple levels across countless domains and sites". The children (and adults) in the three schools were exposed to a range of biopedagogical devices that taught them about health, inactivity, obesity, and fatness at a number of sites and spaces, both within and outside the school (see also Powell, 2015). What *Life Education*, other corporatised resources, and teachers failed to do was to *challenge* these pervasive biopedagogies. The biopedagogies employed to teach children about healthy lifestyle choices were, for the most part, undisruptive to dominant discourses of individualism, health, and obesity.

On a number of occasions, teachers and the external experts appeared to be either unwilling or unable to engage in discussions about the complexities of health and fatness. For instance, during the Year One students' '*Harold's Picnic*' lesson about sugar, teeth, and Macleans toothpaste, Marion asked the whole class: "Why don't we eat sugar?". Leon raised his hand and at the same time shouted back: "Because it makes you fat!". Marion looked at Leon, remained silent, then turned back to the class and asked: "Anybody else?". As a biopedagogical device, ignoring Leon's comment meant that Leon's voice was constrained – Leon was silenced. By Marion choosing *not* to reply, verbally or otherwise, to Leon's response, she employed a *pedagogy of silence*. Silence was joined with discourse in a strategic way (Carrette, 2000) and acted as a "shelter for power" (Foucault, 1978, p. 101). A potential teaching and learning opportunity that may have engaged children and their teachers in a discussion about fatness was shut down, silencing Leon, his classmates, and Mrs Constansa. Through both the said and unsaid, Leon's (and the rest of the Year One's) understanding of fatness, fat people, sugar, and exercise remained undisrupted.

Silence was also used within the healthy lifestyles education programmes in another curious way. Aside from promotional material that talked about crises of obesity and inactivity and the role educational resources would have in teaching children to make healthy lifestyle choices, the actual games, 'fact sheets', lesson ideas, reading resources, and other teaching and learning activities were completely silent about obesity and fatness. In other words, even though some of the programmes were explicitly promoted as being 'part of the solution' to childhood obesity (and others were understood by the participants as playing a role in preventing obesity), the actual resources, workbooks, coaches, and teachers barely mentioned obesity at all. The closest these resources came to mentioning obesity occurred in the *Be Healthy, Be Active* (Nestlé New Zealand, 2011, p. 14) resource which discussed "healthy body weight". Although I can only speculate why fatness or obesity was not explicitly written about in these resources, this pedagogy of silence did little to challenge the dominant discourses that underpinned young people's understanding of fatness or obesity.

This is not to say that children were unable to resist the notion that fat was inherently unhealthy, that all fat people were greedy and lazy, or that someone's fatness was the result of individual failure. For instance, when I asked Leon: "Can fat people also be healthy?", he replied, "Yeah, they can, but if they eat too many lolly-things they won't be". Year Seven Dudley School student Nicole described her mother as "obese", but also healthy. However, even though a number of children admitted that you could be both fat *and* healthy, the consensus was that you would still be *healthier* (and happier, more attractive, and have more friends) if you were skinny or lost weight. Ultimately, whatever the solution to fatness and/or ill health, the success of solutions was almost always directly linked to an individual's *responsibility* to make healthy lifestyle choices.

Transforming informed choice to personal responsibility

The various corporate and charity resources and workbooks drew on the notion that all children needed to do to be healthy was be more responsible for making healthy choices. For instance, the *5+ A Day* resource states that one of its key learning outcomes is for students to learn to "demonstrate *increasing responsibility* for self-care" (5+ A Day Charitable Trust, 2009, p. 3, my emphasis). The prominent rationale for healthy lifestyles education programmes is to govern children to take increased responsibility for their choices and their lifestyles. The outline for *Life Education's 'Warrant of Fitness'* unit, for example, stated: "We look at a variety of issues relating to food and nutrition including: body image, healthy nutrition for growing bodies, media influence, *taking responsibility for a balanced lifestyle*" (Life Education Trust, 2011b, p. 1, my emphasis). In a similar way, three of the ten lessons suggested in the *Iron Brion* lesson plans were based on the following learning outcome: "Students will: describe their nutritional needs for growth and development and demonstrate *increasing responsibility* for what they eat" (New Zealand Beef and Lamb Marketing Bureau, n.d., p. 13, my emphasis).

The use of food and exercise diaries, often in conjunction with goal-setting activities, was a common strategy to transfer the responsibility of (un)healthy lifestyles choices to children themselves (see also Gard 2008; Powell & Gard, 2014). In *Iron Brion*, for example, students were required to "Design a seven-day eating plan that shows meals for Breakfast, Lunch and Dinner", "Check their eating plan against their knowledge of the five food groups" (linked to the *Iron Brion* food pyramid), then "make changes to their food plan if they have identified that it is not balanced in terms of foods they should be eating 'lots of', some of' and 'little of'" (New Zealand Beef and Lamb Marketing Bureau, n.d., p. 19). The monitoring of food choices and consumption was not entirely limited to the self. Students were also asked to confess to classmates "what they have decided to eat for each day of the week" as well as making "recommendations to each other of what they could include" (p. 19). They were required to modify their eating plan in alignment with what their classmates, teachers, *Iron Brion*, The Heart Foundation, and the New Zealand Beef and Lamb Marketing Bureau think they "*should be eating* 'lots of', some of', and 'little of'". Students were then instructed to share this plan with their families and are considered successful by being able to "describe their nutritional needs for growth and development and *demonstrate increasing responsibility for what they eat*" (p. 19, my emphasis). However, complexities around the notion of choice – such as the (in)ability of families or individual children to have the access and finances to take 'responsibility' to choose the 'right' food – was largely ignored. The danger of these types of approaches that are strongly underpinned by the ideology of healthism is that health is conceived "as a responsibility, rather than a right, [repositioning] subjects as at fault if they are deemed to be unhealthy, particularly if they had the information about how to achieve health. (As if it were that formulaic.) (LeBesco, 2011, p. 156).

In a comparable (although more simplistic) self-monitoring activity, the *Life Education* workbook for '*Harold's Picnic*' asked Year One (five-year-old) students to "Draw pictures of everything you ate in one day" – "REMEMBER! Think about food you should eat most, food you should eat some of, and food you should only eat now and then" (Life Education Trust, n.d.-b, p. 5). In addition to the children being required to recall and 'own up' to their (un) healthy choices, they were also required to make judgements about their food according to the *Life Education* 'traffic light' system. Although they were told to 'think' about these foods and how much they should eat of each, the likelihood that most five-year-old children would have any say or control over what they ate that day was not open for discussion. Nor did this prescriptive curriculum cater for one of Mrs Constansa's students, a five-year-old Māori girl called Marama, who regularly did not have anything to eat at school. Marama's so-called choices were either to go hungry, or accept 'charity' from some of her caring classmates.[2]

These types of self-monitoring and self-problematising activities acted as technologies by attempting to make children more responsible and by coercing children to set goals in order to 'make changes' in their everyday lives. For instance, *Be Healthy, Be Active* encouraged students to use Nestlé's downloadable 'Pocket Diary', where children would record their food intake and physical activity over three weeks in order to "check how you are going against recommendations of what you ideally need to be doing, aim to make some changes if you need to. Even small changes can make a big difference to how you feel" (Nestlé, n.d.-a, para. 10).

In the lesson designed to teach students how to use their diaries, the technologies of self-monitoring and self-problematising were linked to the individual student's *responsibility* to set goals, make changes, and be healthier. At the beginning of the lesson, teachers were instructed to "Tell the students that setting and sticking to goals can be a great help in changing eating habits. The diary will help them focus their goal setting and show areas that need work" (Nestlé New Zealand, 2011, p. 16). For the next part of the activity, teachers were then required to "Have the students write their goals in their Online Journals. They can then complete a second week in their diary to see if they achieve those goals, for example, eating a broader range of foods or more vegetables" (Nestlé New Zealand, 2011, p. 16). In other words, food and exercise diaries, goal setting, and the use of 'confessions' were combined strategies that attempted to fuse self-surveillance, predetermined ideal behaviours, and actual improvements in individual conduct.

The final activity in *Life Education's 'Warrant of Fitness'* (WOF) workbook (Life Education Trust, n.d.-a, p. 35) was a 'WOF Sheet', in which students were required to answer 'Pass' or 'Fail' for 19 statements, a selection of which are provided below:

I eat 5+ A day from fruit and vegetables
I choose healthy snacks
I feel good about how I look
I exercise for 30 minutes daily
I choose foods based on their nutritional value
I feel good about myself
I feel in control of the choices I make
I help to make food choices at home
I am aware of healthy choices available in the school

This self-monitoring/self-assessment activity is obviously individualistic, as well as corporeal. Through the extensive use of 'I' statements, students' (un)healthy thoughts, actions and bodies are reduced to individual choices, thoughts, and feelings. However, it is not enough for students to merely identify their (un)healthy conduct – they also need to take responsibility for any failures by devising and recording "strategies to help resolve the problem". In fact, one of the main learning intentions for the *'Warrant of Fitness'* unit was for students to be able to "develop an action plan to meet our own nutritional needs" (Life Education Trust, 2011b, p. 1). If, for example, a student problematised their choices after failing to 'pass' a WOF test statement, such as "I eat 5 + A day from fruit and vegetables" (Life Education Trust, n.d.-a, p. 35), it then became the responsibility of the individual child to be able to create a plan to fix the 'problem'. Of course, the significant influences that shape children's ability to receive or even buy the 'right' amount of fruit and vegetables are mostly, if not wholly, out of their control. The multiple, complex, and broad determinants of children's 'choices' were once again re-imagined as problems that could be solved through personal choice and individual responsibility.

There's something about Natia: fat, unhealthy, irresponsible ... and poor

At St Saviour's School there was one particular noteworthy, and deeply troubling, illustration of how the responsibility for children's health and fatness was shifted onto the shoulders of children. Natia was a 12-year-old Samoan girl in Ms Ellie's class that I built a strong relationship with over six months

I spent at her school. On numerous occasions, both children and adults discussed with me Natia's 'obesity' and fatness, and connected this directly to what they perceived as her unhealthy choices of food, including her poor attitude to her own health (as well as the health of her five-year-old brother who also attended St Saviour's). During one lunchtime I walked into the staffroom and a member of the administration staff called me over to a window, pointing to the concrete steps below. There was Natia, sitting away from the rest of her classmates and sharing a large bag of Twisties chips[3] with her brother. The middle-aged Pākehā women was disheartened with Natia's lunch choice, telling me that she "should know better" and that it was these 'bad' choices that had made Natia "obese". This was not the only time an adult had bemoaned the 'fact' that children *in general* had fat bodies, were lazy, and ate too much 'junk food'. However, what was significant about Natia's case was that adults seemed to pick on Natia as an almost cautionary tale of immorality and ill health. Natia was viewed as an individual with 'unhealthy' conduct, attitude, and corporeality, even though there were a number of other children (and adults for that matter) who were fatter, less active, and who also ate 'junk' food at school. It was not just adults though who shared these thoughts about Natia.

Natia's classmates also made frequent remarks (not in front of Natia) about her health, eating, and fat body. These were not conversations where I had asked the children about Natia or anyone else they thought was fat or unhealthy. Rather (and much like the adults), the children tended to point out Natia as a specific example of the 'abject other' and 'what not to do'. For instance, when I was having a discussion with Mary, Amy, and Peta about the differences between healthy and unhealthy, the girls described Natia as an individual who was unhealthy because she ate 'junk food' at school. Another time I talked with the same three girls about their perspectives of what a 'healthy lunch' might look like. I then asked them: "What does an unhealthy lunch look like?". Amy instantly replied: "Natia's lunch!".

These students (and some other girls in Natia's class) also expressed their frustration and annoyance that Natia tried to 'scab' food from them.[4] Natia had previously told me she sometimes 'scabbed' food because she was hungry, either because she had needed to eat her own lunch before school, or she had given her whole lunch to her little brother, or simply because she had not been provided any food to eat for lunch (or breakfast) in the first place. Some classmates also remarked that on days when Natia did have food for lunch, she tried to swap her 'junk food' for their 'healthier' sandwiches. Natia's tendency to be seen as fat, a 'scab', and a chip-eater resulted in Natia being constructed as unhealthy *and* immoral – lazy, greedy, and irresponsible.

From speaking with Natia on numerous occasions, both informally (usually as I wandered around the playground at lunchtime or before school), and formally (i.e. during recorded interviews), I soon learned that Natia and her family were living in poverty. Natia lived with her mother, father, and four siblings in a three bedroom 'state house' (one provided and funded by the government through the welfare system), but they had all been evicted for allowing their cousins to live in the house, breaking one of the conditions of their tenancy. At the time of my last conversation with Natia, she was living in a car at the rear of another relative's house. Natia told me there was often no food for her to eat at all, never mind make a 'healthy' lunch and bring it to school (as suggested by the school receptionist). Sometimes when Natia received a handful of coins from her parents or other relatives, she would buy potato chips (and occasionally a soft drink) from a small convenience store (or what New Zealanders would call a 'dairy') on the way to school – the supermarket was too far away to walk. She told me that she felt guilty about not being able to provide food for her brother, felt shame when asking classmates for food, and felt embarrassed for not having a healthy lunch like some of her classmates (for a further discussion on school lunches, see Pluim, Powell, & Leahy, 2018).

The choices in Natia's life were highly constrained by political, socio-economic, environmental, historical, and cultural forces largely out of her control. However, Natia's teachers' and classmates' understanding of health was inextricably interconnected to the rationalities of healthism, which acted to place the "responsibility for body vigilance solely on the individual, and deflects attention away from the social and cultural conditions which shape and constrain health" (White, Young, and Gillett, 1995, p. 160). The notion of healthism reinforced the assumption that children like Natia not only *could* take responsibility for their own choices, but *should* (see Gard, 2011). Natia was *obliged* to take responsibility for her health and was *blamed* for making the wrong choices, being irresponsible, and having a fat body.

Careless lifestyle choices or careless lifestyle programmes?

I am not suggesting that the broader influences of children's freedom to choose their lifestyles are completely ignored or silenced by healthy lifestyles education programmes. A number of charitable and corporate resources encourage students to recognise (but not act on) wider forces that shape their choices. However, there are significant tensions when different authorities try to 'educate' children about the broader socio-cultural influences on their health, bodies, lifestyles, and choices, and attempt to create individualistic, self-responsible, citizen-consumers (for an in-depth discussion on education and the citizen-consumer, see Spring, 2003). For instance, in the Life Education Trust's (2011b, p. 1) '*Warrant of Fitness*' unit, even though one of the four learning intentions was for students to "identify the elements that influence our choices re. health", the other three intentions stressed individual responsibility: "take responsibility for our own food choices", "recognise the importance of the key elements in a balanced lifestyle: activity, attitude and appetite", and "develop an action plan to meet our own nutritional needs".

Similarly, in *Be Healthy, Be Active* (Nestlé New Zealand, 2011, p. 14), the aim of the second module 'Food and you' was as follows:

> to support students to develop healthy eating habits that contribute towards maintaining a healthy body weight. As part of this, students need to understand the concept of a balanced diet and healthy eating. They also need to understand the influences (from society, the media, their family/whānau, and their peers) on their eating habits and how they can set goals to work towards balanced eating.

While on one hand the *Be Healthy, Be Active* resource claimed to develop students' understanding of the wider societal influences "on their eating habits", on the other hand children were told to "set realistic goals so they can work towards making healthier food choices" (Nestlé New Zealand, 2011, p. 14). The responsibility for children's food choices and their body weight was once again placed onto children, rather than encouraging students *to take action to* shape media, family, peer, societal, or commercial influences. *The New Zealand curriculum's* aim to develop children's "understanding of the factors that influence the health of individuals, groups and society: lifestyle, economic, social, cultural, political, and environmental factors" (Ministry of Education, 2007, p. 23) was re-crafted to emphasise individual health, individual choice, and individual responsibility. It certainly did not encourage students to use their "skills and understandings to take critical action to promote personal, interpersonal, and societal well-being" (p. 23).

In *Be Healthy, Be Active* students were also required to complete an online journal in which they self-monitored and recorded their food and exercise choices over one week. The follow-up activity for this journal writing was called 'Setting Goals' (Nestlé New Zealand, 2011, p. 16), in which teachers were instructed to begin the lesson by sharing *their own* journals – confessing and problematising their choices – by asking the students questions such as:

- Which food groups did I eat too much of?
- Which groups could I have eaten more of?
- Was I on target with my healthy eating?
- What could I be doing differently? What steps could I take to do that?
- Was there anything that contributed to my eating too much or not enough?

The Nestlé New Zealand (2011, p. 16, my emphasis) resource then provided the following parenthetical note:

> (For some students, this might be an issue related to money or access to food. This could lead to a conversation about how to deal with such issues, for example, suitable substitutes. The focus should be about *making the student responsible* for their learning and actions.)

So even though the resource writers conceded, albeit briefly, that students' choices may be influenced by money, their proposed solution was simple: getting teachers to make the child responsible. The solutions to poverty, hunger, and ill health were rendered technical and non-political. The complex determinants of an individual's health and the impact of social, cultural, environmental, political, historical, and economic forces were re-imagined as insignificant compared to an individual's ability to freely make the 'correct' choices.

These approaches to teaching about food, health, and lifestyles are not merely simplistic; they represent a significant dumbing down of the possibilities of health education. At best, they demonstrate an inability of corporations, charities, and classroom teachers to engage with – or support students to be able to understand – the complex nature of health and how it may be achieved. At worst, they illustrate a deliberate attempt by corporations and their partners to misinform children and to divert children's attention away from significant factors that shape children's health. Either way, the healthy lifestyles education resources and pedagogies are careless. They demonstrate a lack of care for students' learning and a lack of care for students' everyday lives.

Re-shaping 'healthy' resources and pedagogies

Corporate-produced resources and enacted pedagogies are strongly shaped by key tenets of neoliberalism: personal responsibility, autonomy, freedom of choice, and consumerism. As neoliberal pillars of health (Herrick, 2011), they underpin healthy lifestyles education resources and pedagogies in ways that attempted to 'inform' children about making the right food, nutrition, and physical activity choices, as well as the consequences of making the 'wrong' choices, displaying the 'wrong' body, and even having 'wrong' thoughts, attitudes, and beliefs about health. Children's individual responsibility to make the correct healthy lifestyle choices is promoted as a silver bullet solution to children's ill health and fatness. Instead of encouraging children to challenge the 'myth of choice' (Greenfield, 2011), or contest the notion that fat people were fat (or even healthy) simply because they ate too much sugary or fatty food, the outsourced resources and pedagogies merely worked to keep the *status quo* secure and stable.

Rather than corporations and their partners trying to *make* children be healthy, these organisations attempt to coerce children 'at a distance' (Miller & Rose 2008) to *want* to be healthy and be seen to be healthy. As Rose (1999, p. 88) further explains,

> the project of responsible citizenship has been fused with individuals' projects for themselves .... Thus, in a very significant sense it has become possible to govern without governing society – to govern through the 'responsibilized' and 'educated' anxieties and aspirations of individuals.

Teaching children that they may have some responsibility to make healthy decisions is not in itself a bad thing. However, by and large these neoliberal resources and pedagogies exemplify Crawford's (1980) concerns about healthism: they promote a narrow view of what health is (corporeal and individualistic) and how it may be achieved (responsible healthy lifestyle choices). They ignore, mask, downplay, and even subvert significant 'other' determinants of children's health, such as poverty, policy, industry lobbying, and corporate commercialism.

These corporatised healthy lifestyles education resources and pedagogies also represent "strategic attempts to market not a benign conception of health, but a particular brand of health – namely one that conflates health with morality and bodily perfection, and is ultimately connected to consumer culture" (Vander Schee, 2008, p. 5, italics in original). As Rose (1999, pp. 164–165) also argued, with neoliberal forms of governance there are "new forms of consumption ... the regulation of habits, dispositions, styles of existence in the name of identity and lifestyle ... the citizen is to become the consumer". This new 'brand' of health and health education is intimately connected to new lifestyles and new identities for children, where the child-citizen is now shaped into the child-consumer.

This is especially evident when children's alleged 'freedom of choice' and their need to be self-responsible, healthier, active, and non-obese are fused with technologies of 'healthy consumption': the consumption of corporate education, corporate philanthropy, the corporate brand, and corporate products.

Notes

1 MILO is a popular chocolate/malt drink that is heavily marketed by its producer, Nestlé, in New Zealand, Australia, South America, Southeast Asia, and parts of Africa.
2 One morning at Dudley School, Jane, a five-year-old student in Mrs Constansa's class, arrived at school with her mother and gave Mrs Constansa a plastic shopping bag with sandwiches, yoghurt, and an apple inside. Jane's mother explained that Jane had noticed her classmate, Marama, often had no lunch to eat, so Jane wanted to make her some. At lunchtime, Mrs Constansa tried to give Marama the food Jane had made for her. Marama refused to accept it.
3 Twisties are a 'flavoured corn snack' marketed by New Zealand company Bluebird Foods Ltd., a brand owned by PepsiCo.
4 Scab is a common colloquial term that is used as both a noun and a verb to describe either a person who asks to be given food or drink for no payment, or the process of asking for free food or drink (e.g. "Don't be a scab!" or "can I scab some of those chips?").

References

5+ A Day Charitable Trust. (2009). *Primary school teaching resource*. Retrieved from http://www.5aday.co.nz/media/28228/primary-resource-health-well-being.pdf

5+ A Day Charitable Trust. (2011). *Primary school teaching resource: Bright ideas – marketing and advertising fresh fruit and vegetables*. Retrieved from http://www.5aday.co.nz/media/18459/primary-resource-marketing-advertising.pdf

Ayo, N. (2012). Understanding health promotion in a neoliberal climate and the making of health conscious citizens. *Critical Public Health*, *22*(1), 99–105. doi: 10.1080/09581596.2010.520692

Burrows, L., & Wright J. (2007). Prescribing practices: Shaping healthy children in schools. *International Journal of Children's Rights*, *15*(1), 1–16.

Carrette, J. R. (2000). *Foucault and religion: Spiritual corporality and political spirituality*. London: Routledge.

Crawford, R. (1980). Healthism and the medicalization of everyday life. *International Journal of Health Services*, *10*, 365–388.

Foucault, M. (1978). *The will to knowledge: The history of sexuality* (Vol. 1). London: Penguin.

Gard, M. (2008). Producing little decision makers and goal setters in the age of the obesity crisis. *Quest*, *60*(4), 488–502.

Gard, M. (2011). *The end of the obesity epidemic*. Oxon, UK: Routledge.

Greenfield, K. (2011). *The myth of choice: Personal responsibility in a world of limits*. New Haven, United States: Yale University Press.

Harwood, V. (2009). Theorizing biopedagogies. In J. Wright & V. Harwood (Eds.), *Biopolitics and the obesity epidemic: Governing bodies* (pp. 15–30). New York: Routledge.

Herrick, C. (2009). Shifting blame/selling health: Corporate social responsibility in the age of obesity. *Sociology of Health & Illness*, *31*(1), 51–65. doi: 10.1111/j.1467-9566.2008.01121.

Herrick, C. (2011). *Governing health and consumption: sensible citizens, behaviour and the city*. Bristol: The Policy Press.

Leahy, D. (2009). Disgusting pedagogies. In J. Wright & V. Harwood (Eds.), *Biopolitics and the obesity epidemic: Governing bodies* (pp. 172–182). New York: Routledge.

Leahy, D. (2012). *Assembling a health[y] subject*. (Unpublished doctoral dissertation). Deakin University, Melbourne, Australia.

LeBesco, K. (2011). Neoliberalism, public health, and the moral perils of fatness. *Critical Public Health*, *21*(2), 153–164. doi: 10.1080/09581596.2010.529422

Life Education Trust. (2011a). *Harold's Picnic*. Retrieved from http://www.lifeeducation.org.nz/site/lifeedutrust/files/Module_Resource/food_and_nutrition/FN%20Info1%20Curric%20Folder%20Harold%27s%20Picnic%20WALT.pdf

Life Education Trust. (2011b). *Warrant of Fitness*. Retrieved from http://www.lifeeducation.org.nz/site/lifeedutrust/files/Module_Resource/food_and_nutrition/FN%20Info5%20Curric%20Folder%20WOF%20WALT.pdf

Life Education Trust. (2018). *Welcome*! Retrieved from https://www.lifeeducation.org.nz/

Life Education Trust. (n.d.-a). *Warrant of Fitness* – workbook.

Life Education Trust. (n.d.-b). *Harold's Picnic* – workbook.

McDermott, L. (2012). 'Thrash yourself Thursday': The production of the 'healthy' child through a fitness-based PE practice. *Sport, Education and Society*, *17*(3), 405–429. doi: 10.1080/13573322.2011.608942

Miller, P., & Rose, N. (2008). *Governing the present*. Cambridge, England: Polity.

Ministry of Education. (2007). *The New Zealand curriculum*. Wellington, New Zealand: Learning Media.

Nestlé. (n.d.-a). *Be Healthy, Be Active: Online action*. Retrieved from https://www.behealthybeactive.co.nz/online-games/

Nestlé. (n.d.-b). *Online action: The Fuel Up Challenge*. Retrieved from https://www.behealthybeactive.co.nz/the-fuel-up-challenge/

Nestlé. (n.d.-c). *Online action: The Health eDash*. Retrieved from https://www.behealthybeactive.co.nz/online-games/health-edash/

Nestlé New Zealand. (2011). *Be Healthy, Be Active: Teachers' resource.* Wellington: Learning Media.

Nestlé New Zealand. (n.d.-a). *Be Healthy, Be Active: Nestlé Healthy Kids Global Program.* Retrieved from http://www.nestle.co.nz/nhw/behealthybeactive

Nestlé New Zealand. (n.d.-b). *Be Healthy, Be Active: Read and response cards.*

New Zealand Beef and Lamb Marketing Bureau. (n.d.). *Iron Brion's hunt for gold resource kit.* New Zealand Beef and Lamb Marketing Bureau.

Pluim, C., Powell, D., & Leahy, D. (2018). Schooling lunch: Health, food and the pedagogicalization of the lunchbox. In S. Rice & A. G. Rud (Eds.), *Education dimensions of school lunch: Critical perspectives* (pp. 59–74). Cham, Switzerland: Palgrave Macmillan.

Powell, D. (2010). *'Running in circles: Children's lessons in PE, fitness and fatness'.* (Master's thesis, University of Auckland, Auckland, New Zealand). Retrieved from https://researchspace.auckland.ac.nz/handle/2292/6446

Powell, D. (2015). *"Part of the solution"?: Charities, corporate philanthropy and healthy lifestyles education in New Zealand primary schools.* (Doctoral dissertation, Charles Sturt University, Bathurst, Australia). Retrieved from https://researchoutput.csu.edu.au/files/9316089/80326

Powell, D., & Fitzpatrick, K. (2015). 'Getting fit basically just means, like, nonfat': Children's lessons in fitness and fatness. *Sport, Education and Society, 20*(4), 463–484. doi: 10.1080/13573322.2013.777661

Powell, D., & Gard, M. (2014). The governmentality of childhood obesity: Coca-Cola, corporations and schools. *Discourse: Studies in the Cultural Politics of Education, 36*(6), 854–867. doi: 10.1080/01596306.2014.905045

Rose, N. (1999). *Governing the soul: The shaping of the private self.* London, England: Free Association Books.

Spring, J. (2003). *Educating the consumer-citizen: A history of the marriage of schools, advertising, and media.* New York: Routledge.

Vander Schee, C. (2008). Consuming health: Health curricula and the production of a healthy student. In D. Boyles (Ed.), *The corporate assault on youth: Commercialism, exploitation, and the end of innocence* (pp. 1–26). New York: Peter Lang.

White, P., Young, K., & Gillett, J. (1995). Bodywork as a moral imperative: Some critical notes on health and fitness. *Loisir et Société, 18*(1), 159–182.

Wright, J. (2009). Biopower, biopedagogies and the obesity epidemic. In J. Wright & V. Harwood (Eds.), *Biopolitics and the obesity epidemic: Governing bodies* (pp. 1–14). New York: Routledge.

Wright, J., & Harwood, V. (2009). *Biopolitics and the obesity epidemic: Governing bodies.* New York: Routledge.

7

SHAPING THE (UN)HEALTHY
CHILD-CONSUMER

The exploitation of schools as a site to proliferate consumerism is hardly new (Spring, 2003). However, in neoliberal times there are increasingly "new technologies of government that fashion new institutions and modes of delivery within which new social subjectivities are being fostered; extensions of the logic of the marketplace that socialize individualized subjects and discipline the noncompliant" (Peck & Tickell, 2002, p. 390). Technologies of consumption are one group of technologies that re-fashion the educational sphere, extending 'market logic' into schools, and attempting to foster children as consumers (see Miller & Rose, 1997). These are technologies that depend

> upon fabricating delicate affiliations between the active choices of potential consumers and the qualities, pleasures and satisfactions represented in the product, organized in part through the practices of advertising and marketing, and always undertaken in the light of particular beliefs about the nature of human subjectivity. (Miller & Rose, 2008, p. 31)

Technologies of consumption shape resources and pedagogies in an attempt to bring children's identities into line with the goals of neoliberalism, consumer capitalism, and corporations. With this in mind, in this chapter I critically examine the ways in which healthy lifestyles education programmes – in the name of fighting childhood obesity – have employed different tactics and strategies to shape children as a particular kind of consumer citizen (Spring, 2003). To do this I have analysed four technologies of consumption – product placement, transforming children into marketers, sponsorship, and free gifts – and interrogated how each of these technologies has 'congealed' with the resolve of corporations to develop children as lifelong consumers of the corporate brand image and their allegedly 'healthy' corporate products. While some of healthy lifestyles education programmes claim to be 'critical' forms of education, there are certainly limits on how critical (or not) they expect teachers and children to be.

Product placement in educational resources

Product placement was one technology of consumption that endeavours to connect branded and unbranded objects with children's understanding of health and self. Product placement is a term commonly used to describe a form of advertising where corporate logos, products, trademarks, and services are promoted in the context of a television programme, film, video game, or music video (e.g. a character in a movie drinking a can of Coca-Cola). In a number of instances, corporations and their not-for-profit' partners used, or abused, the healthy lifestyles education programmes to market their corporate brand and corporate products directly to students. For example, despite Nestlé New Zealand (2011) explicitly stating in the foreword to the *Be Healthy, Be Active* teacher resource, "The content of the programme is not commercial in nature", some of the resources for students had Nestlé-branded products placed within them. The interactive 'Food Plate' (see Nestlé, n.d.), for example, had links to a 'Snack Time' section where students could view and use recipes for "twelve simple snacks you can make for home or at school", such as 'Sensational Smoothies', 'Muffin Magic', 'Mighty Muesli Bars', and 'Super Noodles'. However, the ingredients of these recipes contained branded Nestlé products. 'Sensational Smoothies' was a banana-chocolate smoothie made with popular brand MILO. 'Muffin Magic' included Milk Melts – a Nestlé brand of cooking chocolate. 'Mighty Muesli Bars' were made with Nestlé's Sweetened Condensed Milk, whereas 'Super Noodles' were to be made with Maggi '2 Minute noodles – chicken flavour'. This form of product placement and branding appeared to contradict one of the central assurances of Nestlé's *Healthy Kids Global Programme:* "NO product branding" (Nestlé, 2014).

Nestlé was not the only organisation to use a programme to market its products. The *Life Education* resources (as well as its promotional materials and mobile classrooms) advertised a number of sponsors' products. In fact, two of the Life Education Trust's named national sponsors – Just Juice and Macleans – *were* products (as opposed to the corporation, Frucor or GlaxoSmithKline, respectively, being named as the sponsor). On the inside cover of the '*Warrant of Fitness*' workbook (Life Education Trust, n.d.-a), the Just Juice logo was displayed twice with the following 'credit': "This book was produced with the generous assistance of Just Juice". In this student workbook, a picture of a Frucor product – a bottle of H2Go water – was conspicuously inserted into one of the food pyramids that informed students about the "recommended fuel for a healthy body" (Life Education Trust, n.d.-a, p. 9). The same bottle appeared in another lesson entitled "Consuming" (p. 20), where children were encouraged to keep hydrated by drinking water. In this lesson, students were also taught how to read a food label (another component of learning how to make 'informed choices'), a label branded: "125 ml Tetra Just Juice Orange and Mango flavour" (p. 23).

The resources and lessons provided to Year One and Two students also contained marketing for Just Juice. The children were sent home with a leaflet that outlined to parents what their children were learning in *Life Education*. At the bottom of the letter, next to a picture of Harold, it read:

A message from Just Juice – did you know …

That one glass (250 ml) of fruit juice counts for one of your daily fruit servings for everyone over 5 years.

This information sheet has been produced with the kind support of one of our national sponsors, Just Juice. (Life Education Trust, n.d.–b, p. 1)

This was an obvious attempt to connect a corporate product – Just Juice – with a government-endorsed, private sector-devised, charity-promoted health imperative to eat a certain number of servings of fruit each day.[1] The decision by *Life Education* to promote this particular product was unusual, given that Marion (the Life Education teacher) spent much time warning the Year One and Two children about the dangers of sugar and soft drinks, yet Just Juice had exactly the same proportion of sugar as Coca-Cola (see Community and Public Health Board, n.d.). We can also see in this example that product placement was not just a tactic to attach a corporate product to children's knowledge of what a healthy product looks like and which specific products they needed to consume, but was a marketing strategy to shape children's and adults' understanding of the corporation's image. Product placement acted as a technology of consumption by attempting to re-invent Just Juice and its producer/marketer Frucor as healthy, as well as educational, "kind", supportive, caring, and "generous" (Powell, 2016).

The products placed within corporatised resources were not always branded products, but sometimes generic products associated with a particular industry group, such as beef and lamb, or fruit and vegetables. For instance, the writers of the *Iron Brion* resources barely mentioned 'New Zealand Beef and Lamb' or its more recent brand name 'Beef + Lamb New Zealand'. Instead they chose to liberally sprinkle terms like 'beef', 'lamb', 'red meat', and 'iron' (see New Zealand Beef and Lamb Marketing Bureau, n.d.). For all but one of the ten prescriptive *Iron Brion* lessons, the aim was to teach students about the healthy consumption of iron, beef, and lamb. Here is a snapshot of some of the learning intentions in the *Iron Brion* (New Zealand Beef and Lamb Marketing Bureau, n.d.) resource materials:

Lesson 1: "Discuss which senses you might use when identifying iron" (p. 13)
Lesson 2: "Discuss and critically reflect on why people need iron in their daily eating plan" (p. 16)
Lesson 3: "Identify the main sources of iron in their weekly food plan" (p. 19)

Lesson 4: "Students choose a beef or lamb product to promote to their class members and design a package and label for this product" (p. 21)

Lesson 5: "Prepare and produce advertising material to develop an awareness of the importance of zinc, iron and protein in our eating plans" (p. 22)

Lesson 6: "Look at the labels on beef and lamb products and discuss the information they contain" (p. 23)

Lesson 7: "Gather a range of recipes that use beef and lamb" (see www.recipes.co.nz)" (p. 25)

Lesson 9: "On an outline of a dinner plate or bowl, students design a meal and identify foods which contain easily absorbed iron and poorly absorbed iron" (p. 28)

Lesson 10: "Discuss how beef and lamb is kept at home" (p. 30)

The ubiquitous placement of beef and lamb in the resource's learning experiences acted as a technology of consumption by trying to fuse children's understanding of beef and lamb consumption with discourses of health: to 'educate' "young Kiwis about healthy eating and the role beef and lamb play in a healthy lifestyle" (New Zealand Beef and Lamb Marketing Bureau, n.d., p. 1).

Inserting product placement strategies into healthy lifestyles education programmes meant that what was supposed to be an *educational* endeavour, transformed into one that represented the *commercial* interests of private sector players and partners (Powell, 2016). It is difficult to see exactly how placing a branded H2Go bottle in a food pyramid, or a Nestlé-branded product into a recipe, worked in the educational interests of children. Product placement was a technology of consumption used by the private sector, with the assistance of voluntary sector organisations, to form relationships between *objects* of consumption – Just Juice, H2Go, beef and lamb, and Maggi 2 Minute noodles – and the *subjects* of consumption: children (see Rose, 1999). It was not the only technology that attempted to achieve this. Product placement was a stealthy marketing strategy that joined with other technologies of consumption in an attempt to align children's desires to make healthy choices with the desire of for-profit players to shape children to be uncritical consumers of their 'healthy' products.

Transforming children into marketers

A number of the corporatised programmes featured a pedagogical strategy that interconnected technologies of sponsorship and product placement, whereby children were required to become marketers of corporate products. For instance, the *5+ A Day* programme (5+ A Day Charitable Trust, 2011, p. 4) aims to raise "awareness, critical thinking and action" about food marketing by providing opportunities for children "to create their own advertising and marketing campaigns to promote fresh fruit and vegetables to their friends and families". Predictably, these marketing 'lessons' exclusively promote products manufactured/sold by the corporate sponsors/partners/developers of the 'educational' programmes and resources; as a tactic to increase consumption of their products. In fact, the 5+ A Day Charitable Trust, an organisation devoted to "increasing the consumption of fresh fruit and vegetables" (5+ A Day Charitable Trust, 2013, para. 1) – one with strong personnel and funding links to the fruit and vegetable industry – produces an entire resource called 'Bright ideas: marketing and advertising fresh fruit and vegetables' (see 5+ A Day Charitable Trust, 2011). One of the intended learning outcomes is for children to be able to "plan for and implement advertising strategies to encourage a greater consumption of fresh fruit and vegetables" (p. 2). For students to meet this outcome, teachers are required to: "Tell children that they have a very important job to do. They have to help 5+ A Day promote fresh fruit and vegetables to other children and their family" (p. 6). One of the activities instructs children to

> draw a picture and write a message that promotes the eating of fruit and vegetables. (Designs could be laminated and posted around the school, or copied and placed into the school newsletter, or used as a school fundraiser, source and print aprons and tea towels and sell to school community). (p. 6)

In other words, the point of this lesson and activities is for children to disseminate the 5+ A Day Charitable Trust's marketing message to their classmates, parents, and the wider community; a message funded and promoted by a number of private sector organisations, including supermarket giants Countdown and Foodstuffs. In a similar vein, the 'Give Me A Go' activity asks students to design a poster to help "launch a new marketing campaign aimed at encouraging children to eat a variety of fresh fruit and vegetables" (p. 8). On the same page, another activity called 'Simply the Best' not only transforms students into marketers of the 5+ A Day slogan, but into health educators and health promoters as well: "Explain that the students are now professional health educators whose job it is to develop campaigns to encourage people to eat 5+ A Day". After conducting research into healthy behaviours and deciding on a "target audience", students are then asked to "prepare a short skit, print ad, or mock TV or radio ad that promotes their health message to their chosen audience". The third marketing 'option' for students crossed over with embedded marketing practices, as students are required to analyse the 5+ A Day logo in order to 'learn' how to effectively use logos in marketing campaigns.

These marketing-focused learning activities act as technologies of 'healthy' consumption in three distinct ways. First, they reinforce the idea that in order to be healthy, children need to increase their consumption of fruit and vegetables to at least five servings a day. Second, they reinforce the 5+ A Day logo/slogan/brand/message as essentially a public health imperative, a regime of truth about health that has been significantly shaped by private sector interests. Third, even though this resource states that it encourages children to think critically about marketing, health, and consumption, by turning children into marketers they attempt to 'teach' children to be *uncritical* of marketing strategies that saturate public and private spaces (see Klein, 2002). In other words, turning children into marketers of corporate products aids in the naturalisation of advertising and consumerism in children's everyday lives, rather than a socio-critical health education that encourages children to challenge or act against the normalisation of marketing to children (Powell, 2016).

This is not to say, however, that children were unwilling to resist or problematise attempts to transform them into advertisers for the corporate sponsors. For instance, in one of the *'Warrant of Fitness'* lessons that I observed in a Year Seven/Eight class at Dudley School, children demonstrated that they were not 'cultural dupes' (Hall, 1981). In this lesson, the children were required to create and perform "a commercial kind of thing" (Eton) for H2Go, Just Juice, and Just Juice Splash (a 'healthier' diluted fruit juice beverage aimed at children). All three are Frucor products. According to the students, the point of the student-created commercials was to entertain the audience, "tell them all about the calories in it" and make the product "look good at the same time" (Eton). However, Eton and Brian (as well as other students) were critical of these lessons as they perceived the educational purpose and value of the lessons or resources as being undermined by the corporate efforts to advertise their products. On the basketball court outside their classroom, Eton and Brian reflected on this 'commercial lesson' and a page in their *'Warrant of Fitness'* workbook which featured product placement for a Frucor-brand of bottled water:

DARREN: What sort of water was it?

BRIAN: Yeah, it was H2Go

ETON: But in our books, instead of like, putting just there a bottle of water … in the food pyramid … it would be like, all the healthy stuff, and at the bottom would be like, bottles of H2Go.

DARREN: Was that a food pyramid in your workbook or in the van?

ETON: In our workbook.

BRIAN: And on the van, like inside.

DARREN: Why do you think they chose Just Juice, not just orange juice?

ETON: Because Just Juice sponsored them and like, they deserve [it]. Just Juice would be like, 'if we sponsor you, you have to put us in your books', so it's like, advertising at the same time to all the kids that they go to.

DARREN: And what do you think about being advertised to in school books and things like that?

ETON: I think it's kind of dumb, because we're there to do our school work.

DARREN: What was the point of talking about advertising and making up your own ads?

ETON: I'm not sure, I reckon it was just another fun game.
BRIAN: I think there might've been a point behind it, but I don't think she got round to telling us.

Eton and Brian were aware of the attempts being made to promote corporate products to them, as well as the reasons why corporate sponsors were able to insert their products into their workbooks, lessons, and classroom spaces. More importantly, they did not just perceive these forms of 'stealthy' (or in this case, not so stealthy) advertising as "dumb", but were sceptical of the educative value of teaching them to be marketers of bottled water and fruit juice.

Sponsorship: 'promoting your products to consumers'

Sponsorship was another technology of consumption that was connected to notions of education, health, and corporate products. For example, in a brochure produced by United Fresh, the writers asserted that the 5+ A Day Charitable Trust "promotes fresh produce, working towards raising consumption for all New Zealanders through ... Sponsorship, Advertising, Public Relations and Communications" as well as "Curriculum linked education material for early childhood centres, schools and health professionals" (United Fresh New Zealand Incorporated, 2014, p. 2). Under the heading "Raising Consumption", United Fresh further stated that its

> Members can link with the 5+ A Day Charitable Trust's high-impact promotional activity to *raise the consumption of their products* and fresh fruit and vegetables in New Zealand. 5+ A Day is very well established and links directly into the national school teaching curriculum, including early childhood education centres. The Trust is a respected provider of practical and fun classroom concepts that *encourage children to learn about and eat, fresh fruit and vegetables* every day. *Promoting your products to consumers through education*, social media, public relations, television, *advertising, marketing and sponsorship*. (p. 3, my emphases)

United Fresh and 5+ A Day Charitable Trust's 'philanthropic' sponsorship provided resources to educate children, yet also acted as a technology – one brought together with multiple technologies – to promote member's products and encourage children to consume these products. The relationship between an ensemble of heterogeneous elements, such as corporations, schools, branded products, discourses of health and sport, and sponsorship, was a cause of tension. One such tension noted by most of the Year Six and Year Seven students I talked with (from all three schools) was the relationship between food and drink corporations and the various school-based 'obesity solutions', health and physical education (HPE) programmes, resources, physical activity initiatives, and sports events. In a lengthy discussion with James, Brian, and Eton, they recognised the multiple and contradictory elements that were cobbled together when 'fast food' companies sponsored healthy lifestyles education programmes and professional sports. I began this part of the conversation by asking the boys about the McDonald's *My Greatest Feat* pedometer programme they had participated in two years earlier:

DARREN: Why do you think McDonald's would be wanting people to measure their steps?

ETON: To try and encourage people that McDonald's is helping people get fit.

BRIAN: (Laughs)

JAMES: But it's not really – look at me! (James points to his own stomach)

BRIAN: [People] have McDonald's, keep fit and then exercise a day later.

ETON: They try to encourage them to go to McDonald's.

DARREN: What do you think the ultimate goal for McDonald's is in doing these programmes in schools?

ETON: Profit?

JAMES: To see who has the most shops.

DARREN: So you think it's like a competitive thing, so against

JAMES: They're fighting against like Wendy's, Burger King, Subway.

DARREN: So do you think that would help McDonald's in some way, to compete against Burger King and Wendy's?

BRIAN: Yeah, because they gave out free things.

ETON: Like Wendy's doesn't or BK or anything, [do not] support like the Olympics. McDonald's [is] sponsored everywhere, but BK and Wendy's doesn't sponsor, like anywhere.

JAMES: Even at basketball, I was watching a basketball game, it was the [Townsville] Croc's versus something else, the [New Zealand] Breakers, and the Crocs had a big M [the McDonald's golden arches symbol] on their shirts.

DARREN: And on the court as well, like at the top of the keyhole.

JAMES: And I was like, 'Dad look, we're having McDonald's right now'.

DARREN: So do you think people are more likely to go to McDonald's because they support sports?

BRIAN: Quite a lot.

ETON: Yes – more advertising, then people will remember about it.

JAMES: They just want to get their name out.

DARREN: Would you consider that the *My Greatest Feat* thing was an education programme?

BRIAN: No.

The students were well aware of the multiple intentions of fast food sponsorship: advertising and branding opportunities; connecting the brand image with sports; to "get their name out" so "people will remember it"; "to encourage [people] to go to McDonald's"; to be competitive; to be seen to be "helping" people "get fit" and "exercise"; and to "profit". They were also conscious of the tensions that arose when corporations – especially those associated with obesity, ill-health, and junk food – tried to make children fit, not-fat, healthy, and informed. In one striking example, Helen (a Year Six student at Dudley School) wrote and delivered a speech to her class (during her literacy lessons) in which she criticised McDonald's sponsorship of sport and the role this played in increasing the prevalence of obesity. A cue card from her speech (with grammatical, punctuation, and spelling errors included) read as follows:

I would just like to say mcdonalds shouldn't sponsor events as

- It gives kids the wrong source of energy to play sports on.
- It will give us kids health problems in the future that can effect our life badly.
- And it will effect our every day life by being 1 of the millions of people being obese
- So now why don't we all say no to mcdonalds sponcering our sports evetns because we like to live a healthy life!!

For Helen, McDonald's sponsorship was inextricably interconnected with the *promotion* of ill health and obesity, rather than being 'part of the solution'.

Many students, particularly the older children, recognised that sponsorship of healthy lifestyles education programmes was a corporate tactic that was not primarily about education or health, but money. Mary, a Year Six at St Saviour's School, believed that the involvement of pokie trusts in school activities was "to raise money" for the gaming industry. When I talked to Leroy and Sam, Year Seven students at Reynard Intermediate School, about *My Greatest Feat*, I asked them for a reason why McDonald's sponsored this physical activity programme, to which they succinctly replied:

LEROY: Money.
SAM: Money – fast money.

Nonetheless, money was not the only answer. The children recognised that a sponsoring organisation's quest for monetary gains and their will to teach children how to be healthy was fundamentally linked to their desire to increase consumption of certain products and improve the brand image of the corporation (Powell, 2016). For example, when I asked Helen and Nicole (Year Six at Dudley School) why McDonald's and their *My Greatest Feat* programme wanted children to be more active, they replied:

HELEN: Make them eat more.
NICOLE: For McD's [McDonald's] to be more popular.

Leroy from Reynard Intermediate School also made a connection between public relations ("being popular"), increasing consumption and improving profit. He talked about the financial losses that corporations suffer when a product, or corporation itself, is seen as unhealthy. I asked Leroy why he thought McDonald's failed to sponsor the *My Greatest Feat* programme for the London 2012 Olympic Games, to which he responded: "Losing too much money. Wanting to spend more on themselves. Some people watch those 'What's really in our food' [television] programmes and stop eating McD's [McDonald's]".

Students were mindful that a corporation's use of sponsorship was closely associated with their desire to develop more positive public relations and increased revenue, especially at a time when corporations (and their goods) were perceived as being unhealthy. In a conversation with a group of Year Six boys from St Saviour's – DJ, Mark, Hone, Carlos, and Afu – I asked them: "Why do you think that a company would want you to be healthy or keep healthy?":

DJ: To be strong.
MARK: To stay fit and stay healthy.
HONE: Because they care about us.
CARLOS: So we can live a longer life and buy more of their products.
DARREN: So you think part of it is–
AFU: –to get more money.
DJ: Yeah, to get more money!
DARREN: How do you think they get more money from doing these sort of programmes?
AFU: They put a vivid image in children's heads so they can go home and tell their parents about the company.

While children were cognisant of the 'money motives' of corporate sponsorship, they were also aware of other technologies of consumption that intersected with sponsorship to help accomplish the profit-seeking intentions of the corporation: the corporation's desire and need to be seen to be caring – to "care about us" and make children fit, healthy, and strong; to teach children about food and to pester parents to buy their food; to foster a positive brand image "in children's heads"; to make children healthier, so they would live longer and "buy more of their products" (see also Powell, 2016). These were elements that were assembled by the overall aim to shape children's (and even their parents') thoughts and actions, their health, lives, and consumption, in ways that strongly aligned with the corporation's business interests.

Free food, free gifts, and free education

An additional technology of consumption that was interconnected with technologies of sponsorship and philanthropy was that of *free gifts*. During a number of lessons and edutainment events, students received free, often

143

branded, gifts that were provided by the corporate sponsors. *Life Education*, for instance, provided a number of sponsors' products free to children. Room Four students at Reynard Intermediate School recalled competing in a *Life Education* quiz and winning a whole-class supply of Just Juice. As described previously, the Year One and Two students at Dudley School received a free Macleans-branded gift bag. Curiously, when I asked *Life Education* teacher Marion about the Macleans gift bag, she claimed that she was "not promoting the bag and what's in the bag itself" but was focused on teaching the children about advertiser's 'tricks':

> I'm doing a unit [on] making choices at the moment, using adver-
> tising. So we get to create an ad so that we can look at the tricks
> and trades of advertising and what they do. And we have Macleans
> toothpaste and we have the other products, so it's a good opportu-
> nity to get the sponsor's product in without actually having to go out
> of my way to promote it.

There are clear contradictions here between Marion's claim that she did not promote the products or the gift bag, but was "definitely happy to promote" Macleans toothpaste and other products as "it pays the bills". In the end, hand-ing out the free gifts was more important to Marion and *Life Education* than the alternative − not receiving funding from Frucor or GlaxoSmithKline. There was also a clear tension between Marion's assertion that she taught the students about the 'tricks and trades of advertising', but did not explicitly point out the use of free gifts (or sponsorship) as 'tricks' that Marion and the marketers of Just Juice and Macleans were employing on the students. For Marion, giving free branded gifts to children was rationalised as "part of the promotion − that's what pays us. And I'm happy to do it if we can work it in and it's not too much of a stretch".

Nestlé also provided free gifts via MILO sponsored and branded cricket coaches who instructed Dudley School students for one session:

ETON: We had some MILO cricket coaches come in … we played a non-stop
    cricket game and they taught us skills and how to catch the ball and how
    to hit the ball, and if you did really well they gave you Raro[2] − no, not
    Raro − MILO sachets.
DARREN: Ok. So that was a reward?
ETON: Yeah.
DARREN: Did they have any other MILO logos or−
JAMES: I think on their T-shirt.
ETON: Yeah, on their jacket they had a MILO symbol, and yeah, the jacket
    was green and had white stripes.

The use of free gifts was a strategy to achieve Nestlé's ambition of increas-ing MILO's brand recognition and improving its brand image. The results were somewhat mixed. Eton recognised the MILO logo, colours, and slogan ("they say that MILO is the 'official drink of play'") and was aware that MILO was re-invented in ways that encouraged consumers to see it as more than just a hot chocolate drink, but "an energy drink". Eton and his classmates, however, were unsure as to whether MILO and its key ingredients were healthy or unhealthy (except for the water).

Children from all three schools frequently challenged the assumption that the gifting and incentive strategies would encourage children or families to make healthier choices. For example, a number of students at Reynard Intermediate School and Dudley School had participated in the *Yummy Apples School Sticker Promo* run by The Yummy Fruit Company (a paid member of United Fresh). This incentive scheme encouraged children and their parents to buy branded Yummy Apple products, collect the stickers attached to apple bags and individual apples, and return the stickers to school in order to help the school gain its "share of the $200,000 free DG Sport sports gear prize pool" (The Yummy Fruit Company, n.d.). During one conversation at Reynard Intermediate School I asked a group of Year Seven students what they thought about the following claim made by Yummy Apples brand ambassador and celebrity footballer Wynton Rufer: "*I couldn't think of a better way to be encouraging our kids to be actively healthier Kiwis. Eating Yummy apples and getting free sports gear in return is an awesome campaign to be proactively supporting*" (The Yummy Fruit Company, n.d., italics in original). The children instantly burst into laughter, then listed a number of ideas they had to improve children's health and lifestyles, such as making fruit cheaper.

This gift of sports equipment is not entirely free. Like most incentive schemes, families have to spend money for schools to receive their 'prize': "The more [stickers] you collect, the more sports gear you get so get going and start collecting" (The Yummy Fruit Company, n.d., para. 1). In other words, a school can only receive the "free DG Sport sports gear" when the parents of students make the 'right' choice of consumption – choosing Yummy-branded apples. The *Yummy Apples School Sticker Promo* attempted to increase consumption of its branded fruit by connecting two ideas: that the company – its marketing scheme, partners, products, *and consumers* – were philanthropic; and that buying these apples would improve children's health.

The children were not convinced that the *Yummy Apples School Sticker Promo* would improve apple consumption. Eton said that although his mother did not buy Yummy Apples, he was "sure some other parents would say 'I don't mind paying thirty cents for these types of apples'". Brian also said that his mother did not want to pay more for this particular brand of apple, so he collected stickers by stealing them off the apples when he was at the supermarket! When I asked Eton and Brian what free sports equipment their school received for participating in this scheme, Brian replied: "I'm pretty sure one year we won and the girl [from the Yummy Apple Company] came up with the big-as hula-hoop bag and every class got one". To these students and their families, the benefits of buying the branded

apples was outweighed by the monetary cost of purchasing what they perceived to be more expensive apples than other brands. Instead, students
found other ways to subvert the promotion (albeit illegally), and still help
their school receive free sports equipment.

The 'charitable' giving by external organisations was translated into a
charitable act made *by the teacher and/or principal* – for the good of their students. For instance, I talked with some Year Six St Saviour's boys about
the *Iron Brion BBQ Roadshow* (when Iron Brion and Beef + Lamb New
Zealand employees cooked and gave out 'healthy' hamburgers at the end
of Iron Brion's edutainment event). The boys believed that their principal,
Mrs Sergeant, who had paid up to $15 per student for Iron Brion's perfor-
mance and the free hamburgers. Students like Hone positioned the private
sector givers as organisations who "care about us", but also saw teachers and
principals in similar philanthropic ways. Students were shaped as both subjects of consumption and objects for charity.

The roles of teachers and principals were also re-configured by the acts
of giving and gifting. The teachers frequently discussed with me their role
as not just about providing educational opportunities, but an array of social,
health promoting, and/or entertaining experiences for their students. This
was especially evident at St Saviour's School, where students and their families lived in a low socio-economic area. I was told on a number of occasions
at St Saviour's that the students lived in poverty, were often hungry, and as
Ms Ellie said, "have nothing". As discussed earlier, Ms Ellie was aware that
the *Iron Brion BBQ Roadshow* was "just a marketing thing", far more "promotional" than educative. Yet it was the marketing aspect of this gift – the
provision of free hamburgers – that convinced Ms Ellie and her students of
its worthiness for consumption. Like Mrs Sergeant and her acceptance of
programmes funded by pokie trusts, Ms Ellie did not want to 'stand in the
way' of her students getting something for free, whether it was free entertainment, free education, or free food. As Ms Ellie explained to me: "Let's
face it, our children are, you know, hungry. And when Iron Brion arrived,
everyone got a hot lunch". Teachers and principals endorsed and sanctioned
free gifts based on an understanding that their children *needed* these free
gifts. Teachers were re-imagined, by themselves and others, as more than
'just' teachers, but charitable givers themselves. Further, through the practice of anti-politics, the policies and politics that had contributed to the
children's hunger (e.g. expensive fruit), to teachers' inexpertise, or a lack of
sports equipment in schools (e.g. government funding), were excluded from
the possibilities for resistance.

A number of teachers further justified their use of the corporatised programmes by drawing on the idea that they had educational benefits for the
students. However, this idea was contradicted by the students who believed
that the act of receiving free gifts far outshone any educational purpose or rel-
evance. For example, when I asked DJ, Mark, Hone, Carlos, and Afu if they
would want Iron Brion to come back to St Saviour's School, all five students

responded with a resounding "Yes!". However, when I asked "Why?", they responded:

AFU: I want the free hamburgers!
DARREN: And would you want [Iron Brion] to do the same sort of talk in the hall?
MARK: Just the free burgers.
HONE: We already know what he's going to say.

Rather than students simply being exploited by the private sector and their technologies of consumption, in some cases there was an element of children being willing to 'exploit' the free gifts and corporate philanthropy for their own gain.

Often the educational purpose for the gifting was unclear. Year Seven students at Dudley School excitedly recalled an occasion when Ronald McDonald and "his assistants" (Brian), wearing red McDonald's branded t-shirts, gave out McDonald's hats, rugby balls, and hacky sacks and taught them a dance. However, the students could not agree on *why* he was there. While most of students thought it was part of the *My Greatest Feat* pedometer programme, some thought it was promoting another health education programme: McDonald's *Road Safety in Schools*. Again, rather than being easily fooled into believing these gifts came with 'no strings attached' and no ulterior motives, a number of students were aware of corporate attempts to govern their thoughts towards consumptive ends. When I asked Helen, Nicole, and Laura at Dudley School why Ronald McDonald gave them free hats and balls at school, Laura replied: "To make you hungry – to make you think of McDonald's".

Although I am unable to say whether or not these free gifts successfully shaped these students' conduct and made them hungry or "think of McDonald's", they did not appear to discourage students from consuming McDonald's products. All three girls (even Helen, who had delivered the speech about the dangers of McDonald's) said they regularly went to McDonald's and enjoyed consuming Big Macs, fries, and Coca-Cola. It was a similar story for the Year Six boys at Dudley School who repeated Beef + Lamb New Zealand's marketing message that Iron Brion's hamburgers had "less fat", "better quality beef" and were "healthier" (DJ) than McDonald's, yet still thought that "McDonald's tastes better" (Afu). When I asked Carlos "which [hamburger] would you rather have?", he grinned and swiftly replied: "I'd have McDonald's".

'Critical' corporate resources?

The various healthy lifestyles education resources provided 'free of charge' to schools are widely promoted as empowering children to live healthy lifestyles for life through teaching them how to be responsible and make informed choices. Some are also marketed as being a form of critical education, one that draws on the socio-critical aims of *The New Zealand curriculum* by critiquing broader influences on children's choices, such as food and drink advertising. For instance, the stated aim of the *5+ A Day* resource 'Bright ideas: Marketing and advertising fresh fruit and vegetables' (5+ A Day Charitable Trust, 2011, p. 4) is to promote "awareness, critical thinking and action" about food marketing by providing "opportunities for children to critically analyse advertisements". There are aspects of this resource that appear to encourage 'critical thinking and action' about advertising and how it may influence health. For example, the resource directs teachers to ask students to "examine how food advertisements affect our attitudes toward and choices of different foods" (p. 2), and suggests a number of activities for students to learn how advertisers used logos, mascots, and cartoon characters to increase consumption.

Similarly, *Life Education's 'Warrant of Fitness'* unit states that the purpose is to teach students to be critical of advertising. In the *'Warrant of Fitness'* workbook (Life Education Trust, n.d.-a, p. 13) there is an 'Advertising is everywhere' activity which endeavours to teach children the differences between two food pyramids: one that represents "diet as recommended by doctors and dieticians" (a 'healthy' food pyramid); and the other which demonstrates "diet as shown by amount of advertising". Students are instructed as follows:

> Think about the types of food we see advertised, are they the sorts of food that would make up a recommended diet? Not really but advertising must work, after all the companies wouldn't pay the big money that they do if it wasn't going to help to sell more of their product now would they? And where do we see this advertising ... not only TV [but also] sponsorship ... So we need to think carefully about what we are seeing and believing. (Life Education Trust, n.d.-a, p. 13).

On the surface, these 'charitable' resources give the impression they are teaching a critical form of healthy lifestyles education. However, they also employ pedagogies of silence to ensure children, teachers, and the external providers remain *uncritical* of marketing messages and tactics that might benefit the business interests of the corporations. The resources and various teachers/educators/coaches/mascots did not attempt to inform students how to negotiate marketing strategies of corporations that are not meant to be seen as advertising, such as free gifts, product placement, or the 'obesity solutions' themselves. For instance, *Life Education* teacher Marion explained to me that the point of the 'You are what you eat' lesson was to "look at how people get tricked into buying junk food, what the advertisers want us to see, want us to buy, why they want, and that it's just money". Marion, however, never asked the students why Frucor, a Japanese-owned company that marketed and sold a range of 'unhealthy' products to young people outside of school, was wanting to teach New Zealand children about healthy choices.

Neither did Marion, the resource writers, or nutrition advisor (Frucor nutritionist Jenny Yee) for *Life Education* encourage students to discuss how Frucor profits from sponsoring the programme, or critique how placing Just Juice and H2Go products in students' workbooks and newsletters was a form of corporate 'trickery'.

The notion of a form of 'critical' education that specifically challenged advertising was added to the healthy lifestyles education programmes as a way to resolve tensions between the need for organisations to market products to children and the need for school to teach children about health. For instance, the 5+ A Day Charitable Trust claims that its resource will teach children how to be critical of the influence of marketing on their "attitudes toward and choices of different foods" (5+ A Day Charitable Trust, 2011, p. 2). At the same time, however, the *5+ A Day* programme employs a number of pedagogical strategies "to help children develop health enhancing attitudes to fruit/vegetables" (p. 3), "to promote fresh fruit and vegetables to their friends and families" (p. 4), and "help make 5+ A Day a way of life for children and their families" (p. 4). In other words, this form of critical education is strongly shaped by the commitment of 5+ A Day Charitable Trust to increase the consumption of fruit and vegetables, not only for children and their families, but for its 'not-for-profit' benefactor United Fresh, and its numerous fee-paying, for-profit members. The *5+ A Day* resources do not ask students to challenge the idea that consuming five or more fruit and vegetables will inevitably make them healthier, or how the 5+ A Day message is not just a health message, but a marketing campaign. Corporatised healthy lifestyles education programmes act as a vehicle to mobilise technologies of consumption that aim to achieve the dual governmental ambitions of the private sector: to shape the uncritical child–consumer, and to increase consumption. The possibilities to disrupt dominant discourses of health, consumption, and marketing remained silent.

Shaping the (un)critical, (un)healthy consumer

By using philanthropic strategies and charitable partners, what the private sector attempts to do is mobilise children 'at a distance' to consume. Corporations employ technologies of consumption to form connections between "very specific features of goods enmeshed in particular consumption practices" (especially in terms of health) and children's "needs, desires, pleasures and terrors" (Miller & Rose, 1997, p. 43). From my numerous conversations with children, it was evident that many children (from 5 to 13 years of age) had clear needs, desires, pleasures, and terrors that were aligned with neoliberal notions of health and fatness. Advertised features of corporate products (e.g. 'low calorie', 'sugar-free', 'gives you energy') are attached to these beliefs about health in ways that fulfil the child's 'desire' to make the right choices, their 'pleasure' in having a thin body, their 'terror' of being fat, and their 'need' to consume healthy, often branded, goods.

The re-invented 'healthy' corporation and their 'healthy' products are articulated as essential solutions to multiple 'problems', such as iron deficiency, a lack of fruit and vegetable consumption, energy levels, sports participation, 'junk food' advertising, unhealthy lifestyles, and obesity. This new brand of corporations, products, and practices are promoted and understood as providing simpler means for children to make healthier choices (e.g. to choose H2Go water over soft drinks); as a way to be active and have more fun (e.g. MILO as the 'official drink of play'); and, to avoid being unhealthy, fat, and disgusting (e.g. McDonald's selling fruit, vegetables, and Weight Watchers products).

It is not only 'healthy' corporate products that children are convinced to consume. These technologies of consumption are also employed in an effort to shape children and teachers to become uncritical consumers of corporate strategies and profit-seeking tactics: advertising, marketing, public relations, and corporate philanthropy. For instance, Mrs Donna dismissed the intent of sponsorship, believing that "they're not using it as advertising to the kids". Mr Woodward stated that profit was not the "prime purpose" of the programmes he allowed into his school and believed to be of value to his students, such as McDonald's *My Greatest Feat*, *Life Education*, and the *Yummy Apples Sticker Promotion*. Mr Spurlock admitted he had "not noticed" the Just Juice and H2Go marketing in the '*Warrant of Fitness*' workbook he asked his students to complete.

However, the success of these technologies to work 'at a distance' and not be seen as obvious, coercive, or ponderous forms of power were rather mixed. For example, when I asked Reynard Intermediate School Year Seven student Sam if he thought McDonald's cared about children's health: "I think McDonald's probably does care a bit … they have like Weightwatchers meals, so it shows they kind of care for health. But then again they mainly deal fast food". Similarly, there was both resistance and acceptance of the official corporate rhetoric that they wanted to make children healthier. I asked Dudley School students Helen, Laura, and Nicole if they thought McDonald's implemented physical activity programmes in schools to make children active, or healthier, or to teach them about health:

LAURA: No.
HELEN: If they're going to teach you about health.
NICOLE: Make your food healthy!
HELEN: But they have healthy food, like apples.

Bringing together the healthy corporate products with the healthy and caring brand image of the corporation acted as an additional technology of consumption, helping to smooth over any perceived contradictions between the aims of a corporation (e.g. to sell junk food, or to make profit) and the impact on children's health or education.

As I hope I have already made clear, I am not suggesting that children were naïve and easily coerced into becoming mindless consumers of corporate brands. Rarely were the students positioned by corporations as consumers who were "largely irrational or foolish, to be manipulated through methods not far removed from those of political propaganda" (Miller & Rose, 1997, p. 3). Like Kenway and Bullen (2001, p. 110), I also found that a number of children "are highly literate when it comes to explicit advertising and [are] well aware of its purpose". Indeed, a number of children actively contested, negotiated, and resisted dominant discourses of health and consumption, as well as more *explicit* forms of marketing (e.g. the placement of an H2Go bottle in the *Life Education* food pyramid) and strategic philanthropy (e.g. the free hamburgers from *Iron Brion*). The children's perception that corporate sponsorship and product placement was mostly about profit contrasted with the ideas expressed by a number of teachers, principals, and external providers. However, despite the students' cynicism towards the intent of some of the technologies of consumption, there was also an acceptance of sponsorship, product placement, and advertising as 'normal'. As Eton recognised, when a corporation sponsored an education programme they "deserved" to promote their brand to children in schools.

However, resistance to more *inconspicuous* and hidden forms of school-based commercialism was mostly absent, as was opposition to marketing and commercialism *in general*. Advertising was perceived, by adults and children alike, as a natural and unproblematic part of children's everyday lives. Indeed, there were a number of occasions when I was talking to Year Six or Seven students about advertising, McDonald's or a specific product, and the children burst into spontaneous song ('I'm lovin' it') or role-played scenes from their favourite (or most hated) television advertisements. Marketing was not just a normal part of everyday life that was merely accepted, but something that children found entertaining, even enjoyable.

Towards a critical approach to health in schools

To state the obvious, corporations and industry groups (as well as their charitable partners) are unlikely to encourage teachers or students to critically examine, or take collective action, against business strategies that attempt to influence children's choices, lifestyles, education, or lives. These corporatised healthy lifestyles education programmes certainly did not attempt to significantly 'empower' or 'inform' children how to take radical or critical action and challenge how corporations and their educational resources may *negatively* influence their own and others' health. Not one of the resources encouraged teachers or students to critique the role of the food industry in shaping rules, laws, and regulations around food production, labelling, marketing, pricing, and selling. Not a single external provider or mascot spoke out against the absence of regulations in New Zealand to restrict marketing in schools and in educational resources. No external providers asked children to question if the private sector should be allowed to advertise to children at all.[3] In this way, technologies of consumption were joined with multiple

151

rationalities (e.g. neoliberalism, welfarism), tactics, organisations, and people through the practice of anti-politics (Li, 2007a, 2007b). Any potential debate about problematic politics and policies relating to marketing to children and targeting children as consumers were shut down. The 'anti-politics machine' (Ferguson, 1994) ensured that the school-based solutions to the alleged problem of children's unhealthy lifestyles and fat bodies, fell within the skills and expertise of the very companies with the most to gain (and lose) from any changes to the *status quo* (Powell, 2018). In this case, it was the private sector who were re-invented as the experts on children's (un)healthy consumption.

Although the anti-politics machine attempts to restrict debate about how to govern, who to govern, and what to govern, looking at healthy lifestyles education as an anti-political device also opens up opportunities to 'unsettle' these corporatised programmes (Youdell, 2011). As Li (2007b, p. 10) reminds us, the employment of expertise to render problems anti-political and technical is an ongoing mission: "Questions that experts exclude, misrecognize, or attempt to contain do not go away". With this, I am encouraged to find ways to ensure these questions remain, and to look for ways to make these questions visible, audible, and teachable; to understand how teachers – as experts in their student's lives – may challenge this new corporate brand of health and education (Powell, 2018). This is an area of research that needs further exploration: how do we enable a counter-politics (see Youdell, 2011), or at least a counter-narrative, to the corporate 'part of the solution' to childhood obesity?

A critical approach to education is vital. In the three primary schools there were some glimpses of critique and resistance. Students, principals, teachers, and external providers were not corporate or political stooges, who uncritically reproduced dominant notions of health, fatness, and consumption. There were moments of contestation, such as five-year-old Leon shouting out that sugar was bad because "it makes you fat", Mrs Sergeant blaming inappropriate pedagogies of external providers on the fact they were not teachers, Ms Ellie identifying *Iron Brion* as promotional. Yet all too often these potential 'openings' to critique or resist programmes were closed off, most often by teachers, principals, charities, and corporations drawing on prevailing discourses of education, health, obesity, and/or philanthropy. The practice of corporations promoting healthy lifestyles education programmes in primary schools remained safe.

One of the most encouraging and rewarding aspects of this research was that children were perhaps the *most critical* out of all the participants I worked with. They regularly challenged the idea that corporate philanthropy was altruistic, that the free programmes and resources were more about advertising than education, or that people could not be fat *and* healthy. However, during my time in these schools, these critiques and debates only occurred in the discussions we had *outside* the classroom. Neither the classroom teachers, the external providers, nor the corporate-friendly educational resources encouraged the children to engage in any meaningful, in-depth critical analysis. Critical approaches to health education were sadly missing.

Ideally, a critical approach to healthy lifestyles education programmes – indeed, education in general – would require teachers to work alongside their students and support them to pose problems that are important to them in their culturally-located contexts, to research and critically examine key evidence that is relevant to their own and others' well-being, spark students' love for learning, and ultimately develop their passion to challenge social injustices by taking transformative social action (see Kinchloe, 2008). This, however, cannot be achieved through one-off lessons, pre-packaged resources, or a few 'critical' pedagogical strategies. Fitzpatrick (2014, p. 184) provides some guidance on a number of ways that teachers can use critical pedagogy to respond to these issues of health and social justice, and expand a form of critical health education:

1 Being focused on health issues (local and global) deemed important by students.
2 Viewing health education as a discipline of study, NOT as a means to make students healthy.
3 Rejecting health-based, rather than education-based, outcomes (such as fitness, Body Mass Index [BMI], eating habits, etc.).
4 Focusing on how health issues in the local community came to be diachronically (i.e. through poverty/wealth, resources/lack of resources/cultural patterns/hierarchies) rather than the all too often synchronous "snapshot".
5 Questioning how health issues intersect with gender, racism, social class, sexuality, and culture.
6 Questioning the inter/national status and social construction of health issues.
7 Viewing health as inherently political.

This is a difficult task. Teachers have to be able to skilfully and thoughtfully balance the need to develop students' knowledge and understanding of complex social, cultural, economic, historical, and political issues with the need for critical social change (Powell, 2018). Some researchers and teachers may argue (and certainly some have already made this point directly to me) that primary school children are 'too young' to understand the cultural-politics of health, or to take meaningful social action. However, the alternative – to continue to 'fill children's heads' with simple facts about how to make responsible healthy choices, live healthy lifestyles, and not be fat – is unpalatable. As bell hooks (2010, p. 185) reminds us: "When we make a commitment to become critical thinkers, we are already making a choice that places us in opposition to any system of education or culture that would have us be passive recipients of ways of knowing". To resist the corporate attempts to passively 'teach' children about health, morality, marketing, and capitalism, we must continue to challenge the damaging discursive practices that are created and maintained (at least in part) by healthy lifestyles education programmes in primary schools (for an excellent book detailing critical perspectives of health education, read Fitzpatrick & Tinning, 2014).

Critical scholars have also highlighted the possibilities of engaging with a critical pedagogy of commercialism and consumption (e.g. see, Boyles, 2005a; Giroux, 2001; Powell, 2018; Sandlin & McLaren, 2010a; Saltman & Gabbard, 2011), as opposed to schools ignoring, avoiding, or banning corporate resources and programmes. Saltman and Goodman (2011, p. 53), for example, recommend that as

> corporate curricula continue to turn schooling into a propaganda ground for their own destructive interests, one solution is clearly to stop using them. Another is to provide teachers with resources for researching the agendas of the corporations that finance and distribute such products in public schools and museums so that the ideological functions of the curricula can be turned against themselves, and the corporation's global agendas will be shown as contextualised and centred within the curricula. In this way, students can be shown how their interests and worldviews actually differ from the way their interests and worldviews are constructed in the curricula.

In other words, just as corporations or charities may exploit concerns about obesity or health or education for their own interests, teachers can also be supported to exploit the relationships between these organisations and their impact (intended or otherwise) on health and education "as object lessons for students' critical analysis" (Boyles, 2005b, pp. 218–219). By doing so, the school and classroom can become "places where students learn to renegotiate their relationships to corporate-sponsored ideologies and to formulate possibilities for oppositional strategies" (Saltman & Goodman, 2011, p. 53).

Sandlin and McLaren (2010b, p. 15) argue in the introduction to their edited book *Critical Pedagogies of Consumption: Living and Learning in the Shadow of the 'Shopocalypse'*, that there is a need to make "better connections between consumption, education, and learning ... explore the consumptive aspects of the everyday educational and learning sites that we teach in or learn in ... explore the educational and learning aspects of various sites of consumption" and "investigate sites of hegemony as well as sites of resistance and contestation". In this respect, there is an opportunity – and a dire need – for teachers, students, and researchers to critically examine the corporate providers (and various partners), the corporate materials, the political rationalities which underpin them, and the everyday practices they shape. As Sandlin and McLaren (2010b, p. 15) further assert: "We need to take consumption seriously within education, and that we need to move towards not only understanding how consumption operates as pedagogy, but also understanding what a resistant 'critical pedagogy of consumption' might look like".

As I have argued recently (Powell, 2018), techniques from *culture jamming* could be one avenue for students "to critique, subvert, and otherwise 'jam'

154

the workings of consumer culture" (Delaure & Fink, 2017a, p. 6), including specific healthy lifestyle education resources, pedagogies, and messages that target children in schools, and neoliberalism more broadly (for critical discussions about culture jamming, see Delaure & Fink, 2017b). This might include the practice of *pranking*: an exaggerated, visible, and mischievous act that produces some type of social change, and a way "to experiment, improvise and interpret pedagogies of consumption" (Powell, 2018, p. 384; see also Harold, 2017). It could also involve techniques of *detournement*, where corporate techniques (e.g. advertising) and messages (e.g. dominant Westernised, biomedical notions of health) are misappropriated, subverted, hijacked, and made strange. The five-year-olds in Mrs Constansa's class at Dudley School, for instance, could have invited Ronald McDonald back to their school, then asked him why his company advertises Happy Meals during children's television programmes every morning, even though they are not old enough to go to McDonald's by themselves (for a detailed description of how a school might go about this, see Powell, 2018).

Teachers in primary schools could encourage their students to question why McDonald's, Nestlé, Frucor, Life Education, or United Fresh promote individualistic understandings of nutrition and physical activity over and above other understandings children may have about health, fatness, eating, and moving. Reynard Intermediate students, for instance, could have written to Nestlé New Zealand and the New Zealand Nutrition Foundation and asked how "making the student responsible for their learning and actions" would solve the "issue related to money or access to food" (Nestlé New Zealand, 2011, p. 16). Teachers might support students to investigate Big Food – their practices (e.g. lobbying, marketing, philanthropy), products, profits, and criticisms; how they try to shape children's bodies, thoughts, and conduct (for an example of students challenging Big Food, see Darts & Tavin, 2010). Mr Spurlock and his Year Seven students could have asked *Life Education* teacher Marion why she said she would teach them about the 'tricks' of advertisers, yet did not point out the ways Frucor was trying to 'trick' students into buying H2Go and Just Juice.

Utilising critical pedagogy as a form of counter-politics can result in forms of resistance that do not solely target specific healthy lifestyles education resources and pedagogies, but look to broader elements that encompass "everyday struggles and resistances enacted by students, teachers or others in the practices of their everyday lives" (Youdell, 2011, p. 15). Critical teachers can work with students to develop a deep, rich, and nuanced understanding of how technologies of consumption, notions of individualism, the rationalities of welfarism and neoliberalism, and multiple 'other' organisations may intersect with and shape the 'everyday lives' and identities of children and adults in schools and outside of schools. For example, teachers could explore how healthism – an ideology that Crawford (1980) described as assuming a non-political agenda – works to privilege certain groups in society more than others, and why obesity rates, life expectancy, and ill health may be worse for those living in poverty and/or from Māori and Pasifika[4] communities. Natia and her classmates at St Saviour's might ask 5+ A Day and United Fresh to answer questions, such as 'Why are you telling us to eat 5+ A Day when we can't afford it?', 'Why are fruit and vegetables in New Zealand so expensive', 'How much do the growers and the supermarkets pay you to promote the 5+ A Day message', or even, 'Is eating 5+ servings a day really going to make me healthy?' Such critical approaches to health and education are vital as they "have the potential to speak back to, or at least unravel, discourses of healthism which ... cause damage to young people and their communities" (Fitzpatrick, 2014, p. 185). They also provide important opportunities for children "to engage in a critique of, and resistance to, the kinds of narrow forms of health education" (p. 185) that are promoted by corporations in schools.

Critical approaches to healthy lifestyles education programmes may also employ counter-politics as a "form of organized lobbying or co-ordinated resistance over particular policy initiatives" (Youdell, 2011, p. 15). In terms of the corporatisation of health and education this could take multiple forms, such as lobbying the World Health Organization to re-think its focus on multi-sector partnerships, or demanding the EU Pledge repeal its policy to allow marketing to children in schools for 'educational purposes'. St Saviour's students, for example, could have set up and promoted their own counter '5+ A Day challenge', where students and the wider community gathered five plus signatures a day to petition supermarkets, growers, and the government to make fresh produce more accessible and affordable for low-income families. Teachers, principals, academics, and unions could work together to lobby the government to re-instate professional development advisors in HPE, to re-distribute Kiwisport funds directly into HPE resources, to reduce the burden of the legacy of National Standards and an increasingly narrow curriculum, and to challenge the politics of the 'creeping privatisation' (Sockett, 1984) of HPE and other 'doesn't matter' areas of learning.

By urging teachers to enact a critical pedagogy of health, children and teachers could be encouraged and supported to recognise the complex interconnections between health, obesity, neoliberalism, and the private sector. Children would not be coaxed into repeating the usual messages about health, where the only route to good health is through taking more responsibility to make the 'correct' choices of consumption; choices based on notions of energy balance, the food pyramid(s), the 'you are what you eat' message, a fear and disgust of fatness, and obediently following the corporate attempts to 'make' children healthier. Rather, teachers and students would question *why* wealthy corporations are 'gifting' free education programmes (and corporate products) to schools and students, and ask *how* these hidden forms of marketing shape the lives of children, families, and the wider community (Powell, 2018). A critical examination of these healthy lifestyles education programmes would provide teachers and their students the chance to discuss, debate, and reflect on what health and healthy bodies mean to them, what shapes their understandings of health, and how they may re-invent health and health education in ways that is meaningful to them and their lives.

Notes

1 Interestingly, the current New Zealand Ministry of Health Food and Nutrition guidelines for children and young people advise the public to find resources on fruit and vegetables via the 5+ A Day website (see Ministry of Health, 2015).
2 Raro is brand of a powdered sugar drink made by Cerebos Foodservice, a division of food and beverage company Cerebos Greggs Limited.
3 In 2014, Brazil's Conanda (National Council for the Rights of Children and Adolescents) passed Conanda Resolution 163, which stipulated that "the practice of directing advertising and marketing communication to children with the intention of persuading them to consume any product or service" is illegal as it is considered "abusive" (Consumer International Group, 2014, para. 2).
4 Pasifika is a common term in Aotearoa/New Zealand for immigrants from Pacific Islands.

References

5 + A Day Charitable Trust. (2011). *Primary school teaching resource: Bright ideas – marketing and advertising fresh fruit and vegetables*. Retrieved from http://www.5aday.co.nz/media/18459/primary-resource-marketing-advertising.pdf

5 + A Day Charitable Trust. (2013). *About the 5+ A day charitable trust*. Retrieved from http://www.5aday.co.nz/5plus-a-day/about-5plus-a-day.aspx

Boyles, D. R. (2005a). *Schools or markets? Commercialism, privatization, and school-business partnerships*. Mahwah, NJ: Lawrence Erlbaum.

Boyles, D. R. (2005b). The exploiting business: School-business partnerships, commercialization, and students as critically transitive citizens. In D. R. Boyles (Ed.), *Schools or markets? Commercialism, privatization, and school-business partnerships* (pp. 217–240). Mahwah, NJ: Lawrence Erlbaum.

Community and Public Health Board. (n.d.). *How much sugar is in drinks?* Retrieved from http://www.cph.co.nz/Files/NUT0007d.pdf

Consumer International Group. (2014). *Advertising to children now illegal in Brazil*. Retrieved from http://www.consumersinternational.org/news-and-media/news/2014/04/advertising-to-children-now-technically-illegal-in-brazil

Crawford, R. (1980). Healthism and the medicalization of everyday life. *International Journal of Health Services, 10*, 365–388.

Darts, D., & Tavin, K. (2010). Global capitalism and strategic visual pedagogy. In J. A. Sandlin & P. McLaren (Eds.), *Critical pedagogies of consumption: Living and learning in the shadow of the 'shopocalypse'* (pp. 237–248). New York: Routledge.

Delaure, M. & Fink, M. (2017a). Introduction. In M. Delaure & M. Fink (Eds.), *Culture jamming: Activism and the art of cultural resistance* (pp. 1–35). New York: New York University.

Delaure, M. & Fink, M. (Eds.). (2017b). *Culture jamming: Activism and the art of cultural resistance*. New York: New York University.

Ferguson, J. (1994). *The anti-politics machine: 'Development,' depoliticization, and bureaucratic power in Lesotho*. Minneapolis: University of Minnesota Press.

Fitzpatrick, K. (2014). Critical approaches to health education. In K. Fitzpatrick, & R. Tinning (Eds.), *Health education: Critical perspectives* (pp. 173–189). Oxon, UK: Routledge.

Fitzpatrick, K. & Tinning, R. (Eds.). (2014). *Health education: Critical perspectives*. Oxon, UK: Routledge.

Giroux, H. A. (2001). *Stealing innocence: Corporate culture's war on children*. New York: Palgrave Macmillan.

Hall, S. (1981). Notes on deconstructing the popular. In R. Samuel (Ed.), *People's history and socialist theory* (pp. 227–239). London: Routledge & Kegan Paul.

Harold, C. (2007). *OurSpace: Resisting the corporate control of culture*. Minneapolis: University of Minneapolis Press.

hooks, b. (2010). *Teaching critical thinking: Practical wisdom*. New York: Routledge.

Kenway, J., & Bullen, E. (2001). *Consuming children: Education-entertainment-advertising*. Buckingham, UK: Open University Press.

Kinchloe, J. (2008). *Knowledge and critical pedagogy: An introduction*. New York: Springer.

Klein, N. (2002). *No logo: Taking aim at the brand bullies*. New York: Picador.

Li, T. M. (2007a). Practices of assemblage and community forest management. *Economy and Society, 36*, 263–293. doi: 10.1080/03085140701254308

Li, T. M. (2007b). *The will to improve: Governmentality, development, and the practice of politics*. Durham, NC: Duke University Press.

Life Education Trust. (n.d.-a). *Warrant of Fitness* – workbook.

Life Education Trust. (n.d.-b). *Harold's picnic* [pamphlet].

Miller, P., & Rose, N. (1997). Mobilizing the consumer: Assembling the subject of consumption. *Theory, Culture and Society, 14*(1), 1–36. doi: 10.1177/026327697014001001

Miller, P., & Rose, N. (2008). *Governing the present*. Cambridge, England: Polity.

Ministry of Health. (2015). *Food and nutrition guidelines for healthy children and young people (aged 2–18 years): A background paper*. Retrieved from https://www.health.govt.nz/publication/food-and-nutrition-guidelines-healthy-children-and-young-people-aged-2-18-years-background-paper

Nestlé. (2014). *Nestlé healthy kids global programme infographic*. Retrieved from http://www.nestle.com/nutrition-health-wellness/kids-best-start/children-family/healthy-kids-programme/nestle-healthy-kids-global-programme-infographic

Nestlé. (n.d.). *Food plate*. Retrieved from https://www.behealthybeactive.co.nz/food-plate/

Nestlé New Zealand. (2011). *Be healthy, Be active: Teachers' resource*. Wellington: Learning Media.

New Zealand Beef and Lamb Marketing Bureau. (n.d.). *Iron Brion's hunt for gold resource kit*. New Zealand Beef and Lamb Marketing Bureau.

Peck, J., & Tickell, A. (2002). Neoliberalizing space. *Antipode, 34*(3), 380–404.

Powell, D. (2016). Governing the (un)healthy child-consumer in the age of the childhood obesity crisis. *Sport, Education and Society, 23*(4), 297–310. doi:10.1080/13573322.2016.1192530

Powell, D. (2018). Culture jamming the 'corporate assault' on schools. *Global Studies of Childhood, 8*(4), 379–391. doi: 10.1177/2043610618814840

Rose, N. (1999). *Governing the soul: The shaping of the private self*. London, England: Free Association Books.

Saltman, K. J., & Gabbard, D. A. (Eds.). (2011a). *Education as enforcement: The militarization and corporatization of schools* (2nd edition). New York: Routledge.

Saltman, K. J., & Goodman, R. T. (2011b). Rivers of fire: BPAmaco's iMPACT on education. In K. J. Saltman & D. A. Gabbard (Eds.), *Education as enforcement: The militarization and corporatization of school* (pp. 36–56). New York: Routledge.

Sandlin, J. A. & McLaren, P. (Eds.). (2010a). *Critical pedagogies of consumption: Living and learning in the shadow of the 'shopocalypse'*. New York: Routledge.

Sandlin, J. A. & McLaren, P. (2010b). Introduction. In J. A. Sandlin & P. McLaren (Eds.), *Critical pedagogies of consumption: Living and learning in the shadow of the 'shopocalypse'* (pp. 1–20). New York: Routledge.

Sockett, T. (1984). The education agenda: a view to the future. *Irish Education Studies, 4*(2), 1–20. doi: 10.1080/0332331840040204

Spring, J. (2003). *Educating the consumer-citizen: A history of the marriage of schools, advertising, and media.* New York: Routledge.

The Yummy Fruit Company. (n.d.). *School sticker promo.* Retrieved from http://www.yummyfruit.co.nz/schoolstickerpromo

United Fresh New Zealand Incorporated. (2014). *Our mission: To provide valuable, relevant services to our members and represent them in good faith on pan-industry issues.* Retrieved from http://www.unitedfresh.co.nz/unitedfresh/assets/PDFs/United%20Fresh%20Profile%20June%202014.pdf

Youdell, D. (2011). *School trouble: Identity, power and politics in education.* New York: Routledge.

8

CONCLUSIONS

At a basic level, this book has been an attempt to tell two interrelated stories: how the global war on childhood obesity has encouraged corporations to be seen as 'part of the solution', and the ways in which corporate healthy lifestyles education programmes are experienced by children and adults in schools. Of course, this is not a simple story to tell. There are a large number of disparate organisations, people, discourses, and tactics that have been deployed as a panacea to children's allegedly unhealthy lifestyles and bodies. By disentangling various elements of healthy lifestyles education programmes – from discourses of health and obesity to technologies of consumption, from the political rationalities of neoliberalism to the actually implemented curricula and pedagogies, from strategies of philanthropy and charity to marketing tactics of product placement and free gifts – I have tried to interrogate how these elements have 'come together', as well as how they may act in tension with each other.

In the end, the point and purpose of this book has been to understand the rationales of those authorities with the will to solve the 'wicked' problem of childhood obesity, and how technologies – such as the healthy lifestyles education programmes – may (or may not) shape the conducts of organisations and individuals 'at a distance'. What I also hope to have achieved is to shed light on how the practice of corporations funding, devising, and implementing school-based 'solutions' to childhood obesity has enabled the interests of a heterogeneous array of players to forge alignments, for often self-serving ends, and how their attempts to guide individuals' conduct towards definite ends has unpredictable, even dangerous, consequences for schools, teachers, and children.

Shaping the (un)healthy child

Political rationalities (in particular, the rationalities of neoliberalism) underpin a variety of business strategies that produce (or at least attempt to produce) certain subjects as 'natural' and 'necessary'. Schools, corporations, intergovernmental organisations (e.g. World Health Organization), industry groups (e.g. International Food & Beverage Alliance [IFBA], United Fresh), governments, non-governmental organisations, charities, and other 'not-for-profits' were all brought together and re-invented through their mutual interest in so-called educational solutions to obesity. This convergence did not happen by accident, nor was it forced. Rather, by sharing interests, 'scratching backs', making compromises, managing contradictions, relieving tensions, and forming partnerships, diverse parties joined forces to make healthy lifestyles education programmes possible in schools. By re-shaping themselves (and each other), and by re-shaping the meaning of health, education, and philanthropy, organisations are able to realise their 'shared' ambitions and transform them into programmes in schools.

Corporations, particularly those from the food and drink industry, appear to have successfully re-invented themselves (or at least their reputations) as 'part of the solution' to childhood obesity by globalising philanthropic programmes that ultimately inform children to be more responsible for their health. Outsourceable healthy lifestyles education programmes act as strategies to promote consumption – healthy or otherwise – but also align public education and public health with the macroeconomic objectives of governments, corporations, and 'not-for-profits'. In this way, the desire of corporations and charities to fund, devise, and implement school-based obesity programmes should not simply be understood as a shift in business strategy but, as King (2006, p. 98) pointed out, "part of a struggle over how and by whom socioeconomic management on a transnational scale should be undertaken". This represents two noteworthy transformations in the governance of contemporary societies. First, the state's responsibility for the health, wealth, and education of the population is shifted to 'others'. Second, the 'non-coercive' strategies that the various authorities employed, such as industry groups making marketing commitments to the World Health Organization and corporations gifting free educational resources to schools, work as a form of "normative coercion" (Turner, 1997, p. xiv). Governments, corporations, charities, and schools come together to construct the 'problem' (e.g. obesity, inexpert teachers) and then provide solutions that fitted their own interests and expertise; solutions that also became normalised. Teachers consider it normal to outsource teaching. Students think it is common to be taught about health by corporate mascots. Charities and their employees believe that it is normal to accept sponsorship and nutritional advice from a soft drink manufacturer. And corporations believe it is natural to be involved in schooling children about health, fatness, and advertising. The fact that private financial interests are able to align with the divergent purposes of governments, public health organisations, charitable trusts, national sports organisations, schools, teachers, and children demonstrates what Ball (2012, p. 2) describes as the "triumph of 'the neoliberal imaginary'".

This is not to suggest, however, that it is solely the rationalities of neoliberalism that re-shapes the invention and implementation of healthy lifestyles education programmes. Not everything that happens in primary schools in the name of promoting healthy lifestyles or fighting childhood obesity are examples of 'pure' neoliberal rationalities. As Li (2007, p. 6) notes, any explicit programme of intervention, although shaped by a will to govern and a will to improve, is not necessarily "the product of a singular intention or will".

While there is a tendency for some commentators to suggest that neoliberalism is wholly responsible for technologies of privatisation, corporatisation, consumption, and commercialisation – the 'neoliberalism did it' argument – the political rationalities of *welfarism* are also clearly evident and influential. Rationalities of welfarism frame healthy lifestyles education programmes in ways that both *justify* the reason corporations, charities, and schools 'gift' healthy lifestyles education programmes to children, and *actualise* (Inda, 2005) the means to transform welfarism into reality (Miller & Rose, 2008). The provision of programmes – whether resources, external providers, sponsorship, or free gifts – features new modes of government that embody a moral form and are articulated by distinctive idioms, such as corporate social responsibility, charity, partnership, and philanthropy. These idioms are more than just the rhetoric of welfare, care, and kindness. They are "a kind of intellectual machinery or apparatus for rendering reality thinkable in such a way that it is amenable to political deliberations" (Rose & Miller, 1992, p. 179). Although neoliberalism may not be solely responsible, it certainly provides a fertile ground on which the philanthropic gift of education programmes can be planted, germinate, and flourish.

The rationalities of neoliberalism and welfarism underpin, and help to connect, a gamut of techniques and tactics: Nestlé's *Global Healthy Kids Programme*; Frucor's partnership with Life Education Trust; Ronald McDonald handing out free pedometers; the IFBA's promise to reduce (but not stop) marketing to children; and the promotion of products in schools for 'educational purposes'. These are all programmes articulated in relation to 'problems' of government – the social and public health consequences of childhood obesity, children's unhealthy lifestyles, and a lack of health and physical education (HPE). In this way, school-based solutions to childhood obesity do not rely solely on a welfare state, nor on a 'corporate-owned' public health imperative. It involves complex relationships between rationalities, technologies of government, and public, private, and voluntary sector organisations; relationships that connect 'at a distance' to the apparatus of the state.

Schools are certainly affected by this distinct form of corporatisation by being re-positioned as more than sites for critical education and the development of democracy (Giroux, 2001). New elements are fused to education (e.g. commercialism, philanthropy, anti–obesity interventions) and old elements re-worked (e.g. the aims and vision of education, the expert status of teachers) in ways that substantially re-articulate the roles of schools, staff, and students. The commercial interests of the private sector and their charitable partners mean that schools become legitimised sites for corporations and industry groups to promote their brands, brand images, products, new-found health statuses, and altruism. Schools re-imagine their role as allowing these profit-seeking organisations and their beneficiaries into their schools for the benefit of their students, and at the same time teachers, principals, and students become active agents of the private sector, proxy marketers, and active consumers of the philanthropic corporation and its 'healthy' products.

The field of HPE is also re-imagined by the convergence of educational resources and pedagogies with key tenets of neoliberalism. The socio-critical aims of *The New Zealand curriculum* are re-posed to represent neoliberal notions of freedom of choice, individual responsibility, autonomy, self-care, self-monitoring, and active consumerism. HPE is re-placed as a certain type of healthy lifestyles education, one that attempts to transfer the responsibility for children's health, fatness, and consumption away from corporations (and the state), and towards children and their families.

Furthermore, the normalisation and naturalisation of outsourcing HPE also work to further enable the neoliberal imaginary to succeed, shifting the responsibility of the state to provide teachers with HPE professional development opportunities, and the responsibility of teachers to teach their students HPE, towards external providers. These are providers that, in the majority of cases, were not qualified, registered, or experienced teachers, and as Petrie (2012) also points out, tend to rely on 'one-size-fits-all' prescriptive teaching approaches. Ideas about the purpose of HPE, what quality HPE looks like, or who the HPE expert should be, are re-imagined to align with the aims, interests, expertise, and ambitions of corporations, charities, pokie trusts, industry groups, and sporting organisations – and rarely the specific interests or needs of the students.

The private sector has, and continues to, benefit considerably from this broad re-invention. The corporations of the IFBA, for example, are re-shaped by grafting the element of education on to their desire (and necessity) to *be seen* to be implementing healthy solutions to childhood obesity and to their marketing practices. Corporations like Danone, Nestlé, and McDonald's have agreed "not to engage in food and beverage product marketing communications to students in primary schools", *except* when it is for "education purposes", charitable donations, fundraising activities, or public service announcements (IFBA, 2014, p. 8). As long as the gatekeepers of children's education are convinced that profit is *not* these programmes' "prime purpose" (Mr Woodward), or that "they're not using it as advertising to the kids" (Mrs Donna), then it is permissible, even encouraged, to reproduce this corporate 'brand' of health and education. The unhealthy, obesity-causing corporation that has been criticised as "greed-driven and uninterested in the wider public good" (Kenway & Bullen, 2001, p. 100) is now re-invented as an organisation that is socially responsible and healthy.

The dangers of healthy lifestyles education programmes

My point is not that everything is bad, but that everything is dangerous, which is not exactly the same as bad. If everything is dangerous, then we always have something to do. So my position leads not to apathy but to a hyper- and pessimistic activism. I think that the ethico–political choice we have to make every day is to determine which is the main danger. (Foucault, 1997, p. 256)

Foucault's notion of danger reminds us that attempts to govern others, such as healthy lifestyles education programmes, cannot be simplistically reduced into binaries of good and bad. Rather than searching for solutions to the problem of childhood obesity, or even the problem of corporate interventions in schools, the idea that there is no certainty that the 'war on obesity' is inherently right or wrong, has enabled me to critique the naturalisation of such programmes in schools; to point out "what kinds of assumptions, what kinds of familiar, unchallenged, unconsidered modes of thought the practices that we accept rest" (Foucault, 1988a, p, 155). One of the main aims of this book has been to challenge two dominant assumptions: that when it comes to childhood obesity 'it's better to do something than nothing'; and that these types of programmes in schools 'can do no harm'.

The ways in which schools, charities, corporations, and HPE are re-shaped by the global war on childhood obesity have a number of potentially dangerous implications for different organisations and people. When teachers re-imagine their role as outsourcers to expert providers, when they watch their students and claim to be 'learning from the sideline', they are inadvertently placing a strain on their relationships with students. The young people I spoke with expressed love, care, and admiration of their teachers, yet perceived their teachers' reluctance to teach HPE as evidence of laziness and their lack of the appropriate skills and knowledge (in comparison to the sports coaches and other external providers). In turn, teachers were positioned, by both others and themselves, as deficient.

As well as contributing to the construction of the classroom teachers as inadequate, the teachers, by their reliance on external organisations to provide educational experiences to their students, are directly implicated in the increasing privatisation of education in New Zealand. As Thrupp (2015, para. 12–13) observed of the New Zealand education context: "Some of the privatisation could be considered hidden but a lot of it is becoming pretty obvious. New Zealand's privatisation of education is through public apathy as well as by stealth". The teachers in the three schools in my study were often vociferous opponents of the more obvious privatisations of education – such as the introduction of charter schools or the outsourcing of the payroll system – but were less opposed to and apparently ignored the 'hidden privatisations' (see Ball, 2007), such as outsourcing HPE to corporations, charities, and other organisations. That is perhaps one of the greatest risks of outsourcing, it has become, or at least will become, the 'new normal' to be embraced, rather than resisted; a privatisation in and of education that is not merely considered a good way of teaching, but the *best* way. As my conversation with Mrs Donna revealed when I asked her about outsourcing:

MRS DONNA: I think it's perfect. I personally think it should happen more often.
DARREN: Do you mean in health and physical education, or do you mean across the board?
MRS DONNA: Across the board.

There are obvious dangers for children who are regularly and ubiquitously informed by the various resources and teachers/instructors/coaches/mascots that health and fatness was their responsibility. In the view of many students, this repeated mantra of personal responsibility to make healthy lifestyles choices was frustrating, boring, and did little to develop their knowledge, skills, or understanding about health in any meaningful way. This health-ist perspective rarely acknowledges the complex lives of children, especially young people like Natia who had little choice in what she ate or how she lived her 'lifestyle'. Instead, these healthy lifestyles education programmes attempted to shift the "responsibility for the politics of health to individuals' inherent 'ability' or capacity to act responsibly and change the ways they live their lives" (Evans, Rich, Davies, & Allwood, 2008, p. 54). Yet, despite some young people's resistance to *some* aspects of these programmes, the children in my research rarely challenged the notion that to be healthy they sim-ply needed to make better choices, continue to self-monitor their attitudes and behaviours, be more responsible, and be less fat. This is hardly surpris-ing given the body of evidence that these responsibilising, individualistic, healthist imperatives are circulated not only in schools, but also in families (Burrows, 2009; Fullager, 2009; Lupton, 2014), the media (De Pian, Evans, & Rich, 2014), and even supermarkets (Colls and Evans, 2008).

Clearly, one of the intended outcomes of a neoliberal approach is that the state and the private sector are absolved of any responsibility for children's ill health or fatness. At the same time, they endeavour to make themselves *appear* to be responsible for children's health and non-fatness. The programmes pro-vided to schools work to gloss over, if not completely obscure, the multiple constraints, forces, drivers, and understandings of health. In many respects, wider determinants of health, such as homelessness, marketing, cost of food, access to public transport, sub-par living wage, unemployment, and poverty, are re-imagined as merely excuses for unhealthy and/or obese children's own moral failure to make the 'correct' choices of consumption. In this way "the issue of choice can be seen as more of a facade as it is understood that a num-ber of oppressive social and structural forces mediate the choices in which one is able to make" (Ayo, 2012, p. 104). One of my hopes for this book is to problematise the 'façade' of informed choice as the foundation for teaching children about health and obesity. The concept of obesity is contested and

165

its 'causes' are complex, yet through the ideology of healthism, it is individual behaviour, emotions, attitudes, and bodies that are re-positioned "as the relevant symptoms needing attention" (Crawford, 1980, p. 368). The fat child, like Natia, is therefore understood by children and adults alike as an unhealthy child, one that is fundamentally immoral, fat, and "unhealthy on purpose" (Crawford, 1984, p. 71). The child who is ill or fat or poor (or all three) is then able to be blamed for their own individual, moral, and corporeal 'choices' (see also Crawford, 1977).

In contrast, a child who is dissatisfied with their health and/or body and desires to be more responsible is also, as Pylypa (1998, p. 27) notes, "good for capitalism as it leads to consumption". The corporate-influenced obesity programmes I have examined in this book, both those in New Zealand and the many others being rolled out internationally, deploy multiple technologies of consumption to not merely shape children to become healthy citizens, but healthy consumers. Numerous mechanisms are employed to achieve the business goals of corporations and charities: the insertion of 'healthy' corporate products into children's resources, workbooks, letters home, and lessons; sponsorship of programmes and resources; re-inventing children as marketers of the sponsors' products; children and schools receiving free products; and, re-imagining a corporate-friendly form of 'critical' health education. Healthy lifestyles education programmes are, therefore, an essential strategy to shape the child–consumer.

Corporations like Nestlé, McDonald's, and Frucor would arguably find it more difficult (although still not impossible) to mobilise their commercialistic strategies if it were not for the promise to schools for education, entertainment, and health promotion. Rather than being a form of education that encourages students or teachers to challenge the *status quo*, take critical action, or to empower students to resist the corporate version of health and health education, this type of healthy lifestyles education is employed as a means to shape children as uncritical consumers of corporations (their brand, image, public relations, products, philanthropy) *and* uncritical consumers of a new 'brand' of education – schooling for 'healthy' consumption.

Future directions: research, teaching, and advocacy

For researchers there is clearly more work to do. Further research needs to be conducted with teachers and principals to help connect the dots between the 'humble and mundane' use of outsourced, corporatised lessons, resources, and providers with the broader social, cultural, political, and economic forces that continue to shape schools' propensity to revert to outsourcing, such as a lack of government-funded professional development, initial teacher education, or curriculum-informed resources. This could include finding effective ways to illuminate how the Global Education Reform Movement (GERM) (Sahlberg, 2006) and other reforms are not just enforced from the 'outside in' or 'top down', but are made possible from the 'inside out' or 'bottom up', and by pointing to the critical role teachers and principals play in (re)producing the ever-present practices of privatisation and corporatisation.

What also requires further investigation are the ways teachers and children – the targets of experts and authorities – are able to (re)create the conditions that enable challenges to expert diagnosis and dominant discourses, make deliberate attempts to de-stabilise the corporate attempts to shape children's thoughts and actions; challenges that authorities cannot contain, control, or close. As Foucault (1984, p. 94) reminds us, power is productive, able to be "exercised from innumerable points" and is not necessarily hierarchical, to be imposed on populations and individuals from above. There needs to be a closer examination of the instances when teachers and/or students refuse to believe the idea that fat is bad, disgusting, or unhealthy, or that health is a five-year-old child's responsibility. More critical, in-depth research needs to be undertaken to examine how teachers may use critical pedagogy to transform educational moments into political questions, new 'truths', critical action, and other forms of counter-politics (see Powell, 2018). Critical ethnographies, such as Fitzpatrick's (2013) ethnographic account of HPE teacher Dan and his students, are central to unearthing the politics, anti-politics, and counter-politics of schooling, as are studies that interrogate the connections between the global nature of the corporate war on childhood obesity and the impact on local contexts. How are similar programmes 'brought into' schools in Australia, Thailand, Lebanon, Russia, or Nigeria? How do teachers, principals, corporate spokespeople, politicians, and children in these contexts understand and experience these efforts to make them 'healthier'?

One aspect of my book that needs to be 'opened up' by future research is for evidence to be collected from a wider range of sources. For instance, when looking at the 'official' plans of corporations and charities I frequently used documents such as annual reports, promotional material, and websites. However, following on from the work of Williams and Lee (2014) and Macdonald, Enright, McCuaig, Rossi, and Sperka (2014), there is space to talk to the organisations and agents who devise and fund these programmes, rather than just those targeted by them. A CEO, for example, could be asked questions about the strategic nature of corporate philanthropy, partnership, and sponsorship. Corporate nutritionists could be asked about the uncertain evidence that 'fat is bad' or that teaching children to be more responsible *will* make children healthier. Advertising agencies might be quizzed about health-washing corporate products and the brand image. Computer programmers could be questioned about their briefs to create interactive 'health education' web games. Charity and corporate board members might be asked about the blurred boundaries between their profit and not-for-profit activities. Pokie trusts should be interrogated about the contradiction between providing funding for health programmes in schools while simultaneously promoting ill health in the same community. By asking critical, unsettling questions we may discover more about the elements that constitute the corporate war on obesity, as well as gaining greater insight into how the 'corporate assault' on obesity, schools, and children may be undermined.

Through developing a deeper understanding of how these programmes work in different contexts, there is an opportunity for many of us to become better advocates and activists, to loudly speak up and speak back to obesity-imbued policies and practices that are corrupted by the influence of private sector organisations, especially those whose self-interests actually oppose and attempt to subdue the 'business' of schools to develop democratic societies and critical citizens.

A healthy lifestyles mis-education

On the surface, the various healthy lifestyles education programmes appear to be 'part of the solution' to childhood obesity. However, it may be more fitting to define these programmes as a type of healthy lifestyles *mis-education*.[1] The healthy lifestyles education resources and pedagogies are mis-educative because they portray the path to good health as making 'good over bad' choices in life – as simple as the click of a mouse button to choose milk instead of a soft drink, or the swish of a pencil to navigate the 'maze' of food choices. They reproduce the dominant assumption that health is primarily one's individual responsibility to make the right choices and that all children have the same freedom to choose between good/bad, healthy/unhealthy, right/wrong foods. This mis-education represents a significant shift to 'teach' children, as young as five years of age, to monitor, judge, and take more control of their health; an attempt to ultimately make children responsible for their (un) healthy conduct and bodies. It is perspective dominated by healthism that mis-educates because it

> does not deny the possibility of other health-threatening factors beyond an individual's sphere of action, such as geographic location, environmental pollution, living and working space, poverty and stress, but by its sharp focus on free will and determination it nevertheless makes it less tenable to see such factors as pertinent.
> (Kirk & Colquhoun, 1989, p. 419)

In other words, healthy lifestyles education programmes are mis-educative because they deny the evidence that a number of children, like Natia, do not have the same freedom to 'choose' what to consume. They consistently downplay the ways that children's choices are constricted, constrained, and moulded by a number of factors that are outside children's (and their parents') control.

This process of 'responsibilisation' (Rous & Hunt, 2004) aligns closely with central principles of neoliberalism and demonstrates an attempt to shape the "ideal subject of neoliberalism" (King, 2006, p. 99): self-responsible, responsible to others, autonomous, competitive, entrepreneurial, consuming, active, and healthy. It also aligns with the neoliberal project to produce the "choosing subject" (Coveney, 2006, p. 141): a child (or future adult) who is educated to be more responsible to make the 'right' healthy choices of consumption. Of course, these choices are now regularly attached to specific 'healthy' products made and marketed by the corporate funders/sponsors/ partners, such as H2Go, Just Juice, MILO, and McDonald's sliced apples.

The corporatisation of healthy lifestyles education programmes also represents a brand of health that is underpinned by 'Western' views of health that privilege biomedical science, individualism, and the non-fat body. It is not the only perspective of health though. In the New Zealand context, for instance, a unidimensional focus on *tinana* (physical dimension) as a main indicator of healthy food and healthy bodies does not align well with Māori knowledge of health and well-being that may also encompass *wairua* (spiritual), *hinengaro* (mental and emotional), and *whānau* (close and wider family), as well as *te whenua* (the land, identity, and belonging), *te reo* (language), *te taiao* (the environment), and *whanaungatanga* (extended family and relationships) (see Cram, Smith, and Johnstone, 2003; Durie, 2004). In many other countries and contexts, there will also be a range of understandings of what health 'is', what health means, what a healthy body looks like, and how a healthy person might act. However, when corporations and their partners privilege one version of health and one type of body over all others, what is actually healthy for 'others' is ignored, silenced, or even subjugated (Powell, 2018). Given that Westernised views of health dominate public health imperatives and children's understanding of health, it is necessary to further examine, critique, and challenge the ways in which the corporate marketing of healthy lifestyles may work to 'Coca-Colonise' the health knowledges, practices, and identities of 'others'.

These for-profit organisations are misusing education as a vehicle to reproduce the idea that for children to be healthy they need to choose certain products from 'generous' and 'caring' corporations. It is these very organisations that claim to teach children about the tricks of advertisers, yet at the same time expose children to a range of stealthy marketing tactics. And it was the same authorities – Beef + Lamb New Zealand, Frucor, Nestlé, McDonald's, United Fresh, 5+ A Day – that exclude the politics of health and marketing from their lessons. Potential challenges to the structure of political-economic connections, such as the relationships between corporations, industry groups, charities, and government agencies are largely ignored. Important political questions about the place of advertising in schools and/or to children are re-posed as questions of technique and responsibility. Corporations and charities use marketing strategies to exploit health education resources, teaching children to 'ignore' and 'not believe' certain forms of marketing, while concurrently trying to convince children to consume their products and public relations strategies.

Overall, these healthy lifestyles education initiatives are mis-educative because they are biased towards the commercial interests of the private sector, and to some extent, the financial interests of their charitable partners. The organisations that continue to develop and implement these programmes in primary schools, in particular those with profit-seeking motives have a vested interest in shaping children into becoming and being a certain type of 'healthy' consumer. Healthy lifestyles education programmes have become not only an important 'part of the solution' to childhood obesity, but also a critical element of the overall strategy to realise the neoliberal imaginary: to ensure that the endeavours of corporations, charities, governments, and schools to govern children to healthy, self-responsible, and actively consuming ends are rendered thinkable, doable, and successful.

The blurred boundaries between corporations, charities, the state, and schools work to mis-educate teachers, principals, children, policymakers, and the public about the role of the private sector in schooling and in our everyday lives. The perceived educational, health, and philanthropic benefits of these programmes act as a type of 'masking agent' that conceals, or at least obscures, the business interests and practices of the corporation – to sell food and drink, profit, improve public relations, build brand loyalty, increase consumption, create a philanthropic image, shape regulatory controls, and divert attention from less agreeable (e.g. obesity-causing, junk-food marketing) practices. As Ball (2012, p. 89) argues:

> Financially and organisationally and morally [an organisation's] status and standing is often, at face value, unclear .... Where the social ends and the enterprise begins, and what not-for-profit means, is sometimes difficult to discern at organisational and individual levels.

More so, these solutions to childhood obesity are inherently political, and are frequently promoted to national governments, the World Health Organization, and other influential organisations as evidence that corporations (especially those of the food and drink industry) are being responsible, health promoting, and even educational. Most of all though, they act as 'proof' (albeit incredibly weak proof) that corporations and their advertisers do not require further regulatory controls and government intervention. For all intents and purposes, for the private sector it is 'business as usual'.

The externally provided programmes do little to teach children in any meaningful way about the means by which their "bodies and souls, thoughts, conduct, and way of being" (Foucault, 1988b, p. 18) are shaped by corporations, philanthropy, charity, and dominant discourses of health and fatness. They certainly do not encourage students to challenge the subversive ways "corporate and commercial interests play ... in shaping personal and social meaning and identity" (Kenway & Bullen, 2001, p. 32), such as what it means to a child to be healthy or non-fat, to drink Milo or eat McDonald's.

Corporate mis-education does more than convince children and their parents to buy their products: it works to shift the responsibility of the state for children's education onto corporations, and the responsibility for children's health onto children. At the same time, the 'unhealthy' corporation has been re-invented as 'part of the solution' to childhood obesity and officially endorsed by the state, charities, and schools as a legitimate organisation to shape the way children think, act, and live. Although corporations, governments, and schools continue to cling to the idea 'everyone is a winner' when the private sector agrees to fight obesity, researchers, teachers, parents, and children must continue to challenge the assumption that the corporatisation of healthy lifestyles education programmes – indeed, education in general – is normal, natural, necessary, or harmless. After all, the 'war on childhood obesity' is not an innocuous public health imperative. It is a battle that is causing significant collateral damage to schools, children, and childhood.

Note

1   The term 'mis-education' does not mean that there is (or that I believe there is) one particular 'right' way to be educated. What the concept of a healthy lifestyles mis-education refers to is how certain institutions in our society (e.g. corporations) have manipulated (by design and by accident) public education in a way that reproduces certain régimes of truth (e.g. health as a personal responsibility), while concurrently marginalising alternative discourses and silencing opposing voices (e.g. the idea that marketing negatively impacts children's well-being). Healthy lifestyles mis-education is, therefore, a form of neoliberal education that employs mis-direction, attempting to divert students' and teachers' attention from the profit-seeking motives of the private sector, and towards the re-invention of the new, 'caring', healthy corporation of the 21st century.

References

Ayo, N. (2012). Understanding health promotion in a neoliberal climate and the making of health conscious citizens. *Critical Public Health*, 22(1), 99–105. doi: 10.1080/09581596.2010.520692

Ball, S. J. (2007). *Education plc: Understanding private sector participation in public sector education*. New York: Routledge.

Ball, S. J. (2012). *Global Education Inc.: New policy networks and the neoliberal imaginary*. Oxon, UK: Routledge.

Burrows, L. (2009). Pedagogizing families through obesity discourse. In J. Wright & V. Harwood (Eds.), *Biopolitics and the obesity epidemic: Governing bodies* (pp. 127–140). New York: Routledge.

Colls, R., & Evans, B. (2008). Embodying responsibility: Children's health and supermarket initiatives. *Environment and Planning*, 40(3), 615–631.

Coveney, J. (2006). *Food, morals and meaning: The pleasure and anxiety of eating* (2nd edition). Abingdon, Oxon: Routledge.

Cram, F., Smith, L., & Johnstone, W. (2003). Mapping the themes of Maori talk about health. *New Zealand Medical Journal*, 116(1170), 1–7.

Crawford, R. (1977). You are dangerous to your health: The ideology and politics of victim blaming. *International Journal of Health Services*, 7(4), 663–668.

Crawford, R. (1980). Healthism and the medicalization of everyday life. *International Journal of Health Services*, 10, 365–388.

171

Crawford, R. (1984). A cultural account of "health": Control, release, and the social body. In J. McKinley (Ed.), *Issues in the political economy of health care* (pp. 66–103). London: Tavistock.

De Pian, L., Evans, J., & Rich, E. (2014). Mediating biopower: Health education, social class and subjectivity. In K. Fitzpatrick, & R. Tinning (Eds.), *Health education: Critical perspectives* (pp. 129–141). Oxon, UK: Routledge.

Durie, M. (2004). Understanding health and illness: Research at the interface between science and indigenous knowledge. *International Journal of Epidemiology, 33*(5), 1138–1143.

Evans, J., Rich, E., Davies, B., & Allwood, R. (2008). *Education, disordered eating and obesity discourse: Fat fabrications.* Oxon, UK: Routledge.

Fitzpatrick, K. J. (2013). *Critical pedagogy, physical education and urban schooling.* New York: Peter Lang.

Foucault, M. (1984). *The history of sexuality, volume 1: An introduction.* London, England: Penguin.

Foucault, M. (1988a). Practicing criticism. In L. Kriztman (Ed.), *Michel Foucault: Politics, philosophy, culture: Interviews and other writings 1977–1984* (pp. 152–158). London: Routledge.

Foucault, M. (1988b). Technologies of the self. In L. H. Martin, H. Gutman & P. H. Hutton (Eds.), *Technologies of the self: A seminar with Michel Foucault* (pp. 16–49). Amherst, MA: University of Massachusetts Press.

Foucault, M. (1997). On the genealogy of ethics: An overview of work in progress. In P. Rabinow (Ed.), *Michel Foucault: Ethics, subjectivity and truth: The essential works of Michel Foucault, Vol. 1* (p. 253–280). New York: The New Press.

Fullager, S. (2009). Governing healthy family lifestyles through discourses of risk and responsibility. In J. Wright & V. Harwood (Eds.), *Biopolitics and the obesity epidemic: Governing bodies* (pp. 108–126). New York: Routledge.

Giroux, H. A. (2001). *Stealing innocence: Corporate culture's war on children.* New York: Palgrave Macmillan.

Inda, J. X. (2005). Analytics of the modern: An introduction. In J. X. Inda (Ed.), *Anthropologies of modernity: Foucault, governmentality, and life politics* (pp. 1–19). Carlton, Victoria: Blackwell.

International Food & Beverage Alliance (IFBA). (2014). *Letter to WHO DG.* Retrieved from https://ifballiance.org/uploads/media/59de15d6039fb.pdf

Kenway, J., & Bullen, E. (2001). *Consuming children: Education-entertainment-advertising.* Buckingham, UK: Open University Press.

King, S. (2006). *Pink Ribbons, Inc.: Breast cancer and the politics of philanthropy.* Minneapolis, MN: University of Minnesota Press.

Kirk, D., & Colquhoun, D. (1989). Healthism and physical education. *British Journal of Sociology of Education, 10*(4), 417–434. doi: 10.1080/0142569890100403

Li, T. M. (2007). Governmentality. *Anthropologica, 49*(2), 275–281.

Lupton, D. (2014). The reproductive citizen: Motherhood and health education. In K. Fitzpatrick, & R. Tinning (Eds.), *Health education: Critical perspectives* (pp. 48–60). Oxon, UK: Routledge.

Macdonald, D., Enright, E., McCuaig, L., Rossi, T., & Sperka, L. (2014, December). *Fuelling global health issue networks.* Paper presented at the Australian Association for Research in Education conference, Brisbane, Australia.

Miller, P., & Rose, N. (2008). *Governing the present.* Cambridge, England: Polity.

Petrie, K. (2012). Enabling or limiting: The role of pre-packaged curriculum resources in shaping teacher learning. *Asia-Pacific Journal of Health, Sport and Physical Education, 3*(1), 15–32. doi: 10.1080/18377122.2012.666196

Powell, D. (2018). Culture jamming the 'corporate assault' on schools. *Global Studies of Childhood, 8*(4), 379–391. doi: 10.1177/2043610618814840

Pylypa, J. (1998). Power and bodily practice: Applying the work of Foucault to an anthropology of the body. *Arizona Anthropologist, 13*, 21–36.

Rose, N., & Miller, P. (1992). Political power beyond the state: Problematics of government. *British Journal of Sociology, 43*(2), 172–205.

Rous, T., & Hunt, A. (2004). Governing peanuts: The regulation of the social bodies of children and the risks of food allergies. *Social Science & Medicine, 58*(4), 825–836. doi: 10.1016/S0277-9536(03)00257-0

Sahlberg, P. (2006). Education reform for raising economic competitiveness. *Journal of Educational Change, 7*(4), 259–287.

Thrupp, M. (2015). Listen up and learn from critiques. *The New Zealand Herald.* Retrieved from http://www.nzherald.co.nz/

Turner, B. (1997). Foreword: From governmentality to risk, some reflections on Foucault's contribution to medical sociology. In A. R. Petersen & R. Bunton (Eds.), *Foucault, health and medicine* (pp. ixx–xxviii). London: Routledge.

Williams, B., & Lee, J. (2014, December). What is your health and fitness age? Part one. In B. Williams (Chair), Health and physical education. Brisbane, Australia: Symposium conducted at the Australian Association for Research in Education conference.

METHODOLOGICAL APPENDIX
A critical ethnography

On a particularly warm Wednesday afternoon in late October, I sat on the concrete netball courts outside St Saviour's School; an area that also doubled as a car park. The Year Six and Seven students from Ms Ellie's class had begun their *Small Sticks* hockey lesson with their coach Andrea and were being instructed on how they needed to hold their hockey sticks. Some students listened intently. Others were busy swinging their sticks as hard as they could, as though they were teeing off in a game of golf. I winced as Mary, one of the Year Six girls, narrowly missed being struck in the head by one of the boy's wayward swings. I looked back down to read over some of the *Small Sticks* resources and promotional material, when I noticed that the providers and funders of this programme – New Zealand Post and Hockey New Zealand – had made a somewhat curious claim. In an outline of what *Small Sticks* aimed to achieve, one of the benefits was that the programme included "the teacher being trained" (New Zealand Post, 2012, para. 4) in hockey coaching. I looked around and noticed that Ms Ellie was not being trained. In fact, Ms Ellie, was nowhere to be seen. I scribbled down in my research journal: "No evidence of [teacher being trained] occurring, especially when a reliever is being used to cover the teachers while [children] are at hockey – so [teachers] could be doing planning for next year" (Journal entry, 24th October, 2012). This event was not the only one like it. Over the course of my research, there were multiple occasions when what actually happened in schools contradicted the 'official' plans; when the rhetoric of the external provider did not appear to match children's or teachers' experiences; when claims made by a corporation about their genuine attempt to improve children's health acted in tension with their desire to profit (for further details, see Powell, 2015).

To help me understand these tensions and contradictions, I needed a research approach that allowed me critically examine two broad areas: the rhetoric, rationales, and proposed techniques of those who claimed to be 'part of the solution' to childhood obesity; and what actually happened when the authorities and their plans to govern met their intended targets. I used a critical ethnographic research approach to gather and analyse evidence within and across multiple school sites, as well as to compare and contrast the disparate ways in which healthy lifestyles education programmes were experienced, understood, and, in some instances, resisted by teachers and adults.

My approach to research and my collection of evidence in three schools shared a number of features with 'traditional ethnographies'. As qualitative research technique, ethnography is useful for eliciting people's perspectives in an attempt to understand their world, where the researcher participates by "watching what happens, listening to what is said, asking questions-in fact, collecting whatever data are available to throw light on the issues that are the focus of the research" (Spradley, 1979, p. 1). In this way, I was encouraged by the potential of ethnography to allow me to have close interactions with students, teachers, and others in their school lives (Walters, 2007). However, while searching for a particular ethnographic method to emulate, I realised there was not one particular path or system to trace. I therefore embraced a cluster of ethnographic methods – a combination of spending time in schools, conversing with participants, observing participants 'in action', and collecting documentary evidence – in order to research the various strategies, mentalities, technologies, practices, subjects, and their 'actual effects'. As a type of qualitative social research that privileges context and engagement with participants in their everyday relations (Falzon, 2009), critical ethnography provided an opportunity to understand how healthy lifestyles education programmes 'worked' in specific contexts.

Three primary schools in Auckland, New Zealand

Before I describe in more detail my critical ethnographic research approach, I need to introduce the three primary schools I spent time in from July 2012 to December 2012: St Saviour's School, Dudley School, and Reynard Intermediate School.

St Saviour's School

Located in suburban Auckland, St Saviour's is a co-educational Catholic school with approximately 140 students and is a 'full primary school'. A full primary school enrols students from New Entrants to Year Eight (5–13 years of age), whereas a 'standard' primary school only enrols children from New Entrants to Year Six (5–11 years of age). St Saviour's was categorised as a decile two school, and received total annual funding of NZD $770,000, equating to just over NZD $4800 per student.[1] Of the 140 students, 77% of the students identified as Pasifika, including Tongan (38%), Samoan (35%), Cook Island Māori (2%), Fijian (1%), and other Pacific (1%). Additional ethnic groups included Asian (6%), Māori (5%), Pākehā/New Zealand European (5%), Indian (2%), and 'other' (5%). The principal was Mrs Sergeant, a Pākehā woman. Of the six classroom teachers, five were woman. All of the full-time teaching and administrative staff were Pākehā, with the exception of one British teacher. As a Catholic school it is classed as an 'Integrated School', so although the school receives the same funding as state schools, the buildings and land are privately owned (by the Catholic church) and the school is able to charge compulsory 'attendance dues' to families.[2] St Saviour's School uses *The New Zealand curriculum* (Ministry of Education, 2007) alongside "religious instructions and observances, [exercising] the right to live and teach the values of Jesus Christ" (see www.chchceo.org.nz).

During the latter half of 2012 I spent time with two classes whose teachers agreed to participate in the research. Room E was a mixed Year Six/Seven class (aged 10–12) with 23 students (14 with permission) taught by Ms Ellie, a teacher of 20 years' experience. Room B was a mixed Year One/Two class (aged five to six) with 20 students (eight with permission), taught by Miss Black, a 'beginning teacher' (in her first year of teaching). As 'generalist' classroom teachers, both Miss Black and Ms Ellie were responsible for teaching all eight Essential Learning Areas of *The New Zealand curriculum*: English, mathematics, the arts, health and physical education, learning languages, science, social sciences, and technology. The research evidence I draw on in this study comes from the 21 full days I spent in both these classes (one day a week for two terms), as well as time spent before school, morning tea time, lunchtime, and after school (in the playground, school grounds, and staffroom) – approximately 150 hours in total. The specific programmes that had either previously been used or were implemented over the course of my time in the school were *Life Education, Iron Brion, Get Set Go, ActivePost Small Sticks Hockey, ASB Football in Schools, moveMprove, Fruit in Schools,* and *5+ A Day.*

Dudley School

Dudley Primary School is a state, co-educational, full primary school with just over 400 students. It is located in a small rural community approximately one hours' drive from Auckland CBD. The majority of students lived either in the local village or on a 'lifestyle' farm, and 63% of students identified as Pākehā/New Zealand European. The next largest ethnic group was Māori (20%), followed by 'Asian' (10%), Pasifika (3%), and 'other' (3%). It was a decile eight school and received slightly over NZD $1,800,000 of total funding per year, at just under NZD $4200 per student (an amount bemoaned by the principal, Mr Woodward, as inadequate in comparison with the funding given to low decile schools). As a state school, Dudley School implements *The New Zealand curriculum*. Three teachers and their classes took part in this research: Mrs Constansa, a teacher with 13 years teaching experience in New Zealand and overseas who taught Room 2 – a class of 24 Year One students (eight with permission); Mrs Donna, a teacher with "over twenty years" New Zealand teaching experience who taught Room 5 – a class of 16 Year Two students (six with permission); and, Mr Spurlock, the only male teacher in the school, who was responsible for teaching Room 17 – a combined Year Seven/Eight class with 29 students (18 with permission). All three teachers were responsible for teaching all eight Essential Learning Areas of *The New Zealand curriculum*. The data I draw on are from 16 full days (112 hours) I spent at Dudley School, with the majority of the mornings spent observing and conversing with Mrs Constansa and the students of Room 2. I spent a shorter amount of time with the six students from Room 5, while most afternoons were with Room 17. The specific programmes that had either previously been used or were implemented over the course of my time in the school were *Life Education, moveMprove, Yummy Apples Sticker Promotion, My Greatest Feat,* and *MILO cricket.*

Reynard Intermediate School

Reynard Intermediate School caters for Year Seven and Year Eight students only (11–13 years of age). In New Zealand, intermediate schools are classified as primary schools. I asked Reynard Intermediate School to participate in the research after another school withdrew from the study two days before research was to commence. This led to a long delay while I attempted to find another school suitable to participate and gain consent from principals, teachers, parents, and young people. By the time ethical consent had been received (13 of 29 students) I was only able to spend six days with the students and teachers to collect evidence. Furthermore, the school policy was for all students to be 'mixed' into different classes at the start of Year Eight, meaning I was unable to 'follow' the class again at the beginning of 2013. Hence, my time at Reynard Intermediate was brief, although my conversations with Miss Knight and the students provided useful evidence about the different healthy lifestyles education programmes they had experienced: *Life Education, Yummy Apples Sticker Promotion, My Greatest Feat, MILO cricket,* and *Be Healthy, Be Active.*

Reynard Intermediate School is situated in suburban Auckland. It is a decile nine school that received just below NZD $4000 per student, and just over NZD $3,100,000 total funding from the Ministry of Education per annum. The principal was Mrs Ross. There were over 780 students (including 22 international, fee-paying students) and 35 full-time classroom teachers and senior managers (20 women and 15 men). The largest number of students that identified as belonging to one ethnic group was Pākehā (44%). The next largest ethnic group was Chinese (20%), Korean (6%), British (5%), Indian (5%), African (3%), South East Asian (2%), Māori (2%), Filipino (2%), Sri Lankan (1%), 'other European' (5%), 'other Asian' (2%), and 'other' (3%). Reynard Intermediate School utilises *The New Zealand curriculum*. Three teachers agreed to participate in the research – all connected to the same Year Seven class – Room 14. They were Mrs Peterson, the classroom teacher; Miss Hendrix, a student teacher on exchange from the United States; and Miss Knight, a specialist 'sports teacher' with school-wide responsibilities for leading sports and the health and physical education learning area.

A critical ethnographic research approach

Katie Fitzpatrick's (2010, 2013) critical ethnography of Kikorangi High School (also in Auckland) provided a useful starting place for designing my own research approach. I was drawn towards her use of critical ethnographic methods to explore and critique health and physical education, an approach that Fitzpatrick (2010, p. 21) noted was somewhat rare compared with traditional ethnographic accounts of schools, and "almost unheard of" in the field of health and physical education research. Her research did not just focus on health and physical education practices in a New Zealand school, but enabled her "to provide a deep and nuanced account of [her] experiences with students ... in order to attend directly to the ongoing, complex and shifting workings of power in schools today". As a critical ethnographer, she attended to both the micro and macro relationships of power that framed and shaped culture, ethnicity, sexuality, gender, class, teaching, bodies, identities, and young people's lives within a school context. This approach aligned with Foucault's recognition of the importance of 'micro' level techniques of power: "the point where power reaches into the very grain of individuals" (Foucault, 1980, p. 39). Indeed, one of the main aims of my research was to interrogate the micro level practices that congealed with macro influences. Although a number of scholars had critically examined the phenomenon of corporatised resources and programmes in schools, few employed either a conventional or critical ethnographic approach.

I used a range of familiar ethnographic methods (e.g. observations, research conversations, documentary evidence) to provide thick accounts of "ethnographic moments" (Fitzpatrick, 2010, p. 32) across three sites, but hesitate to describe my research as a 'traditional' or 'conventional' ethnography for three reasons. First, traditional ethnographies generally take place in one setting. Although I was interested in the ways in which the various school-based 'solutions' to childhood obesity and unhealthy lifestyles were understood and experienced within a particular site and context, I was also aware of the criticism that traditional ethnographies attempted to 'silo' complex social phenomena within a single site (for discussions, see Falzon, 2009; Marcus, 1995). By choosing a *multi-site* ethnographic approach, it allowed me as an ethnographic researcher to examine and sometimes compare the types of relationships that were formed between the macro (e.g. government policy) and specific micro, localised sites, subjects, relationships, and situations. By employing a multi-sited ethnographic approach, I was also able to move spatially (between classrooms and schools), methodologically (between different forms of evidence collection), and conceptually (between different analytical and theoretical devices) (see also Falzon, 2009).

The quantity of time I was able to spend in each school was my second source of hesitation in defining my research as a traditional ethnography. A conventional ethnography is usually conducted for a long duration, where the ethnographer participates "in people's daily lives for an extended period of time" (Hammersley & Atkinson, 1995, p. 1). There are, however, no hard or fast rules on precisely how long an 'extended period of time' is. Jeffrey and Troman (2004), for instance, suggest 12 months is a suitable length, while Falzon (2009) argues that conventional ethnographies typically take place for several months or more. Although I conducted my research over a six-month period, I was not in each school every day. Instead, I utilised a "selective intermittent time mode" approach (Jeffrey & Troman, 2004, p. 540), where I was present at each of the three schools for at least one day a week, and arranged with the school to conduct research on additional days when there were specific, relevant events (such as staff meetings or school trips) or programmes (e.g. a *Life Education* lesson).

Finally, my methodological approach was distinct from conventional ethnographies through my endeavour for this to be a *critical* project. This has, in part, been influenced by my engagement with Foucault, the adaptable and malleable analytical tools developed by governmentality scholars, and a "certain ethos of investigation" (Rose, O'Malley, & Valverde, 2006, p. 101; see also Foucault, 1982). My understanding and use of the term 'critical ethnography' reflects this ethos and Foucault's notion of 'critique': "the right to question truth as truth operates through power and to question power as it operates through truth" (Madison, 2005, p. 6). Indeed, my interest in critically examining the role of corporations 'teaching' children about health and obesity began with a concern that corporate programmes represented the profit-seeking mentality of powerful corporations and may work to reproduce certain discourses and potentially 'dangerous' practices. The reason why a critical ethnographic approach was necessary to investigate this phenomenon was the desire to search for possibilities to confront and dispute the *status quo*: the place and power afforded to dominant institutions (e.g. multinational corporations and schools), regimes of truth, and the practices that attempt to shape choices, identities, and communities (Madison, 2005).

Research conversations

My research approach elicited the 'voices' of children and adults in order to gain an insight into the 'really-lived worlds' of each person I spoke with and listened to. I collected, analysed, and reflected on participants' voices through a number of methods, including conducting all formal research conversations (approximately 70 hours of recorded research conversations), informal research conversations (i.e. random, spontaneous, unplanned dialogue, sometimes recorded in my research journal), as well as observations of interactions between participants.

Even though interviewing is recognised as an effective research tool to understand the experience of others from their perspective (see Kvale, 1996; Patton, 2002), interviews also have limitations. One is the propensity for children and young people to feel that they are expected to have the 'right' answers to questions they have had little or no time to consider (see Eder &

Fingerson, 2002). Formal one-to-one interviews and focus group formats, although common research methods, can also impose "an interrogative, threatening, and uncomfortable atmosphere on participants" (Fitzpatrick, 2010, p. 84). This may have been the case for Sonny, a five-year-old Māori boy at St Saviour's who I included in three research conversations, yet never spoke a single word.

By acknowledging the problem of power and power imbalances between interviewer and interviewee, I used what Fitzpatrick (2010) labelled *research conversations* (see also Fine & Weis, 2003, for a discussion about 'extraordinary conversations'). According to Fitzpatrick (2010, p. 86), this is a practice that allowed students a freedom to express and explore issues of power and equity:

> I also felt that conversations held greater potential for building rela-
> tionships and reciprocal trust, and might allow a less formal and
> more natural environment for students to express their ideas ....
> Unlike interviews and focus groups, however, conversations are pro-
> duced through two or more people talking, not one asking questions
> and others answering.

Social hierarchies and power imbalances were not only present between the participants themselves, but also seemed to be present between me as a researcher and the participants. This was obvious in my initial research conversations, where students tended to wait for me to ask a question, provide me with a short answer (or look at each other to see who was 'brave enough' to give a response), and then wait for the next question. One way I tried to address this power imbalance (in addition to building trusting relationships and adapting the interview guides) was encouraging the participants to 'steer' the conversations towards experiences, understandings, and interests that they were more familiar with and knowledgeable about. Using this 'auto-drive' (Clark, 1999) technique, the research conversation was 'driven' by the participants. I felt that this technique allowed participants to guide the topic of conversation towards their own interests and knowledges, as well as set the pace, linguistic level, and tone of the conversation. Encouraging students to steer the conversation and explain their own 'really-lived worlds' enabled the children to be 'experts' and provided rich ethnographic moments (Clark-Ibáñez, 2008).

In addition to the group research conversations with children, I also conducted one-to-one research conversations with teachers, principals, and external providers. Some children were also selected for one-to-one research conversations when it became evident that they had specific, in-depth knowledge, ideas, opinions, and/or experiences that were relevant to my research. The aim of these one-to-one conversations was to develop a deeper understanding of participants and their understanding of the various healthy lifestyles education programmes they had implemented/resisted/experienced (as well as other related issues). It was also used as a technique that allowed participants to talk and share in a more private and personal setting. This latter point proved to be important when connecting participants' experiences and understanding of issues, programmes, resources, organisations, and people to their 'actually existing lives' outside of the school context. This was certainly the case in my one-to-one conversations with Natia (see Chapter 6).

There were also a number of research conversations that were 'informal' (i.e. not recorded by digital voice recorder) and unstructured (i.e. without a prepared interview guide or questions). For instance, I regularly ate lunch with the students and had discussions and debates about: what they had (or did not have) in their lunch box; which foods were healthy, 'junk', yummy, yucky, expensive, or cheap; or why boys didn't eat 'Dora the Explorer' yoghurt.[3] By encouraging children and adults to talk about various topics from their own frame of reference, this informal approach provided greater depth of evidence. This type of malleable (and perhaps less intimidating) approach to research conversations was a crucial aspect of my data collection and analysis, encouraging me to regularly reflect on and contextualise my everyday experiences of listening to the voices of students and adults in the playground, staff room, and classroom.

Throughout my research I was aware that the concept of voice is "slippery, shifting, knowable, unknowable, certain, uncertain, audible, inaudible, and certainly unstable" (Mazzei, 2009, p. 45). In this way, I did not try to present participants' voices to the reader as a simple articulation of the 'truth' or a reflection of the 'real' meaning of an experience (see Mazzei & Jackson, 2009). Voice, like an observation or piece of documentary evidence, must not be conflated with pure, clear, 'concrete' evidence; voices are socially constructed, fluid, discursively formed, and constantly negotiated. The participants I chose (or was able to choose) to listen to, the questions I asked (or did not ask), the lines of conversations I chose to explore or ignore, how I listened to and interpreted participant's voices, and the voices I accepted as 'true', all shaped the representation of voices in my research. Throughout my research and analysis, I reflected on how conversations could act to 'gag' certain voices and I became more critical of how I conducted my conversations. I attempted to elicit and listen to voices other than those that were easy to categorise and respond to, such as those voices that obviously related to my research questions or which agreed with my own view of the corporate 'part of the solution' to obesity. Mitchell's (2009, p. 78) advice for researchers to listen "to the voices of participants with 'soft ears' – or ears that are malleable and opened to subtle understandings and interpretations" helped me to seek those voices that escaped easy classification.

School time: observations and journals

At the beginning of my research I was mindful that trying to see, record, and capture 'everything' that occurred in each school was an ineffective, somewhat pointless, and wholly impossible exercise. With this in mind I chose to use 'selective observations' (see Murtagh, 2007) in which I focused on specific healthy lifestyles education programmes that were sponsored, funded, designed, and/or implemented with the financial assistance of the private sector. However, this approach proved to be challenging. The vast majority of, if not the entire school day, had little to do with the corporatised 'solutions' to obesity or unhealthy lifestyles. At times I felt frustrated that useful ethnographic moments would never occur, or that my time would be better spent in another class or another school where something 'relevant' might be happening. However, these 'dead spots' were valuable. They provided insights into how classroom teachers taught, and how students learned, in a range of subjects, often showcasing the teacher's pedagogical expertise. They illuminated the importance of the classroom teacher-student relationship, in particular the ways in which teachers used their knowledge of their students' wants, needs, and lives to teach and care for their students. And it gave me time and space to observe, talk to, form relationships with, and discover more about the students and teachers who were participating in my research.

Throughout my time in schools I used what some ethnographers refer to as journaling to take notes of my 'observations'. Instead of attempting to be a 'fly-on-the-wall' researcher, one that would be neutral and detached from my observations, I took on a number of active 'roles' during the day and took journal notes either during or afterwards. I engaged in numerous, spontaneous conversations in a variety of contexts, took students out of class for research conversations, and used journaling as a means to reflect on my thoughts, experiences, interactions, and emotions. The decision whether, or how, to participate in any one lesson or experience was rarely predetermined, but dependent on the context – the school, teacher, students, a specific lesson, or the general 'mood' of the class. Often my decision to participate, observe, or take journal notes was in response to spur-of-the-moment events; those unstructured and unplanned moments that were common in a busy classroom with up to 30 children.

I usually made entries in my journal immediately after or a short time after specific moments occurred, rather than recording them in 'real time' (i.e. as they happened). One reason for this was, at times, my notebook and pen seemed to form a barrier between the participants and myself. I recall one situation when I was sitting at a desk with three Year Seven girls at Dudley School, when they began to complain (in hushed tones) that their teacher never listened to them. As soon as I picked up my pen (to make a note about teacher-student relationships), all three girls stopped talking and looked at me – in fact, looked at my pen and journal – anticipating what I was about to write *about them*. Noticing their apprehension, I placed the pen on the desk and engaged in conversation about their relationship with their teacher. It was one of a number of situations in which *talking with* participants was far more rewarding (both in terms of research evidence and building relationships with participants) than *writing about* them. It was also an example of how participants may at times have felt as though they were being monitored, surveilled, judged, or even criticised, and perhaps more likely to change their words, thoughts, actions, and opinions to what they thought I wanted to see or hear or think.

My observations and journal entries were valuable as they encouraged me to reflect on the processes by which I gathered evidence. They allowed me to be more reflexive and self-aware as a researcher, to consider my relationship with participants and school contexts, and to connect me personally and affectively to my evidence, research questions, and analytics. While I did not attempt to use observations and journaling as a means to capture 'everything' in the staffroom, playground, or classroom, it allowed me to consider how different rationalities, authorities, and technologies of government 'fused' with actual subjects. These journal entries also helped me reflect on the ways in which healthy lifestyles education programmes were not just imagined, but enacted in actual spaces, sites, and points in time.

Documentary evidence

Gathering documentary evidence alongside other ethnographic methods (i.e. journaling, research conversations, and observations) proved to be especially rewarding. They assisted me in collecting rich evidence and helped me reflect on and analyse how these 'official' documents (themselves an assemblage of rationalities, technologies, and discourses) were 'actually' enacted, understood, and experienced by the children, teachers, principals, and external providers who used them.

The documents I collected were not neutral objects or artefacts that reflected 'reality', but were an expression of power relations and the social, political, cultural, and economic contexts that helped construct them. They provided evidence of the discursive nature of healthy lifestyles education programmes, particularly how the rationale of neoliberalism was "made thinkable" (Miller & Rose, 2008, p. 59) through language. For instance, I noticed and collected a number of documents that contained a range of idioms, rhetoric, and 'truths' that were underpinned and reproduced by the ideology of healthism, with terms like 'healthy body weight', 'informed choices', 'individual responsibility', and 'healthy lifestyles'.

In some instances, I collected documentary evidence on an *ad hoc* and opportunistic basis, such as students' work, a teacher's instruction written on the whiteboard, a copy of a school newsletter, and a *Life Education* 'information letter to parents' left lying in a rubbish bin. At other times I was more deliberate and purposeful in collecting documentary evidence. I conducted numerous internet searches, delving into documents produced by corporations and charities, such as annual reports, Education Review Office reports,[4] educational resources, media releases, news articles, blogs, and other websites created by schools, charities, foundations, media, and government departments. I looked at school policies, library books, children's PowerPoint presentations, school resources, student workbooks, and government documents.

Written documents also included my own journal entries and transcripts of research conversations, where I frequently reflected on the rhetoric of the corporations and their partners, particularly the instances when their claims (e.g. to fight obesity, to educate, to help children make informed choices, to not use scare tactics) appeared to contradict what I was seeing and hearing when these programmes were enacted and experienced.

For instance, in a section called 'Why the movement approach?', the writers of *moveMprove's Educator's guide* made a number of educational claims, such as that the coaches utilise "a learner-centred approach", "flexible delivery models", and would "adapt equipment to suit the activity … and to continually challenge children" (GymSports New Zealand, n.d., para. 4–5). Yet when I observed the *moveMprove* programme being taught by two different gymnastics clubs and four different coaches in two different contexts – St Saviour's School and Dudley School – I was struck by the inconsistencies between the 'official rhetoric' of GymSports New Zealand, the pedagogies and practices experienced by the children, and the perceptions of teachers and principals. For example, despite the claims of flexible, adaptable, challenging activities, a number of the students thought the activities were too easy (such as six-year-old Anita at Dudley School who said they were "all easy"), and some students appeared to be bored, often ending up doing their own activities. Yet when I asked Antia's teacher, Mrs Donna, what she thought about the *moveMprove* session, she described it as not only "great", but thought "it was better for the children" to be taught by externally provided coaches, rather than their classroom teacher. This was just one of a number of instances where I observed tensions and contradictions as they happened, as well as how these tensions and contradictions were later resolved and managed.

Analysing and 'writing up' research

I approached the analysis and writing up of my empirical materials by trying to do two things: disentangling individual elements of healthy lifestyle education programmes; and searching for discursive connections, tensions, and contradictions. Before I set foot in the primary schools I had already sourced and read a variety of documentary evidence and had begun to note some key components of healthy lifestyles education, such as discourses of individualism and technologies of consumption. This process of collecting and analysing evidence continued as I spent time in the primary schools and conducted multiple research conversations with children and adults, observed lessons and other moments in the school day, wrote in my journal, and accessed more documentary evidence. I repeatedly gained new evidence to analyse and reflect on. This was not only useful in terms of the quantity of data I was able to analyse, but provided me with constant opportunities to critically reflect on my evidence, often pointing to new sources of information (including participants, resources, and programmes), new lines of questioning, and unseen elements that constituted the global corporate 'war on obesity'.

Once I was in the schools and had conducted initial research conversations, I began my process of analysis by repeatedly listening to my research conversations, transcribing the conversations, then 'free-associating' (Alldred & Burman, 2005) with the text and searching for a variety of discourses, perspectives, topics, and relationships. I expected certain themes to appear, such as dominant discourses of obesity, however, a number of unexpected themes developed, such as children's resistance to corporate messages about health.

It was obvious from early on in my analysis that the phenomenon of healthy lifestyles education programmes and their connections to corporations was complex, multi-faceted, and messy. Despite the messiness, my somewhat *ad hoc* approach to analysis helped me to analyse some of the commonalities and differences between the rationales, understandings, and experiences expressed by the participants. Through this process I was also able to consider the 'silences' (Powers, 1996), those discourses that were not defined, described, or discussed by participants. For instance, there were multiple occasions when I felt that teachers and external providers could (or should) have talked to children about notions of obesity or fatness, but remained silent. Although healthy lifestyles education programmes were promoted by corporations and understood by the adults in schools as 'part of the solution' to childhood obesity, there was an apparent unwillingness to explicitly talk to children about obesity or fatness. The discourses of obesity that underpinned teaching and learning in the three schools were just as much about the 'unsaid' as the 'said'.

In the end, this research was an attempt to tell a relatively straightforward story: how corporate-friendly healthy lifestyles education programmes represented the official *plans* to govern, as well as what *happened* when these plans met their intended targets. However, as Hartmann (2016, p. 215) explains, the *art* of "grasping and conveying the proper iterative dialogue between case and context, between particularities and generalities, one of the greatest methodological changes" in research such as this. Given the disparate nature of global and local contexts, the complex array of rationalities, technologies, institutions, discourses, agents, knowledges, truths, relations of power, and 'humble and mundane' practices in schools, and the idiosyncrasies of each and every school, teacher, and child that I conducted my research with, the story was not a simple one to articulate. The corporate war on childhood obesity is convoluted, ever-shifting, and multi-faceted. It cannot be reduced to a single story, single context, or single villain. My hope for this critical research project, something only the reader can judge, was to provide a challenge to the *status quo*: to contest the idea that corporate solutions to childhood obesity are uncomplicated, unproblematic, and harmless.

Notes

1 Total funding = Operational funding + teacher salaries. I have not given the exact amount of total funding as this would identify the school.
2 State schools in New Zealand are not allowed to charge any compulsory fees, and can only request for voluntary donations.

3   During one lunchtime at Dudley School I was told by the five-year-old children in Mrs Constansa's class that only girls ate 'Dora the Explorer' yoghurt and only boys ate 'Diego' (Dora's cousin) yoghurt. I tested this 'norm' by bringing 'Dora' yoghurt to school and eating it in front of the children. Some of the boys looked at me oddly, some with wry smiles, whereas the girls laughed hysterically. Two girls even tried to physically stop me from eating 'girl' yoghurt. I had never before considered that children's food could be so gendered.

4   The Education Review Office (ERO) is a government department which reviews, evaluates, and reports on the education of children in schools and early childhood services across New Zealand (see www.ero.govt.nz).

References

Alldred, P., & Burman, E. (2005). Analysing children's accounts using discourse analysis. In S. Greene & D. Hogan (Eds.), *Researching children's experiences: Approaches and methods* (pp. 175–198). London: Sage.

Clark, C. D. (1999). The autodriven interview: A photographic viewfinder into children's experience. *Visual Studies, 14*(1), 39–50. doi: 10.1080/14725869908583801

Clark-Ibáñez, M. (2008). Gender and being 'bad': Inner-city students' photographs. In P. Thomson (Ed.), *Doing visual research with children and young people*. London: Routledge.

Eder, D. & Fingerson, L. (2002). Interviewing children and adolescents. In J. A. Holstein & J. F. Gubrium (Eds.), *Handbook of interview research: Context and method* (pp. 181–201). Thousand Oaks, CA: SAGE.

Falzon, M. (2009). *Multi-sited ethnography: Theory, praxis and locality in contemporary research*. Farnham, UK: Ashgate.

Fine, M. & Weis, L. (2003). *Silenced voices and extraordinary conversations: Re-imagining schools*. New York: Teachers College Press.

Fitzpatrick, K. J. (2010). *Stop playing up! A critical ethnography of health, physical education and (sub)urban schooling*. (Doctoral dissertation, University of Waikato, Hamilton, New Zealand). Retrieved from http://researchcommons.waikato.ac.nz/handle/10289/4429

Fitzpatrick, K. J. (2013). *Critical pedagogy, physical education and urban schooling*. New York: Peter Lang.

Foucault, M. (1980). Prison talk. In C. Gordon (Ed.), *Power/knowledge: Selected interviews and other writings, 1972–1977* (pp. 37–54). New York: Pantheon Books.

Foucault, M. (1982). The subject and power. *Critical Inquiry, 8*(4), 777–795.

GymSports New Zealand. (n.d.). *Educator's guide*. Retrieved from http://www.gymsportsnz.com/files/mMp_EducatorsA5_v9_HR.pdf

Hammersley, M., & Atkinson, P. (1995). *Ethnography: Principles in practice* (2nd edition). London: Routledge.

Hartmann, D. (2016). *Midnight basketball: Race, sport, and neoliberal social policy*. Chicago: University of Chicago Press.

Jeffrey, B., & Troman, G. (2004). Time for ethnography. *British Educational Research Journal, 30*(4), 535–548. doi: 10.1080/0141192042000237220

Kvale, S. (1996). *Interviews: An introduction to qualitative research interviewing*. Thousand Oaks, CA: SAGE.

Madison, S. (2005). *Critical ethnography: Method, ethics, and performance*. Thousand Oaks, CA: Sage.

Marcus, G. E. (1995). Ethnography in/of the world system: The emergence of multi-sited ethnography. *Annual Review of Anthropology, 24*, 95–117.

Mazzei, L. A. (2009). An impossibly full voice. In A. Y. Jackson & L. A. Mazzei (Eds.), *Voice in qualitative inquiry: Challenging conventional, interpretive, and critical conceptions in qualitative research* (pp. 45–62). Oxon, UK: Routledge.

Mazzei, L. A. & Jackson, L. Y. (2009). Introduction: The limit of voice. In A. Y. Jackson & L. A. Mazzei (Eds.), *Voice in qualitative inquiry: Challenging conventional, interpretive, and critical conceptions in qualitative research* (pp. 1–13). Oxon, UK: Routledge.

Miller, P., & Rose, N. (2008). *Governing the present.* Cambridge, England: Polity.

Ministry of Education. (2007). *The New Zealand curriculum.* Wellington, New Zealand: Learning Media.

Mitchell, R. (2009). 'Soft ears' and hard topics: Race, disciplinarity, and voice in higher education. In A. Y. Jackson & L. A. Mazzei (Eds.), *Voice in qualitative inquiry: Challenging conventional, interpretive, and critical conceptions in qualitative research* (pp. 77–95). Oxon, UK: Routledge.

Murtagh, L. (2007). Implementing a critically quasi-ethnographic approach. *The Qualitative Report, 12*(2), 193–215.

New Zealand Post. (2012). *Small Sticks.* Retrieved from http://www.activepost.co.nz/programmes/small-sticks/

Patton, M. Q. (2002). *Qualitative research and evaluation methods.* Thousand Oaks, CA: Sage.

Powell, D. (2015). 'Part of the solution'?: Charities, corporate philanthropy and healthy lifestyles education in New Zealand primary schools. (Doctoral dissertation, Charles Sturt University, Bathurst, Australia). Retrieved from https://researchoutput.csu.edu.au/files/9316089/80326

Powers, P. (1996). Discourse analysis as a methodology for nursing inquiry. *Nursing Inquiry, 3*(4), 207–217. doi: 10.1111/j.1440-1800.1996.tb00043

Rose, N., O'Malley, P., & Valverde, M. (2006). Governmentality. *Annual Review of Law and Social Science, 2*(1), 83–104.

Spradley, J. (1979). *The ethnographic interview.* Fort Worth, TX: Harcourt Brace.

Walters, S. (2007). 'Case study' or 'ethnography'? Defining terms, making choices and defending the worth of a case. *Methodological Developments in Ethnography (Studies in Educational Ethnography), 12*, 89–108. doi: 10.1016/S1529-210X(06)12006-9

INDEX

Printed in Great Britain
by Amazon